NEW FRONTIERS IN HISTORY

series editors

Mark Greengrass
Department of History, Sheffield University

John Stevenson
Worcester College, Oxford

This important series reflects the substantial expansion that has occurred in the scope of history syllabuses. As new subject areas have emerged and syllabuses have come to focus more upon methods of historical enquiry and knowledge of source materials, a growing need has arisen for correspondingly broad-ranging textbooks.

New Frontiers in History provides up-to-date overviews of key topics in British, European and world history, together with accompanying source material and appendices. Authors focus on subjects where revisionist work is being undertaken, providing a fresh viewpoint, welcomed by students and sixth-formers. The series also explores established topics which have attracted much conflicting analysis and require a synthesis of the state of debate.

MANCHESTER
UNIVERSITY PRESS

Published titles

Jeremy Black The politics of Britain

Paul Bookbinder Weimar Germany

Michael Braddick The nerves of state:
taxation and the financing of the English state, 1558–1714

Michael Broers Europe after Napoleon

David Brooks The age of upheaval: Edwardian politics, 1899–1914

Carl Chinn Poverty amidst prosperity

Conan Fischer The rise of the Nazis

T.A. Jenkins Parliament, party and politics in Victorian Britain

Keith Laybourn The General Strike of 1926

Frank McDonough Neville Chamberlain, appeasement and the British road
to war

Evan Mawdsley The Stalin years: the Soviet Union 1922–1956

Alan O'Day Irish Home Rule 1867–1921

Panikos Panayi Immigration, racism and ethnicity 1815–1945

Daniel Szechi The Jacobites

David Taylor The New Police

John Whittam Fascist Italy

Forthcoming titles

David Andress French society in revolution 1789–1799

Ciaran Brady The unplanned conquest: social changes and political conflict in
sixteenth-century Ireland

John Childs The army, state and society 1500–1800

Barry Coward The Cromwellian protectorate

Simon Ditchfield The Jesuits in early modern Europe

Bruce Gordon The Swiss Reformation

Susan-Mary Grant The American Civil War and Reconstruction

Tony Kushner The Holocaust and its aftermath

Alan Marshall The age of faction

Keith Mason Slavery and emancipation

Alan O'Day Irish Home Rule

Michael Turner British politics in the age of reform

Alexandra Walsham Persecution and toleration in England 1530–1660

Change, continuity and class

Labour in British society 1850–1920

Neville Kirk

Manchester University Press

Manchester and New York

Distributed exclusively in the USA by St. Martin's Press

The right of Neville Kirk to be identified as the author of this work has been asserted by him in accordance with the Copyright, Designs and Patents Act 1988.

Published by Manchester University Press
Oxford Road, Manchester M13 9NR, UK
and Room 400, 175 Fifth Avenue, New York, NY 10010, USA

Distributed exclusively in the USA by
St. Martin's Press, Inc., 175 Fifth Avenue, New York,
NY 10010, USA

Distributed exclusively in Canada by
UBC Press, University of British Columbia, 6344 Memorial Road,
Vancouver, BC, Canada V6T 1Z2

British Library Cataloguing-in-Publication Data
A catalogue record for this book is available from the British Library

Library of Congress Cataloging-in-Publication Data
Kirk, Neville, 1947–
  Change, continuity and class: labour in British society, 1850–1920/Neville Kirk.
    p. cm. — (New frontiers in history)
  Includes bibliographical references and index.
  ISBN 0-7190-4237-2. — ISBN 0-7190-4238-0 (pbk.)
    1. Labor movement–Great Britain–History.   2. Working class–Great
Britain–History.   3. Great Britain–Social conditions.   4. Working class–Great
Britain–Political activity–History.
I. Titl.e   II. Series.
HD8390.K49   1998
331.88'0941–dc21   97-47406

ISBN 0 7190 4237 2 *hardback*
      0 7190 4238 0 *paperback*

First published 1998

05 04 03 02 01 00 99 98   10 9 8 7 6 5 4 3 2 1

Typeset
by Best-set Typesetter Ltd., Hong Kong
Printed in Great Britain
by Bell & Bain Ltd, Glasgow

Contents

v

Acknowledgements

The Department of Economics and Economic History at Manchester Metropolitan University kindly granted me a term's study leave during 1996 which allowed me to concentrate more fully upon the book. Vanessa Graham and her colleagues at Manchester University Press have been most helpful, good-humoured and efficient. And my ventures into the Pennines, often in the company of Charlie Brown, have once again helped me to clear my mind and focus my thoughts.

1

Introduction

Developments and debates since the 1960s

The period since the early 1960s has witnessed significant growth
in popular and academic interest in, and publications concerned
with, the social and labour history of modern Britain. Indeed,
given the voluminous and seemingly ever-expanding nature of
the relevant academic literature, the widened nature of student
curriculum choice, and the mounting financial and 'managerial'
demands being made within the British educational system, it
has become increasingly difficult for students, and indeed many
teachers, to keep abreast of developments within a specific discipline or even sub-disciplinary subject area. A key purpose of this
book is accordingly to provide students and interested general
readers with an up-to-date critical guide to, and analysis of, what
I consider to be the main books and articles dealing with the
position of labour in British society between the mid-Victorian
period and the immediate post-World War I years.

The numbers of such books and articles have not only mushroomed in the relatively recent past, but have also frequently
been characterised by fierce debates and conflicts. For example,
during the 1960s and 1970s Marxists such as E.P. Thompson, E.J.
Hobsbawm and John Saville frequently locked horns with the
anti-Marxists A.E. Musson, W.H. Chaloner and R.M. Hartwell.[1]
Debates concerning class and class consciousness and the effects
of the industrial revolution upon the living standards of the British people, and theories of society revolving around conflict and

consensus and continuity and change became important features of journals such as the *Economic History Review, Past and Present* and *Society for the Study of Labour History Bulletin.* Since the late 1970s Conservative triumphs, labour movement defeats and the rise (resurrection?) of 'radical–liberal' New Labour have provided an added edge to debates about class and social change. Furthermore, underpinned variously by the rise of 'new' black and feminist social movements and the ideas of post-structuralism and postmodernism, and as reflected in the pages of journals such as *Social History, History Workshop Journal, Gender and History, Race and Class* and the *International Review of Social History,* notions of identity structured around ethnicity, race, gender and nation have increasingly come to engage with, and in some instances to overshadow, the traditional concern of British social and labour historians with expressions of class.[2] In addition a small, if vocal, number of British social historians have embraced explicitly postmodernist linguistic 'turns' to the study of identity. These historians have loudly, and at times somewhat messianically, proclaimed the supreme importance of subjectivity to the construction of reality; and, as a corollary, the 'death' of long-established 'modernist' or 'realist' forms of social and labour history which posit the existence of a structured and partially unintended social reality, such as class structure, 'out there', as simultaneously related to and possessing an independent presence from human consciousness and intention.[3]

A second major purpose of the book is further to familiarise the reader with, and offer some critical comments upon, aspects of the historiographical and theoretical debates outlined above which have relevance to the period under study. In so doing, it is important immediately and briefly to alert the reader to a marked divergence in the responses of, on the one hand, social and, on the other hand, labour historians of Britain to the political, social and intellectual changes and challenges of the past fifteen years or so.

Notwithstanding their manifest internal disagreements, social historians of modern Britain have, as amply demonstrated in recent issues of their national journal, *Social History,* shown an enthusiastic desire to investigate and assess the relative strengths and weaknesses of the 'linguistic turn', the epistemological claims of realism and anti-realism, and the historiographies of class, race and gender. In stark contrast, at least as reflected in the pages of their national journal, *Labour History Review*, and taking into account important counter-currents and examples, the responses of labour historians of Britain to political and intellectual defeats and challenges have generally been characterised more by silences, seeming indifference and complacency, and the dogged pursuit of traditional subject areas and areas of debate than by the kinds of intellectual and political curiosity and engagement that placed labour history at the forefront of the discipline of history in the 1960s and 1970s. As recently observed by a leading labour historian, David Howell, the overall failure of labour history sufficiently to *engage* with new forces and its continued rootedness in Eurocentrism, empiricism, even antiquarianism, and its dominant concern with institutions, leaders and white, skilled and male workers have induced a current crisis of conservatism and a loss of intellectual cutting edge. Arguably, unless British labour history shows a tough-minded determination to regenerate itself (much in the manner of US labour history[4]), its future appeal will probably diminish and its subject matter will be in danger of becoming of little more than antiquarian and specialist interest. As Howell has concluded, 'The response to the crisis must combine advocacy and listening, defending the massive achievements of labour historians both substantive and theoretical, but considering criticisms and making new connections.'[5] In providing a critical commentary upon old and new approaches and debates within the social and labour history of the period from 1850 to 1920 and in indicating directions for future research, this book aims to make a contribution to the immediate regeneration and future development of British labour history.

It is suggested that in order to demonstrate its continued relevance and future promise labour history must cast its historiographical, theoretical, substantive and methodological nets wide and deep. In accordance with this statement of belief the focus of this book rests upon more than the institutions and personnel of organised labour. The experiences and values of the unorganised as well as the organised, the unskilled as well as the skilled, women as well as men, and immigrants as well as the native born, merit close attention. Similarly, the institutions of organised labour must be set within their wider societal context. And the achievement of this ambitious goal involves due attention to theory: to the study of the nature and degrees (if any) of correspondence between different levels of abstraction; and between the various levels and practices – linguistic and cultural as well as economic, political and ideological – which constitute society.

One might justifiably argue that in point of fact the *combined* traditional wisdom of such leading labour historians as E.P. and Dorothy Thompson, Eric Hobsbawm, Asa Briggs and John Saville has embraced, indeed in many instances established, the wide substantive and theoretical briefs for the subject outlined in the preceding paragraph. One thinks immediately in this context of Briggs's study of the nineteenth-century languages of 'classes' and 'masses', E.P. Thompson's central concern with culture and meaning, Dorothy Thompson's studies of class, gender and ethnicity with respect to Chartism, Hobsbawm's 'totalising' history and Saville's focus upon politics. Similarly, labour historians such as E.P. Thompson have been concerned to explore the complex relations between politics, culture and economics rather than to reduce values, languages and ideas to a determining economic base.[6]

We must therefore be careful not to reject cavalierly all past labour historiographies as relics of an outmoded modernist past. Equally we must not necessarily assume that current linguistic and other fashions are either entirely novel or necessarily constitute better history than offered by the conventional wisdom. Simultaneously, however, we must, as indicated above, endeavour to arrest and reverse British labour history's current *general* malaise, and especially its retreat from the pioneering, wide-ranging and challenging intellectual frameworks of its founding men and women. Following the lead of some of the labour historians of the United States, we must also more fully incorporate the best insights of feminist, black and other historiographies into the subject of labour history.[7] Finally, the precise and changing nature of the historical interactions between, on the one hand, structure and, on the other, chronology, context, agency and meaning and between intentions and outcomes, and the economic and extra-economic demand renewed historical study. It is by means of a synthesis and further development of the best elements in both traditional and new approaches that the labour history of Britain

4

can reinvigorate itself and advance confidently into the twenty-first century.

Historiography: Marxism and revisionism

In moving from a general concern with the past, present and likely future state of labour history to the specific subject matter, chronological focus and organisational structure of this book, it should be observed that the work is informed by a number of guiding assumptions and principles. First, discussion of events, institutions, value systems and norms, and structures and processes, is consistently set within the framework of different historiographical approaches. The aim – whether in terms of the subjects of trade unionism, working-class politics, the world of work or culture – is not only to describe and chronologically narrate but also to contextualise, analyse and evaluate. Evaluation is carried out according to the historian's established 'rules of method': careful scrutiny of the adequacy of the evidence and concepts, theories and hypotheses on offer; and the making and breaking of concepts and competing hypotheses and historiographies against the full complexities of the evidence (the never-ending fact–theory dialogue).[8]

Second, much of the text is given over to a discussion of the relative strengths and weaknesses of two extremely important, developing and sharply conflicting approaches and traditions, Marxist and revisionist, which have exerted a major influence upon the writing of British labour history during the past thirty-odd years. The core, and in some instances changing, preoccupations, characteristics and findings of these two traditions will be observed throughout the course of the book. At this point it is appropriate to acquaint the reader with the key points of difference and disagreement.

As Jon Lawrence observed in his 1992 article 'Popular Radicalism and the Socialist Revival in Britain', by the 1960s a three-stage model of nineteenth-century working-class development and politics had 'become entrenched in both the liberal and Marxist historiographies of the period'. This new orthodoxy, expressed and consolidated most clearly in the work of the Marxists E.P. Thompson and E.J. Hobsbawm, largely came to supersede the conventional wisdom of the Whig interpretation of history. Both in the classroom and in student texts emphases upon the centrality to the historical process of social and political conflicts and major ruptures, or 'discontinuities', in class experience (rooted in, but not confined or reduced to, the material aspects of life) and class consciousness (as seen in the expression of similar or common interests, ideas and values and opposition to other social classes) successfully challenged the traditional Whig common sense of 'the gradual, but uninterrupted, evolution of democratic principles and institutions' and 'the inexorable triumph of reason and progress'.[9]

More precisely, this newly hegemonic Marxist and *marxisant* historiography divided the labour and social history of nineteenth-century Britain into three interconnected, but simultaneously distinct, periods. The first, the classical age of the industrial revolution, from the 1780s to the 1840s, became the period of 'making', as seen in the making of both the middle and the working classes. For example, just as the Reform Act of 1832, the Municipal Corporations Act of 1835 , the formation of the Anti-Corn Law League in 1838 and the subsequent repeal of the corn laws by a Conservative Prime Minister, Peel, in 1846, constituted important moments in the growth of the class consciousness and drive for power of the middle classes, so the mushrooming of radical political, economic and cultural popular protest movements (Luddism, Peterloo, Owenism, trade unionism, the battle for a cheap radical press, and so on) which climaxed in Chartism (1838–58), bore witness to the growing depth and strength of class consciousness among labouring people. Simultaneously, the process of the making of class involved a decline in the importance of, even the unmaking of, those languages, habits and customs of status, rank, order, loyalism, paternalism and deference which had predominated in eighteenth-century English society. The processes of making and unmaking were both, it was claimed, closely related to the economic disruption attendant upon the accelerated growth of indstrial capitalism. However, as witnessed particularly in the work of Thompson, political and cultural, as well as economic, factors were identified as having played an important role in the processes of class formation.[10]

Just as the birth and development of mass Chartism were

closely identified with the flowering of the consciousness of class among workers, so were the movement's faltering momentum (from the mid-1840s onwards) and decline (from the late 1840s to the late 1850s) cited as crucial pieces of evidence in the unmaking of that class consciousness. This process of unmaking, claimed to have taken place during the mid-Victorian years (from the mid to late 1840s to the 1870s), constituted the second, and far less dramatic or heroic, period of working-class history. E.P. Thompson, for example, while recognising important political, economic and social gains on the part of sections of the working class and the labour movement during these decades, and the persistence of (often acute) industrial conflict, nevertheless portrayed the period as a whole as one of retreat from the wide-ranging class consciousness and totalising radical vision of the Chartist years. Formerly united or linked political and industrial actions and groups were seen increasingly to pull apart, independent working-class politics to decline, and cross-class political and cultural ties (with, for example, middle-class Liberals and Conservatives) to develop, both in frequency and in strength. Sectional and private attitudes and practices spread. The labour movement as a whole became more narrowly based or 'aristocratic' in character and more pragmatic and reformist in outlook – that is to say, more concerned with immediate and limited gains and reforms than with a sudden 'revolving of the whole system'. Furthermore, reformism took root against the backdrop of a working class more fragmented along the lines of skill, purchasing power, ethnicity, occupation, geographical place, gender and general life style and values than during the Chartist years.[11]

Once again, changes in class consciousness and social relations were closely linked with developments in material life, and especially with the scope provided by mid-Victorian economic dynamism and expansion for partial improvements in working-class living standards and greatly enhanced state and class manoeuvres, concessions and all manner of accommodations. But, equally, the working classes were not portrayed as the passive and unmediated cultural bearers of vast, impersonal economic and other determinations taking place behind their backs in concealed and uncontrollable ways. For example, Thompson, arguably more so than Hobsbawm, was as much concerned with an exploration of the cultural, sociological and political influences of agency and conscious choice and intention upon the growth of reformism and the ebbing of class as with the effects of underlying economic or other determinations.[12]

The third period – dating from the 1880s down to the immediate aftermath of the First World War – was held by Hobsbawm to have witnessed the making of the modern, traditional working class 'of cup-finals, fish-and-chip shops, palais-de-danse and Labour with a capital L' (suggesting a remaking of the working class of our first period). The development of a mass labour movement, especially the massive extension of trade unionism ('new unionism') to the non-skilled, significant periods of 'labour unrest' (the late 1880s, 1910–14 and 1918–20), the revival of socialism and the birth and development of the Labour Party were seen by Hobsbawm to be indicative of a growing sense of workers' independence and feelings of 'us and them', a revival of class. This revival was in turn explained with reference to a number of distinct but related developments: intensified international economic competition and employer pressures to reduce labour costs, de-skill and increase control over labour; judicial and employer attacks on trade unionism; the seeming inability of the Liberals and Conservatives adequately to defend labour's pereceived interests; and the growth of a more standardised and segregated working-class culture than that of the mid-Victorian years.[13] The perceived experiences of total war – most notably the failures of individualism and the successes of collectivism, the antisocial and profiteering activities of a section of the rich, and the sacrifices of the many, combined with raised expectations, increased political citizenship and militancy in the immediate post-war years, further moved many workers to the left and underpinned the rise of Labour during the 1920s.[14]

As indicated earlier, even during the predominantly radical 1960s and early 1970s the new orthodoxy of Thompson and Hobsbawm was by no means uncontested. For example, some economic historians, such as A.E. Musson, made a spirited and by no means implausible case in favour of a nineteenth-century British working class continuously more divided and sectional, frequently less class-conscious, in some periods (such as the 1830s and 1840s) less revolutionary and militant and in others (such as the mid-Victorian years) less in retreat and quiescent than many advocates of the new orthodoxy wished to argue. In addition, political and social historians such as Brian Harrison, Patricia Hollis and Henry Pelling identified points of cultural and ideological agreement between Chartists and Liberals and Liberals and Labourites which posed serious questions for advocates of discontinuity.[15]

The criticisms offered in the 1960s and 1970s in many ways prefigured the more widespread and increasingly self-confident challenges to the discontinuous three-stage model which have developed strongly in the more recent past. We may suggest that these more recent challenges, which we will bring together under the umbrella term 'liberal revisionism', embrace a range of determinedly empirical, postmodernist and radical–feminist historians whose points of difference and conflict (especially between the empiricists of the first kind and the theorists of the second and third) are often substantial. However, we may further suggest that the overall *effect* of this internally differentiated revisionism has been to provide comprehensive alternative models or readings to those offered by Thompson and Hobsbawm. Above all, as observed by Lawrence, in direct opposition to advocates of the three-stage model, the new liberal revisionists attach fundamental importance to the notion of continuity, especially political continuity, and the limited nature of class consciousness among nineteenth and early twentieth-century workers.

By way of specific illustration of the general case, revisionists such as Lawrence himself, Gareth Stedman Jones, Alastair Reid, Eugenio Biagini and Patrick Joyce have thus drawn our attention to a long-established tradition of popular political radicalism which, it is claimed, maintained its powerful inter-class appeal throughout the nineteenth century and beyond. Addressing itself to the interests of the independent-minded, respectable, progressive and productive of all sectors of society rather than to a specfic class, popular radicalism explained poverty and exploitation in predominantly political and, at a secondary level, economic exchange-based ways rather than in more Marxian economic production- or class-based terms. It was therefore the unfair and exacting state – of high taxation and parasitic landowners, usurers, placemen and sinecurists (of Old Corruption) – and exclusion from the vote and political citizenship in general, rather than exploitation within production, which allegedly underlay many of the ills of the people. Furthermore, it is argued that as political radicalism manifested itself in a variety of contexts – in, for example, Chartism and mid-Victorian Liberalism and in late nineteenth and early twentieth-century 'new' Liberalism and the Labour Party – it did indeed powerfully promote cross-class political continuity, social integration and cultural and ideological consensus.[16]

In ways strongly reminiscent of Musson, Alastair Reid has been most prominent among the revisionists in drawing our attention not only to enduring features of nineteenth and early twentieth-century politics and ideology but also to continuities in trade unionism and in social structure and consciousness.[17] For example, just as Musson argued in favour of the overall domination of workers' lives between the second and third quarters of the nineteenth century by profound differences and divisions and the weak presence of class, and of workers' economic movements by highly sectional but determined craft and skilled trade unions, so Reid has developed a strikingly similar agenda for the later period. The contention of the Webbs, Hobsbawm and others that there existed important differences and divisions between the craft and skilled 'new model' and the mass 'new' unions is rejected, as are Hobsbawm's emphases upon the development of a more homogeneous working class and, in the face of growing foreign competition and declining prices, greatly intensified employer attempts to deskill and transform labour into the more pliant servant of capital. In general terms Reid sees divisions and conflicting interests, rooted in different levels of income, skill and occupation, different cultures and so forth, as natural features of working-class social structure and culture. As a corollary, the shared or common experiences and articulations of class are viewed as rare moments in the history of British workers.[18]

It is also important to note within this socio-cultural context that many recent radical feminist or 'patriarchy first' studies of gender – of the historical construction of notions of femininity and masculinity – and of relations between the sexes within the working class have shared Reid's 'liberal individualistic' emphases upon diversity, divisions, competition and conflict. For example, Sylvia Walby, Sonya Rose and Anna Clark argue that a 'struggle for the breeches' (Clark) – for resources, power and control, with the odds tilted heavily in favour of the male breadwinner, characterised male–female relations in nineteenth-century working-class families. The pendulum thus appears to have swung away from the socialist-feminist emphases of Sheila Rowbotham, Jill Liddington, Dorothy Thompson and Angela John upon the shared, if unequal, relations which, they suggest, existed between the sexes in these very same families.[19]

Finally, those revisionists, such as Joyce and Stedman Jones, who have taken the linguistic turn have argued that the languages of workers revolved far less around class identity (as employed in a Marxist way to signify the articulation of the primacy and necessity of exploitation within production) than, as noted earlier, around the radical discourses of political exclusion and opppression and the natural unity of productive manual workers and employers (profit being seen as a just reward for honest endeavour) against parasitical landowners and speculators (rent and excessive interest being condemned as ill-gotten gains of an unnatural monopoly position in the market place).[20]

In sum, in opposition to advocates of the class-based three-stage model, the liberal revisionists thus present us with a picture of continuity rooted in the enduring inter-class appeal of political radicalism, in chronic divisions and conflicts among the labouring people, and in articulations of identity of a predominantly non-class-based kind. Also, in part as a reaction against the alleged economic 'reductionist assumptions about politics that underpin the three-phase model' (Lawrence), and notwithstanding Alastair Reid's attention to the worlds of work and trade unionism, most liberal revisionists have elevated politics and political discourse to a position of supreme importance in the forging of identities, values and norms, ways of looking at the world and social practices. Lawrence claims that his approach is concerned to stress 'the relative autonomy of the political' since it 'rejects both the determinist straitjacket of the traditional emphasis ... and the countervailing tendency to focus purely on the interplay of political ideas or the conjuring tricks of high politics'. But it may be argued that, in practice, both Lawrence and those other liberal revisionists primarily concerned with popular politics fail sufficiently to link and *engage* the political and the economic and social in the complex ways employed by E.P. Thompson and other alleged determinists.[21]

Introduction

Chronology, structure and arguments

As demonstrated above, the first and second guiding principles of this book – that analysis should be combined with description and that due attention should be paid to relevant historiographies – lead necessarily to central concern with the issues of change, continuity and class: hence the title. The third and final guideline is that these same issues have largely shaped the chronological focus and organisational structure of the study.

In terms of chronolgy the mid-nineteenth century constitutes the book's point of departure, for a variety of reasons. Above all, perhaps, many of the past and present debates about continuity and change in trade unionism, working-class politics, culture and ideology have focused upon the period from the mid to late 1840s to the 1870s. This period is, of course, bounded on one side by late Chartism and on the other by the onset of the great depression. Given this point of focus, it appeared sensible to exclude from the study detailed discussion of the Chartist movement in its early and middle years. Chartism between 1838 and 1848 has often been treated in the historical literature as a discrete area of study. Furthermore, in view of the amount of published material available to students of Chartism, combined with the relative neglect of the post-Chartist years, it seemed important to make a contribution towards filling some of the gaps in our knowledge of the latter period. Moreover, and notwithstanding their less romantic and heroic appeal, events and processes which took place during the mid-Victorian period were arguably of far more importance than Chartism in setting the modern British labour movement's traditions of gradualism, reformism and the common sense of pragmatism, accommodation combined with the 'bloody-minded' pursuit of its modest goals, and suspicion of theory, the middle classes and plans for revolutionary change.[22]

As indicated earlier, debates concerning the extent to which the late nineteenth and early twentieth-century experience of socialist revival, trade union expansion and labour unrest, the birth of the Labour Party and of war marked continuities or significant breaks in class consciousness and related matters continue to excite the passions of historians. As such they command much of our attention in, and determine the chronological boundaries of, the second part of the book. Beyond the upsurges in immediate post-

World War I labour militancy and radicalism, which climaxed in 1919 and 1920, we are moving into a period – the inter-war years – which, in a manner similar to Chartism, has been treated by historians as constituting a largely self-contained area of study. The chronological focus of this study ends accordingly in 1920.

The book is organised in the following way. Part I traces and explains patterns of change and continuity and organised labour's and workers' advances and retreats during the mid-Victorian years. The first chapter in Part I makes the general case in favour of discontinuity and identifies relevant areas of explanation in relation to the growth of reformism. The following three chapters offer more detailed investigations of some of the general issues raised in Chapter 2. In Chapter 3 the development of reformism is linked with material changes in the fortunes of trade unions, co-operative and friendly societies, and the labour leadership. Such changes are set within the broader context of trends in the the economy, in living standards, in patterns of social mobility and in the values and policies of the state, employers, labour leaders and workers. Chapter 4 moves to an examination of the structure and character of politics and ideologies in these years, concentrating particularly upon the decline of Chartism and the growing popular support extended to both the Liberal Party and the Conservative Party. Questions concerning the interplay of both class- and extra-class-based influences upon politics inform this chapter. These questions are in turn broadened and developed in Chapter 5's examination of the main features of working-class culture in this period. Discussion of sources of unity and fragmentation in workers' lives, including due attention to the issues of employment, gender and respectability and 'roughness', constitutes the core of Chapter 5. In conclusion, Part One's dominant emphasis rests upon the overall importance of change and class fragmentation to the period in question.

Part II investigates the continuing interplay between patterns of continuity and change and between working-class challenges and accommodation to the dominant social order, and the extent to which the sharp intra-class divisions of the mid-Victorian period diminished in importance between the 1870s and 1920. The overview summarises our findings in favour of change and the revival of class consciousness of a predominantly constitutional and reformist kind. Socialist and even revolutionary ideas and aspirations constituted an undoubted element in this process of class remaking. However, strong feelings of 'us' and 'them' were set, for the most part, within predominantly non-revolutionary organisations and cultures. The following three chapters trace the various ways in which the general themes of challenge and accommodation, continuity and change, class and other forms of identity, worked themselves out, with specfic reference to developments at the workplace and workplace relations, in politics and ideology, and in workers' cultures.

An attempt is made in the selected documents to reflect the dominant concerns and themes of the book. The reader's attention is thus directed not only to aspects of the development of the labour movement, but also to relevant features of working-class life and the attitudes and policies towards workers and organised labour of those in positions of power and authority.

In conclusion, it will be evident from this brief outline of organisaton, structure and key arguments that the author's sympathies lie more with proponents of the three-stage model than with the liberal revisionists. This means neither that I express uniform and uncritical endorsement of all the arguments of the former nor that I erect blinkered, preconceived and unyielding ideological barriers against the arguments of the latter. I make my case and argue my conclusions upon the basis of the 'historical rules of method' outlined earlier. We must remember, as historians, that the seeming novelty and fashionable appeal of ideas and trends do not in themselves constitute self-evident truths. Rather we must continue to pay close attention to conceptual rigour and consistency and set hypotheses into engagement with complex and contradictory evidence. It is with reference to these tried and tested disciplinary rules of method that the reader is invited to judge the strengths and weaknesses of this study.

Notes

1 For reviews of such debates see R. Glen, *Urban Workers in the Early Industrial Revolution* (Beckenham, 1984), chapter 1; J. Rule, *The Labouring Classes in Early Industrial England 1750–1850* (London, 1986), pp. 383–93.

2 See, for example, S.O. Rose, 'Gender and Labor History: The

Nineteenth-century Legacy', *International Review of Social History*, 38, supplement 1 (1993) 145–62; K. Boyd and R. McWilliam, 'Historical Perspectives on Class and Culture', *Social History*, 20:1 (January 1995) 93–100; K. Lunn (ed.), *Race and Labour in Twentieth Century Britain* (London, 1985); C. Hall, *White, Male and Middle Class: Explorations in Feminism and History* (London, 1992); P. Gilroy, *There aint no Black in the Union Jack: The Cultural Politics of Race and Nation* (London, 1987).

3 See, especially, Patrick Joyce's most recent book, *Democratic Subjects: The Self and the Social in Nineteenth-century England* (Cambridge, 1994), introduction; and James Vernon's *Politics and the People: A Study in English Political Culture c. 1815–1867* (Cambridge, 1993), introduction.

4 For developments in US labour history see D. Brody, 'The Old Labor History and the New: In Search of an American Working Class', *Labor History*, 20 (winter 1979) 111–26; A. Kessler-Harris, 'Treating the Male as "Other": Redefining the Parameters of Labor History', *Labor History*, 34 (spring–summer 1993) 190–204; D. Roediger, 'Race and the Working-class Past in the United States: Multiple Identities and the Future of Labor History', *International Review of Social History*, 38, supplement 1 (1993) 127–43.

5 See the editorial in *Labour History Review*, 60:1 (1995) 2.

6 A. Briggs, 'The Language of "Class" in Early Nineteenth-century England', in A. Briggs and J. Saville (eds), *Essays in Labour History*, I (London, 1967 edn); D. Thompson, *Outsiders: Class, Gender and Nation* (London, 1993); E.P. Thompson, *Customs in Common* (London, 1991), especially chapter 1; E.J. Hobsbawm, *Worlds of Labour: Further Studies in the History of Labour* (London, 1984); J. Saville, *1848: The British State and the Chartist Movement*, (Cambridge, 1987).

7 Roediger, 'Race and the Working-class Past'; M J Buhle, 'Gender and Labor History', in J.C. Moody and A. Kessler-Harris (eds), *Perspectives on American Labor History: The Problems of Synthesis* (De Kalb, Ill., 1990).

8 See E.P. Thompson, 'The Poverty of Theory', in his *The Poverty of Theory and Other Essays* (London, 1978), pp. 222–42.

9 J. Lawrence, 'Popular Radicalism and the Socialist Revival in Britain', *Journal of British Studies*, 31 (1992) 163.

10 See, for example, the preface and concluding chapter of E.P. Thompson's *The Making of the English Working Class* (Harmondsworth, 1980).

11 E.P. Thompson, 'The Peculiarities of the English', in *The Poverty of Theory* (London, 1981 edn), pp. 280–1 ; N. Kirk, *The Growth of Working Class Reformism in Mid-Victorian England* (Beckenham, 1985), especially chapter 1 and conclusion.

12 Thompson, 'Peculiarities'; E.J. Hobsbawm, *Industry and Empire* (Harmondsworth, 1969), chapter 6.

13 Hobsbawm, *Worlds of Labour*, chapter 11.

14 N. Kirk, *Labour and Society in Britain and the USA*, II, *Challenge and Accommodation 1850–1939* (Aldershot, 1994), pp. 110–15, 150–1, 325–31.

15 A.E. Musson, *British Trade Unions 1800–1875* (London, 1972); A.E. Musson, *Trade Union and Social History* (London, 1974); B. Harrison and P. Hollis, 'Chartism, Liberalism and the Life of Robert Lowery', *English Historical Review*, 82 (1967) 503–35; H. Pelling, *The Origins of the Labour Party 1880–1900* (Oxford, 1965 edn); H. Pelling, *Popular Politics and Society in Late Victorian Britain* (London, 1968).

16 See, for example, G.S. Jones, 'Rethinking Chartism', in his *Languages of Class: Studies in English Working Class History* (Cambridge, 1983); E.F. Biagini and A.J. Reid (eds), *Currents of Radicalism: Popular Radicalism, Organised Labour and Party Politics in Britain 1850–1914* (Cambridge, 1991), especially chapter 1; D. Tanner, *Political Change and the Labour Party 1900–1918* (Cambridge, 1990), introduction and conclusion; P. Joyce, *Visions of the People: Industrial England and the Question of Class 1848–1914* (Cambridge, 1991), chapter 2.

17 Musson, *Trade Unions*; Biagini and Reid, *Currents of Radicalism*; A.J. Reid, 'The Division of Labour and Politics in Britain 1880–1920', in W.J. Mommsen and H.G. Husung (eds), *The Development of Trade Unionism in Britain and Germany 1880–1914* (London, 1985); A.J. Reid, 'Marxism and Revisionism in British Labour History', *Bulletin of the Society for the Study of Labour History*, 52:3 (1987) 46–8; A.J. Reid, *Social Classes and Social Relations in Britain 1850–1914* (London, 1992).

18 For a similar view see J. Benson, 'Work', in J. Benson (ed.), *The Working Class in England 1875–1914* (Beckenham, 1984), especially pp. 75, 78. For a considered critique of Reid's work see D. Howell, 'Reading Alastair Reid: A Future for Labour History?', in N. Kirk (ed.), *Social Class and Marxism: Defences and Challenges* (Aldershot, 1996), pp. 214–35.

19 See, for example, S. Walby, *Patriarchy at Work: Patriarchal and Capitalist Relations in Employment* (Cambridge, 1986); S.O. Rose, *Limited Livelihoods: Gender and Class in Nineteenth-century England* (London, 1992); A. Clark, *The Struggle for the Breeches: Gender and the Making of the British Working Class* (London, 1995); D. Thompson, 'Women and Nineteenth-century Radical Politics', in her *Outsiders*; S. Rowbotham, *Hidden from History* (London, 1973); J. Liddington and J. Norris, *One Hand Tied Behind Us: The Rise of the Women's Suffrage Movement* (London, 1978); A.V. John (ed.), *Unequal Opportunities: Women's Employment in England 1800–1918* (London, 1986).

20 Jones, 'Rethinking Chartism', pp. 117, 134–7, 143, 145, 153–4; Joyce, *Visions of the People*, chapter 5.

21   N. Kirk, 'In Defence of Class', *International Review of Social History*, 32:1 (1987) 2–47.

22   E.J. Hobsbawm, 'Trends in the British Labour Movement since 1850', in his *Labouring Men: Studies in the History of Labour* (London, 1964).

Part I

Advances and retreats in the mid-Victorian period 1850–70s

2

The case for change

There is general agreement among historians that the middle years of the nineteenth century saw the decline of Chartism, the expansion of the economy and the growth of a more stable society in Britain. However, as indicated in the introduction, beyond these points of general consensus there have long existed, and continue to exist, profound differences among historians as to the extent, nature and causes, if any, of changes in four interrelated areas: the character and aims of the post-Chartist labour movement; the social structure of the working class; forms of popular consciousness; and social relations between workers and other social groups.[1] For example, questions concerning the novelty or otherwise of 1850s cautious and conciliatory 'new model' skilled and craft trade unionism, sparked off by the Webbs' pioneering *The History of Trade Unionism* in the 1890s, have persisted and provoked sharply conflicting responses throughout much of this century. Debates relating to a host of other issues – the character and aims of the co-operative movement; the nature, extent and meaning of workers' 'improving' endeavours (in, for example, the fields of education and temperance); the movement of former Chartists into the Gladstonian Liberal Party; the extent to which mid-Victorian economic improvement and (at least in the eyes of many economic historians) its frequently assumed offshoot, social harmony, replaced 1840s distress and social conflict; and the nature and overall balance of fractured as opposed to common experiences and patterns of consciousness among workers and labour movement activists – have likewise proved to be equally

21

enduring and sharp. While concerned primarily with specific features of working-class experience, these debates have also frequently addressed, directly or indirectly, general questions concerning continuities and breaks ('watersheds') in the political, economic, social and cultural history of workers between the second and third quarters of the nineteenth century. In addition, a wide range of factors – economic stabilisation and growth; more widespread general improvements for the people and their institutions and cultures; the emergence and growing influence of a moderate and privatised 'labour aristocracy'; a more cautious, moderate and sectional labour movement; employer paternalism and worker deference; inter-class cultural and ideological consensus; and softened and more accommodating sentiments and practices on the part of the state and the established political parties towards the working class – have been advanced to explain enhanced social stability in the post-Chartist period.[2]

As a teacher of courses in modern working-class history I have observed the apprehension which students often initially display towards the battery of competing facts, historiographical debates and explanations outlined in the previous paragraph. Reassuring words on the part of the teacher about allowing sufficient time and space for students to familiarise themselves with key developments and debates, and about the user-friendly, if (of course!) rigorous, nature of the lectures and the final examination tend, at least over time, to produce soothing and confidence-boosting effects. Nevertheless, in these modern times of the growth of 'self-standing' 'modules', instant 'packages of knowledge' and disappearing special subjects, in which questions of coherence and progression have lost much of their erstwhile centrality to the undergraduate curriculum, it becomes increasingly difficult to convey to students, and enable them to get to grips with, the necessary depth, complexity and contested character of the subject of history and of the most fruitful historical theories and explanations. Faced with such difficulties, I have increasingly resorted to the long-established device of presenting students with a summary of my main evaluations and conclusions before delving into the largely empirical subject matter of the course. I have undertaken this course of action in order to make clear to students my own positions and to give them one particular perspective, or 'handle', upon the mass of substantive and historiographical material to which they are exposed. Subject to certain caveats being made explicit – that the conclusions reached have arisen out of, rather than preceded, an engagement between 'fact' and theory, and that my interpretations must, like those of any other historian, be subjected to the rules of the discipline – this approach has enjoyed a fair amount of success in enabling students to find their way more confidently and securely through the maze of conflicting views. It is with this experience in mind that this chapter outlines what I consider to be the arguments which tip the balance in favour of the case for change rather than continuity. This summary is followed by a brief discussion of the various explanations of change put forward by historians. The themes and arguments raised at a general level in Chapter 2 are subjected to more detailed treatment in the following three chapters of Part I.

As observed by Royden Harrison and Eric Hobsbawm in the 1960s, whether or not one discerns a watershed in the development of the labour movement, workers' consciousness and action, and social relations at mid-century depends very much upon the topic under consideration and the evidence selected. In terms, for example, of trade unionism and workplace relations the Webbs drew attention, in important ways, to the increasing centralisation and bureaucratisation of 'new model' unions, such as the Amalgamated Society of Engineers (established in 1851), and to the growing desire of leading trade unionists to cultivate more harmonious relations with capital.[3] However, the Webbs' overriding interests – in the formal organisation and structures of trade unionism and the origins and development of a modern system of institutionalised collective bargaining in which reasonable trade union officials and employers met together rationally and peacefully to settle matters of mutual concern – did somewhat channel and limit their historical researches. As Musson, Hobsbawm and Harrison have argued, more comprehensive attention to mid-Victorian trade unionism and workplace relations, including due attention to informal and grass-roots practices and attitudes and to behaviour as well as stated intentions, reveals a far less discontinuous and harmonious picture than suggested by the Webbs. 'New model' features and characteristics have thus conclusively been shown to be present within pre-1850s trade unionism.

23

Furthermore, notwithstanding their oft stated principled opposition to strikes and their sincere wish more effectively and widely to develop a shared moral discourse with honourable employers, mid-Victorian trade union leaders continued to encounter sufficient examples of employer dishonour and tyranny to sanction numerous strikes and to view conflict at the workplace between labour and capital as a hard, if unfortunate, fact of life. Indeed, industrial conflict persisted, often at high levels of intensity and bitternesss, throughout the 'golden years'.[4]

With respect to politics, the once fashionable, if partial, view that independent working-class politics died with the fiasco of the Chartists' meeting on Kennington Common in April 1848 and the rejection of the third petition by Parliament has conclusively been shown to be false. Musson, Kate Tiller, Anthony Taylor and Paul Pickering have clearly demonstrated that in certain parts of the country, such as the West Riding of Yorkshire, London and to a lesser extent the cotton districts of Lancashire, Chartism continued to exert a significant influence throughout the 1850s.[5] A further defence of the continuity thesis, albeit put forward from a very different position, is that proponents of discontinuity have often understated the importance of ideological links between the Chartists and middle-class reformers around, as noted in the introduction, notions of the progressive and morally upright 'people', or producing classes, united in opposition to aristocratic reaction, decadence and privilege. In related fashion non-socialist or non-utopian features of the co-operative movement (such as the immediate practical concern with the provision of cheap and unadulterated food) and differences and divisions within the working class based on temperance, ethnicity, self-help and respectability are held to have antedated the alleged mid-Victorian processes of reformism and working-class fragmentation.[6]

In the light of such important continuities, a number of revisionist historians have suggested that there is little or no reason to resort to ambitious explanations of discontinuity in order to understand the labour, social and political history of the mid-Victorian period. Indeed, the most common explanation of discontinuity held by historians in recent times – that of the supposed emergence during the mid-1840s of a moderate and respectable stratum of economically privileged workers, the labour aristocracy, keen to divorce itself from the masses and to preach class reconciliation and harmony – has been shown, by many revisionists and non-revisionists alike, to rest upon methodologically suspect and empirically weak foundations. Not only can we detect the presence of an elite of better-paid, more privileged, more autonomous (in the workplace) and more secure workers in the pre-1850 years, but we can also observe in the post-1850 period that the presence, security, sense of collective identity and influence of such an elite varied greatly from place to place. In sum, even if we allow that a shift did take place from class-conscious Chartism to status-conscious mid-Victorian reformism, the labour aristocracy thesis still constitutes far too narrow and unsatisfactory an explanation of such wide-ranging and profound change.[7]

We must, in view of the overall tenor of the foregoing paragraphs, pay proper attention in our discussion to the full range and complexity of the evidence, and take care to reveal and fully to present aspects of continuity as well as change. Is it, however, possible to move beyond this somewhat eclectic and pluralistic method of investigation? Can we, as a result of studying their various and changing manifestations and interactions, attribute overall dominance to either the forces of continuity or those of change at mid-century? In the event of a judgement being made in favour of the forces of change, can we rearrange our long list of explanatory factors into a more rigorous order of priority? As indicated in the introduction, we can offer an affirmative response to all three questions. Let us first make the general case in favour of discontinuity and the proceed to the issue of causation.

It would be foolish to deny the presence, indeed varying degrees of importance, of elements of continuity at mid-century. However, the *dominant* picture to emerge is one in which, as argued by Harrison and Hobsbawm, the balance of change outweighs that of continuity. For example, there was indeed a marked decline in the appeal and *de facto* anti-capitalist content of independent working-class politics during the third quarter of the century. Thus:

> Independent working-class politics did not suddenly die in 1848 . . . However . . . by the mid-late 1850s Chartism had become a pale shadow, both in members and wider appeal, of its former self . . . independent working-class politics increasingly came into

being in relation to much more limited aims (to enable workers to 'rise in the social scale' rather than to 'knock property on the head') . . . erstwhile Chartist activists and supporters were, by the end of the 1860s, to be found as supporters of Liberalism or Conservatism.[8]

In moving into Liberalism and Conservatism former Chartists did not suddenly or totally abandon their class-based concerns. But there did occur, however unevenly and initially somewhat unconsciously, a narrowing of aims, a growing concern less with the oppressive and exploitative features of the political, economic, social and cultural features of the system as a whole than with specific features of oppression and with the ways in which the policies of gradualism and limited reform would assuredly remove such features and enhance working-class influence and power. The Chartist outsiders of the 1830s and 1840s were, as signified by the passage of the Second Reform Bill in 1867, transforming themselves and being transformed into respectable citizens, possessed of the right and duty to exercise their newly acquired political manhood in a responsible manner.

By the 1860s the implicitly anti-capitalist social programme of Chartism had become greatly diluted. As James Epstein has observed in relation to the 1830s and 1840s,

for many working people the demand for democratic citizenship implied, at the very least, arresting the emergent force of industrial capitalism: regulation of factory hours, repeal of the new Poor Law, some form of state intervention to guarantee a 'fair' wage for labour, a redistribution of land, and a balance between the claims of agricultural and industrial production . . . *the rejection of prevailing notions of political economy defined a fundamental difference between Chartists and middle-class radicals . . . Chartists refused to shake loose the social from the political.*[9] [Emphasis added.]

By the 1860s radical workers were to be found adopting far more accommodating, if by no means on all occasions uniformly favourable, attitudes towards both orthodox political economy and involvement with middle-class reformers. Criticisms of capitalist tyranny did not disappear from the lips of Ernest Jones and other late Chartist leaders. But such criticisms were voiced far less frequently and loudly. The aristocrat, rather than the capitalist, became the main target of attack. Jones himself greatly modified his views. He moved from 1850s outspoken advocacy of independent working-class politics and opposition to an alliance with middle-class reformers to 1860s accommodation with Liberalism. In the parliamentary elections of 1868 Jones stood as a Liberal Party candidate for Manchester alongside many of his erstwhile political opponents in the Manchester bourgeoisie. In the same year Jones declared:

> Seventeen years ago each class in this country was fighting single-handed, and perhaps in antagonism to others. We then called our opponents hard names, and our opponents called us the same. But that has changed, and we have learned not to abuse but to reason together; and the result of that reasoning is that rich and poor, employer and employed, moderate Liberal and advanced, now stand united upon the same platform for one common object, the prosperity of each through the good of all.[10]

Finally, by the 1860s working-class radical politics and workplace issues and conflicts had become far more separate and compartmentalised than during the peak periods of early Chartism. In 1839 the demand for enactment of the Six Points of the charter was backed, in the event of Parliament's refusal, by widespread calls for a stoppage of work (the Sacred Month) and by other 'physical force' activities (culminating in the Newport rising of November). Similarly, the mass strikes of 1842, involving some 500,000 workers, were frequently informed by demands for the charter as well as opposition to reductions in wages. By the 1860s the formal 'no politics' rule in trade unionism had hardened. And even though working-class leaders could, in defence of their own 'respectable' reputations and 'reasonable' demands, resort to mass demonstrations during the widespread Reform Bill agitation of 1866 (culminating in the Hyde Park riots of July), nevertheless attempts to unite political and workplace forms of agitation in support of profoundly transforming goals became increasingly rare during the mid-Victorian period.[11]

Labour's narrowed and more moderate focus was reflected not only in its politics but also in its trade unions, in the co-operative and friendly societies and in the attitudes, values, norms and practices of the working population at large. Notwithstanding the persistence of industrial conflict and the undoubted weaknesses of the Webbs' unqualified watershed thesis, a picture of substan-

tial, if qualified, changes in trade unionism and workplace relations is in accord with the evidence. As I have argued elsewhere,[12]
during the post-1850 years unions, whether of the skilled or non-
skilled variety, generally made far more strenuous efforts than
during the 1830s and 1840s to translate moderate and class-
conciliatory goals into practice, and to relegate strike action
to a position of last resort, even in the face of continued and at
times widespread and bitter employer opposition to the wrong-
headedness of trade unionism *per se*. It is true that a minority
of 'new model' employers came to appreciate the benefits – in
terms of workplace harmony, uninterrupted production, healthy
profit levels and enhanced social stability and cohesion – of recognition of unions and bargaining with 'reasonable' union officials.
But, as the Webbs astutely observed, it was the much maligned
unions which constituted all too often the patient and long-
suffering tutors of recalcitrant employers, both paternalist and
non-paternalist, in the development of a modern system of
institutionalised collective bargaining. And the development of
such a system was given a considerable fillip during the mid-
Victorian period by the fact that the balance of power within the
world of national trade unionism shifted away from the beleaguered trades and occupations (such as hand-loom weaving,
shoemaking, tailoring, mule spinning, power-loom weaving and
sections of the building, mining and metalworking industries)
which had often provided industrial militancy and support for
independent politics during the 1830s and 1840s. By the 1860s the
more secure, better-paid and better protected and treated workers
in engineering and the metal trades in general, in buildng, in
printing and other traditional craft enclaves of male privilege, and
to a lesser extent in cotton and coal mining dominated the increasingly respectable, responsible, 'aristocratic' (i.e. aloof and sectional) and more narrowly based trade union movement.[13]

Questions concerning the 'extent to which the ideals of the pre-
Rochdale co-operators were abandoned', or to which 'the dividend replaced the "New Moral World" in the minds of many
working-class co-operators and that the movement thus aided the
largely unconscious "drift into reformism"', have recently been
revisited by Peter Gurney and John Walton.[14] The conventional
wisdom, associated most closely with Sidney Pollard's pioneering article 'Nineteenth-century Co-operation: From Community

Building to Shopkeeping', published in 1960 in Volume One of Briggs and Saville's *Essays in Labour History*, had indeed at its core the suggestion that, in the midst of post-1850 growth and commercial success, co-operators increasingly, if somewhat unknowingly, lost sight of, or relegated to a position of diminishing importance, the original goals of the movement to build alternative communities upon the basis of co-operative values and relations. Success bred growing concern with profit levels and dividends upon purchases, which in turn increasingly became an end in themselves rather than the means to by-pass industrial capitalism; the wider ideals of the movement thus faded into misty vagueness. However, in raising the possibility that democratic, egalitarian, solidary, community-based and anti-competitive values may have been less peripheral to the succesful co-operative movement of the second half of the nineteenth century than is suggested by the conventional wisdom and inviting us to quarry the evidence in more depth and breadth, Gurney and Walton are both providing timely reconsiderations and setting a potentially productive research agenda for future students of nineteenth-century co-operation. After all, there were close connections between the Rochdale Pioneers and Chartism. And, as John Cole has written, the Pioneers were 'a unique blend of idealism and common sense'. Strict opposition to credit and support for a dividend upon purchases were combined with equally strong support for the extremely advanced principles of equality of membership for men and women, one member one vote, and 'a fixed percentage of profits to be devoted to educational purposes'.[15] Nevertheless, as we shall observe in Chapter 3, the available evidence is still weighed heavily in favour of the conventional wisdom of co-operative discontinuity.

The nature and aims of mid-Victorian friendly societies have aroused much less debate than that surrounding co-operation.[16] From the 1830s onwards the friendly societies, designed to provide a modicum of security and financial support against the many and chronic insecurities of working-class life, grew rapidly. By the end of the 1850s the majority of societies, and especially the popular and powerful affiliated orders such as the Manchester Unity of Oddfellows and the Ancient Order of Foresters, had cast off earlier associations with secrecy and subversion. Indeed, during the mid-Victorian period the friendly societies not only prospered in terms of new members and legal protection (earlier being vulnerable to embezzlement of their funds) but also became widely recognised as 'models of self-help, respectability and sound, moderate habits'. As was the case with prominent figures in trade unionism and the co-ops, mid-Victorian friendly society leaders made every effort, as 'good conservers of the constitution', to demonstrate their patriotism and loyalty to the throne.[17]

The trade unions, co-operative societies and friendly societies constituted the main institutional expression of post-Chartist, and predominantly male-based, independent working-class culture. A key factor in the case for discontinuity is that, in contrast to the overall defeats, failures and setbacks of the Chartist period, such institutional examples of collective self-help among workers registered major advances and successes during the third quarter of the century. As we will demonstrate in Chapter 3, the remarkable progress made by the co-ops and friendly societies and increased trade union strength and recognition, combined with the political enfranchisement of sections of the working class, induced the widespread feeling among labour activists that the movement and its constituency were achieving a stake, however ambiguous and at times tenuous, in the system. In contrast to the Chartist outsiders, working-class leaders of the 1860s (many of whom were themselves former Chartists) were thus to be found speaking the language of 'success' and 'advancement', of 'rising in society', of the proven virtues of 'self-help' and 'respectability', of the 'duties of citizenship' and of advice to 'the poor' to 'reform themselves'.[18]

The language and practice of self-help and respectability undoubtedly appealed to a large and varied number of mid-Victorian workers beyond the ranks of the labour activists and the 'aristocratic' elite of the craft and skilled.[19] Contrary to the impression sometimes given to students, such languages and practices were neither a novel creation of the 1850s and 1860s (Samuel Smiles's famous book of 'Victorian values', *Self-help*, was published in 1859), nor did they necessarily signify working-class acceptance of middle-class values and a process of *embourgeoisement*. Concern with self-help, self-respect, personal and collective independence, earnest and moral behaviour, knowledge, temperance, thrift and those other values and habits often subsumed under the term 'respectability' had long issued from within working-class experience itself, rather than simply being imposed upon passive workers by outside forces. Moreover, as exemplified by the Chartist movement, self-help and respectability were sometimes seen as a means of both individual and class empowerment, as the means of enabling the membership, as conscious agents of history, to develop sufficient powers of reason, organisation, independence and confidence to fashion their own destinies, irrespective of the attitudes and actions of those beyond the movement. Furthermore, on a daily basis, many workers, and especially working-class women, routinely practised industry, thrift and sobriety as a necessary safeguard against the chronic threats, and all too frequent realities, of economic insecurity and poverty. Indeed, resort to self-help as an individual and familial defence against poverty and/or to collective self-help as a means of mutual protection and advancement for groups of workers (as seen in the co-ops, trade unions and friendly societies) was far more prevalent among nineteenth-century workers than self-help undertaken purely as a means of *individual* advancement, either within or out of the ranks of the working class.[20]

We must accordingly be careful not automatically to read off unchanging and uniform meanings from the words 'self-help' and 'respectability'. Meanings were frequently complex, changing and socially and politically contested. Much depended upon the experiential context in which such language, practices and values arose and the relations and balance of social forces at a particular point in time.

As we will shall see in some depth in Chapters 3 and 5, as between the Chartist and post-Chartist periods there were continuities of cultural meaning and practice. Numerous examples of workers' daily and institutionalised forms of self-help are thus to be located in both periods, as are instances of cultural and other conflicts and disagreements among 'respectables' from different social classes. In addition, identifications of respectability with corporate, even on occasion class, pride by no means disappeared entirely in the post-Chartist years. With respect to these years, the socially soothing and consensual features and functions of respectability have tended to be exaggerated in much of the relevant historical literature.[21] Notwithstanding such exaggeration

31

and the continued association of respectable workers with struggle, conflict and collective organisation and pride, self-help and
respectability were harnessed increasingly to more private,
status-conscious and patriarchal ends in the 1850s and 1860s.
'Respectability' in home life became associated far less with mutuality between the (albeit unequal) sexes and far more extensively and deeply with hardened notions of female inferiority, of
a woman's 'place', of women's exclusion from public space and
the public institutions of workers, and with male superiority and
sole breadwinner standing. (The fact that concrete reality was
often at odds with such widely prescribed gender roles should
not be allowed to obscure or diminish the powerful influence of
the patriarchal domestic ideal among working-class men *and*
women.[22]) There is, furthermore, strong evidence to suggest that
working-class 'respectables' showed a much greater desire than
in the Chartist period to divorce themselves from the assumed
'non-respectables' within the labouring population, to build
firmer bridges to respectables across the class structure, and far
more extensively to identify poverty and inequality less as a
result of the structural workings of the system than as an indica-
tor of character failings, of a 'want of ideas', initiative and individual and collective self-help on the part of the poor.[23] In sum,
this increasingly narrowed, more conservative and status-conscious perspective was indicative, both of the extent to which
cultural changes and fragmentation had come to overshadow
continuity and class feeling, and of some of the means whereby
workers accommodated themselves to the consolidation of bourgeois hegemony in mid-Victorian Britain.

These various discontinuities in mid-Victorian working-class
life took place against the wider backcloth of greatly enhanced
class toleration and social stability – as opposed to complete
class harmonisation and consensus. As suggested by Antonio
Gramsci's notion of hegemony, mid-Victorian social conflict was
largely contained within the prevailing political, economic, cultural and ideological 'common sense'.[24] By the 1870s a divided
and reformist working class had come to regard industrial capitalism as a given, as a seemingly permanent fact of life, and its
ruling bloc of landowners, merchants, financiers and industrialists as more favourably disposed to acceptance of labour's moderate inclusionary demands. And leading figures in the labour

movement contrasted the 'wild' and 'visionary' failings of 'revolutionary' Owenism and Chartism with the successes of piecemeal gradualism.[25]

Why had this transformation – from Chartism's 'bitter discontent' (Thomas Carlyle in 1839) to a growing popular concern with '"Co-ops." . . . and their shares in them, or in building societies' (Thomas Cooper in 1870) – taken place? At the most general, structural level a convincing answer has recently been provided by Robert Hall. Hall views the acute social and political conflicts of the Chartist years as stemming from a convergence of crises in the economy, the labour process, society and politics.[26] The extremely unstable and tempestuous character of early nineteenth-century industrial capitalist development was reflected in a volatile mixture of heady, if narrowly based, economic growth (rooted largely in cotton textiles) combined with increasingly frequent cyclical fluctuations and serious depressions. During the latter (as seen especially between 1837 and 1842) employers experienced acute downward pressure upon the process of capital accumulation and their rates of profit, and made intensified and increasingly concerted efforts to gain total control (real as well as formal) over the labour process, to destroy workers' combinations and to reduce unit costs of production, including labour costs. Rapid, if uneven, technological change and de-skilling, and the attempted imposition by a growing number of employers of new patterns of work, authority, power, and values and norms (market-based as opposed to moral economic) upon increasingly threatened and dependent artisans and others further fuelled conflict. Workers in many occupations and geographical settings adopted the language of class, damning the new capitalist employers as purely self-interested, profit-maximising and exploitative 'dishonourable tyrants', and bemoaning the marked decline in customary notions of reciprocity and fairness between masters and men and their own descent into wage slavery.[27]

The maturation during the 1830s of the tradition of popular, and increasingly working-class, political radicalism, struggles surrounding the passage of the 1832 Reform Bill, the widespread sense of betrayal felt by working-class radicals at the exclusionary terms of the 1832 Act, and outrage at the Whigs' blatant class legislation of the 1830s meant that by the mid to late 1830s largely class-based popular critiques of political exclusion and oppression were closely allied to those of economic and social exploitation. In addition, the open hostility, indeed contempt, displayed by increasing numbers of the middle class, as well as of the traditional elite, towards the culture of working people – seen as 'animalistic', 'without culture', 'wild', 'too easily predisposed towards riot and subversion', and 'wrongheaded' and in need of 'due correction' in relation to the natural laws and truths of the workings of the market and political economy – compounded feelings of class separation, antagonism and cultural apartheid.[28] The turn to independent, class-based Chartism represented workers' active response to these interlocking economic, social, political and cultural crises.

As argued further by Hall, the third quarter of the nineteenth century saw a substantial easing, as opposed to complete resolution, of these points of crisis. The massive development of overseas markets and of the capital goods industries provided a much more secure, stable and broadly based platform for sustained economic growth than had earlier been the case. Along with their growing political and social power (especially at the urban level[29]) and the triumph of the political economy of free trade, the material fortunes of the middle classes showed substantial improvement. Pressures upon capital accumulation slackened considerably, especially among the wealthier and better-established employers. Attitudes towards the strict application of the principles of *laissez-faire* and economy could, albeit unevenly, be softened somewhat. Employers became more accepting of the benefits of factory regulation and even of hated trade unionism (if for pragmatic rather than ideological reasons), far more widely disposed towards the adoption of paternalistic practices at work and in the community, and more intent upon presenting themselves less as ruthlessly cost-efficient capitalists, whose actions and attitudes were inexorably driven by impersonal economic laws, than as caring and responsible private and public figures, sensitive to the moral and spiritual as well as material needs of 'their' workers and communities.[30] Notwithstanding continued middle (and indeed working) class concern to watch the purse strings, the mid-Victorian years also witnessed the far more extensive involvement of the 'middling sort of people' in schemes for civic improvement and reform (the provision of libraries, parks, museums and town halls and growing concern with improvements in educational provision and public health).[31] Sections of the mid-Victorian middle class also made far more positive, sensitive and extensive efforts than in the past to hold out the hand of reconciliation and friendship to the respectable within the working class and to invite them to share in their improving and civilising mission – to march in the van of progress. Former Chartist outsiders, externally perceived to be lacking in culture and 'sound reason', were being discursively and experientially transformed into very pillars of mid-Victorian morality and stability. Finally, we can observe greatly diminished middle class fears of economic stagnation (the dreaded 'stationary state') and/ or collapse and chronic social instability and turmoil. Confidence in the future of industrial capitalism and the socially soothing and integrating effects of sustained economic growth had grown apace since the hungry '40s.

As originally claimed by John Foster in his book *Class Struggle and the Industrial Revolution* in 1974, the softening of middle-class attitudes and behaviour, outlined above, was indicative of a wider process of liberalisation at work in the state and upper echelons of society in the post-Chartist period.[32] The extent, pace, practice and effects of liberalisation should not be exaggerated. For example, as John Saville, Dorothy Thompson and other historians have argued, the case in favour of the centrality of the liberalisation of the state to the decline of Chartism in the 1840s (a view associated most closely with Gareth Stedman Jones) has tended to be asserted rather than conclusively demonstrated. Coercion remained a central feature of state policy towards popular unrest during the 1840s, and concrete improvements in, for example, public health and educational provision and in relations between masters and men frequently failed to match mid-Victorian discursive constructions and expectations of progress, success and harmony.[33]

However, if in all probability more uneven in its character and more limited in some its effects (especially upon 1840s Chartism) than suggested by Stedman Jones and Foster, the very notion of liberalisation does merit continued use by historians. The threats and fears raised by revolutionary sentiments in Ireland and Europe and, especially, by Chartism at home – the latter as revealing the extent and profundity of popular discontent and the dangerously exposed position of property in an increasingly proletarian country – combined with the growing respectability of seemingly larger sections of the working class, induced a more widespread feeling among the propertied classes that wealth carried with it duties as well as rights, and that more must be done to accommodate the interests and satisfy the needs of the people. For example, while necessary amounts of force were used to defeat the Chartist and wider insurgencies of 1839, 1842 and 1848, and while coercion remained at the centre of state strategies to deal with popular unrest beyond mainland Britain, nevertheless there were, as argued by Stedman Jones and Foster, important instances from the 1840s onwards of movements away from the blatant class legislation of the 1830s towards far more accommodating and conciliatory examples of state practice. The unexpected decision not to mount a show trial at Lancaster in 1843, in the wake of the Plug Plot riots of 1842, and the leniency shown to O'Connor and the other defendants provided early evidence of a possible softening of thought and practice on the part of a section of the establishment. Peel's reduction of taxes on consumption, the Mines Act of 1842, the Ten Hours Act of 1847, the legal protection and official recognition afforded by the state towards the collective institutions of labour from the 1850s to the 1870s, and the Second Reform Act of 1867 provided full confirmation that an official change of heart had indeed taken place.[34] As noted by Hobsbawm, by the 1870s organised labour was 'enmeshed in the web of conciliation and collaboration' with the state to a much greater extent and much sooner than in many European countries or the United States.[35] And growing recognition by, and involvement with, the state machinery provided a major spur to the mid-Victorian labour movement's increasing reformism. Similarly, as we shall see in Chapter 4, both of the established political parties made greatly accelerated attempts from the 1840s onwards to root themselves in working-class communities and to develop their popular bases of support.

The stabilisation and expansion of the economy had undoubtedly provided greater scope for manoeuvre on the part of, and for concessions and accommodations to be made by, Britain's rulers towards the people. However, economic factors in themselves did not constitute a sufficient guarantee of softened practice. In order fully to understand the motivations underlying, and the nature of, liberalisation we must accordingly attend in ensuing chapters to political, ideological and cultural influences and their interaction with the economic.

Liberalisation was crucially accompanied by significant changes in workers' lives. As I suggested in my book *The Growth of Working Class Reformism in Mid-Victorian England,*

> Changes 'from above' were, however, of extremely limited effect unless accompanied by developments in working-class 'experience' which promoted moderation and reformism. Indeed, it can plausibly be argued that concessions 'from above' often came about more *as a response* to the new-found 'moderation and restraint' of the working class rather than as the direct consequence of working-class militancy and struggle.[36]

As will already be evident from this chapter, to provide a satisfactory explanation of the key developments and changes in working-class experience we must extend our focus beyond narrow concentration upon the labour aristocracy. It is true that moderate skilled and craft workers did increasingly mould the character and outlook of mid-Victorian labour; and that those among the beleaguered 'artisans and others' who managed to survive the depredations of capitalist tranformation of the workplace during the second quarter of the century, such as cotton spinners and some of the London trades, found themselves in a more secure, stable and often prosperous economic environment during the third quarter. The spinners, for example, re-established much of their former control and bargaining strength at the workplace; and, as observed by Marriott, the greatly slackened nature of capitalist transformation among London's trades and the tenacity and success with which groups of craft and skilled workers fought to re-establish and consolidate their workplace influence accounted, in part, for the decline of Chartist influence in the metropolis.[37] However, the labour aristocratic factor must be set within a wider explanatory framework. For example, the serious decline of outworking groups, such as hand-loom weavers, which had provided much of the radical and even revolutionary impetus behind Chartism, combined with the more solid and routinised character of the economic and social systems and more widespread and necessary worker accommodation to the structures and rhythms of daily life under capitalism, constituted factors of manifest importance. And, as I suggested further in *The Growth of Working Class Reformism,*

> the defeats suffered by Chartism in 1848 and the falling away of mass support; the successes increasingly attendant upon other forms of organised working-class endeavour; the substantial improvements in the material conditions and status of labour leaders, and the less substantial, but nevertheless real and 'felt' material gains made by the mass of operatives ... within a generally dynamic economy – were of major importance in initiating and/or reinforcing the drift into reformism and in convincing workers of the new-found viability of the capitalist system ... Finally ethnic and cultural divisions within the post-1850 working class worked against attempts to build labour solidarity and the appeal of independent working-class politics. By the late 1860s the majority of 'respectable' labour leaders had moved into Liberalism; and Conservatism had developed a mass base around the issue of 'No Popery'.[38]

It is to an elaboration and discussion of the issues raised in the first part of the above quotation – of questions concerning defeat, failure, and collective and individual gains and successes; and the ways in which these experiences both shaped and were influenced by inherited and newly constructed values, norms and ideologies – that we will proceed in Chapter 3.

Notes

1 The most recent discussion of these areas is to be found in M. Hewitt, *The Emergence of Stability in the Industrial City: Manchester 1832–67* (Aldershot, 1996), especially the introduction, chapter 7 and the conclusion. Hewitt presents the novel and interesting thesis that workers retained much of their class-based radicalism *throughout* the period from 1832 to 1867, but that there occurred, during the post-Chartist years, important changes in the tactics and strategies employed to achieve enduring goals. Hewitt's book appeared too recently to be considered in this chapter. I would, however, suggest that Hewitt underestimates the extent of changes in working-class radicalism during the mid-Victorian period, as manifested in the languages and actions of trade unionists, co-operators, radicals and working-class 'respectables'.

2 *Ibid.*, introduction; N. Kirk, *The Growth of Working-Class Reformism in Mid-Victorian England* (Beckenham, 1985), chapter 1.

3 S. and B. Webb, *The History of Trade Unionism* (New York, 1920 edition), chapters 3 and 4; R. Harrison, *Before the Socialists: Studies in Labour and Politics 1861–1881* (London, 1965), chapter 1; E.J. Hobsbawm, 'The Labour Aristocracy in Nineteenth-century Britain' and 'Trends in the British Labour Movement since 1850', in his *Labouring Men: Studies in the History of Labour* (London, 1964).

4 Kirk, *Reformism*, chapter 6.

5 A.E. Musson, 'Class Struggle and the Labour Aristocracy, 1830–1860', *Social History*, 3 (1976) 335–56; K. Tiller, 'Late Chartism: Halifax 1847–58', in J. Epstein and D. Thompson (eds), *The Chartist Experience: Studies in Working-class Radicalism and Culture 1830–1860* (London, 1982), pp. 311–44; A.D. Taylor, 'Modes of Political Expression and Working-class Radicalism, 1848–74: The London and Manchester Examples' (Ph.D. thesis, University of Manchester, 1992); P.A. Pickering, *Chartism and the Chartists in Manchester and Salford* (London, 1995).

6 A.E. Musson, *British Trade Unions 1800–1875* (London, 1972); A.E. Musson, *Trade Union and Social History* (London, 1974); Hewitt, *Emergence of Stability*, introduction and chapter 7.

7 T. Lummis, *The Labour Aristocracy 1851–1914* (Aldershot, 1994), introduction, chapter 1 and conclusion; Kirk, *Reformism*, pp. 4–11.

8 Kirk, *Reformism*, pp. 2–3.

9 J. Epstein, 'National Chartist Leadership: Some Perspectives', in O. Ashton, R. Fyson and S. Roberts (eds), *The Duty of Discontent: Essays for Dorothy Thompson* (London, 1995), p. 37.

10 Kirk, *Reformism*, pp. 156

11 Hewitt, *Emergence of Stability*, p. 245; Pickering, *Chartism and the Chartists*, chapter 3; R. Sykes, 'Early Chartism and Trade Unionism in South-east Lancashire', in Epstein and Thompson, *Chartist Experience*, pp 152–93; G.S. Jones, 'The Language of Chartism', in *ibid.*, especially pp. 39–52; Kirk, *Reformism*, pp. 57–8.

12 Kirk, *Reformism*, chapter 6.

13 R.Q. Gray, *The Aristocracy of Labour in Nineteenth-century Britain c. 1850–1914* (London, 1981).

14 P. Gurney, 'Heads, Hands and the Co-operative Utopia: An Essay in Historiography', *North West Labour History*, 19 (1994–95) 3–23; J.K. Walton, 'Co-operation in Lancashire, 1844–1914', in *ibid.* 115–25; P. Gurney, *Co-operative Culture and the Politics of Consumption in England 1870–1930* (Manchester, 1996).

15 J. Cole, *Conflict and Cooperation: Rochdale and the Pioneering Spirit 1790–1844* (Littleborough, 1994), p. 45.

16 P.H.J.H. Gosden, *The Friendly Societies in England 1815–1875* (Manchester, 1961); D. Neave, *Mutual Aid in the Victorian Countryside: Friendly Societies in the Rural East Riding 1830–1914* (Hull, 1991).

17   Kirk, *Reformism*, p. 160.

18   Kirk, *Labour and Society in Britain and the USA*, I, *Capitalism, Custom and Protest 1780–1850* (Aldershot, 1994), pp. 169–75.

19   Kirk, *Reformism*, chapter 5.

20   M. Savage, *The Dynamics of Working Class Politics: The Labour Movement in Preston 1880–1914* (Cambridge, 1987); Lummis, *Labour Aristocracy*, chapter 2.

21   For balanced approaches see P. Bailey, ' "Will the real Bill Banks please stand up?" Towards a Role Analysis of mid-Victorian Working-class Respectability', *Journal of Social History*, 12 (1978–79) 336–65; G. Crossick, 'The Labour Aristocracy and its Values: A Study of mid-Victorian Kentish London', *Victorian Studies*, 19:3 (1976) 301–28.

22   W. Seccombe, 'Patriarchy Stabilized: The Construction of the Male Breadwinner Norm in Nineteenth-century Britain', *Social History*, 21 (1986) 53–76.

23   Kirk, *Reformism*, pp. 226–9; Hewitt, *Emergence of Stability*, pp. 195–205.

24   Q. Hoare and G.N. Smith (eds), *Selections from the Prison Notebooks of Antonio Gramsci* (London, 1971), pp. 12–13, 59–61, 104–6, 206–8, 323–33.

25   Kirk, *Reformism*, pp. 157, 167.

26   R.G. Hall, 'Work, Class and Politics in Ashton-under-Lyne 1830–1860' (Ph.D. thesis, Vanderbilt University, 1991), especially chapter 3.

27   *Ibid.*, pp. 59–60; Kirk, *Capitalism*, pp. 38–78; P.F. Taylor, *Popular Politics in Early Industrial Britain: Bolton 1825–1850* (Keele, 1995), chapter 5.

28   D. Thompson, *The Chartists: Popular Politics in the Industrial Revolution* (Aldershot, 1986).

29   See, for example, Taylor, *Popular Politics*, chapters 3 and 4; S. Gunn, 'The "Failure" of the Victorian Middle Class: A Critique', in J. Wolff and J. Seed (eds), *The Culture of Capital: Art Power and the Nineteenth-century Middle Class* (Manchester, 1988); R.J. Morris (ed.), *Class, Power and Social Structure in British Nineteenth-century Towns* (Leicester, 1986); T. Koditschek, *Class Formation and Urban Industrial Society: Bradford 1750–1850* (Cambridge, 1990); J.A. Garrard, *Leadership and Authority in Victorian Towns 1830–1880* (Manchester, 1983).

30   Taylor, *Popular Politics*, chapter 6; Kirk, *Reformism*, pp. 291–300; P. Joyce, *Work, Society and Politics: The Culture of the Factory in Later Victorian England* (Brighton, 1980), chapter 4.

31   See, for example, Hall, 'Work, Class and Politics', chapter 7; Hewitt, *Emergence of Stability*, chapter 9; Koditschek, *Class Formation*, chapter 18; Kirk, *Capitalism*, pp. 184–91.

32   J. Foster, *Class Struggle and the Industrial Revolution: Early Industrial Capitalism in Three English Towns* (London, 1974).

33 J. Saville, *1848: The British State and the Chartist Movement* (Cambridge, 1987).

34 G.S. Jones, 'Rethinking Chartism', in his *Languages of Class* (Cambridge, 1983), pp. 175–8.

35 Hobsbawm, *Labouring Men*, p. 336.

36 Kirk, *Reformism*, p. 25.

37 J.W. Marriott, 'London over the Border: A Study of West Ham during Rapid Growth 1840–1910' (D.Phil., University of Cambridge, 1984).

38 Kirk, *Reformism*, p. 25.

3

Material changes
and Victorian values

In his celebrated article 'The Peculiarities of the English', published in 1965, E.P. Thompson declared that the workers, 'having failed to overthrow capitalist society', proceeded, from the mid-1840s onwards, 'to warren it from end to end'. For it was during the years from the 1840s to the 1870s that 'the characteristic class institutions of the Labour Movement were built up – trade unions, trades councils, T.U.C., co-ops, and the rest – which have endured to this day'. Furthermore, these institutions and the fortunes of their leaders and members developed within the context of an increasingly stable, prosperous and dynamic industrial capitalist economy. Capitalism no longer appeared to most contemporaries as an unnatural phenomenon, as prone to severe instability and on the possible verge of collapse: rather the 'system' had become a hard and seemingly permanent fact of life, as something to be lived with, negotiated, and variously warrened, accepted or changed rather than simply by-passed (as in the schemes of Robert Owen) and/or ignored. The very existence and future development of labour's institutions were thus becoming intimately bound up with the continued viability of industrial capitalism. As Thompson continued,

> It was part of the logic of this new direction that each advance within the framework of capitalism simultaneously involved the working class far more deeply in the *status quo*. As they improved their position by organization within the workshop, so they became more reluctant to engage in quixotic outbreaks which might jeopardize gains accumulated at such cost. Each assertion of working-

class influence within the bourgeois-democratic state machinery simultaneously involved them as partners (even if antagonistic partners) in the running of the machine. Even the indices of working-class strength – the financial reserves of trade unions and co-ops – were secure only within the custodianship of capitalist stability.[1]

Of equal importance was the growing belief among workers that, unlike the the failures and defeats suffered by visionary movements such as Chartism and Owenism and by the upsurges of mass industrial and political militancy (as in 1842), the more limited, cautious and reformist aims and practices of the mid-Victorian co-ops, trade unions and other institutions of working-class self-help did 'bring evident returns' in terms of enhanced membership, financial and organisational strength, and recognition from and influence within the wider society.

Thompson drew two conclusions from the evidence. First that, if the mid-Victorian labour movement signified a retreat from the wide-ranging class-based appeal and constituency of movements during the Chartist period, nevertheless it also achieved important advances for sections of the working class within the confines of capitalism. Second, that while such advances did not result generally in labour's unmediated adoption of the individualistic and competitive norms, values and practices of deregulated capitalism (Mrs Thatcher's invented system of 'Victorian values'[2]) and total incorporation into the system, they did, along with the strengthened nature of capitalism and the weakened nature of general working-class solidarity, strongly reinforce and further promote the inclination towards piecemeal gradualism. Therein, argued Thompson, lay 'the formation of the extraordinarily deep sociological roots of reformism'. The nature of such sociological roots, combined with the wider material and ideological under-pinnings of reformism, constitute the subject matter of this chapter.

Advances and successes

James Hinton has traced the formation of a mass labour movement in Britain to the period between the 1870s and the First World War.[3] It was, of course, during this period that 'new' unionism and the Labour Party were born, that socialism revived, that trades councils spread rapidly, that syndicalism rose and declined dramatically, and that the membership of the co-operative movement expanded impressively. In comparison, the appeal and independent, class-conscious character of mid-Victorian working-class movements were, on the whole, far more limited. However, as indicated in the introduction to this chapter, solid organisational foundations were laid and advances registered by working-class institutions during the post-Chartist years which have been unduly neglected in much of the historical literature and which provided, in many cases, a secure basis for the more spectacular expansion of the labour movement during the late nineteenth century.

During the 1840s such foundations and advances were often constructed pragmatically, with unremitting endeavour and against great odds, out of the experiences of the defeats suffered by radical movements and the harsh realities of class power. Such experiences routinely involved loss of employment and blacklisting and, for many leaders and activists, imprisonment and/or exile. It is, for example, instructive to note that what was to become possibly the most famous early to mid-Victorian example of successful working-class self-help, the Rochdale Equitable Pioneers' Society of 1844, counted among its immediate formative influences the failures of local Chartist and industrial agitation, combined with employer tyranny and severe unemployment in the weaving industry. Similarly, the development of more cautious and moderate trade unionism from the mid-1840s onwards was, in part, a pragmatic response to the heavy defeats suffered in the strikes of 1842. During and in the wake of the latter workers had been taught that there was indeed a heavy price to pay for militancy, especially failed militancy. Thus Mick Jenkins:

> The scale of repression which followed the strike was probably unmatched in the nineteenth century, and in terms of numbers arrested and imprisoned has no equal until the next general strike of 1926. In the North West alone over 1,500 strikers were brought to trial . . . [4]

And in 1848, as in 1839 and 1842, the state employed calculated and sufficient doses of 'the stick' (albeit alongside increasingly more conciliatory measures) to halt insurgent popular radicalism in its tracks. As John Saville has perceptively remarked, it must be remembered that 1848 was not the first but the third occasion in this decade when the various arms of the state used their repressive mechanisms. The turbulent events of 1839–40, 1842 and 1848 each evoked similar reactions: cool, ruthless calculation . . . What happened in these three main periods of repression was that while some national leaders moved away . . . more important was the elimination of sections of the middle-range leadership; and most of those who suffered prison sentences did not return to the movement.[5]

It was, therefore, far more within this determining context of 'classed' power relations (centrally involving failure and defeat, and increasing divisions and demoralisation) than within the context of a continuous and largely consensual tradition of inter-class radicalism that 1840s and early 1850s Chartists and other radicals pondered their future strategies and realistic options. In the event there occurred a turning away from the threatening mass agitational platform , independence and insurrectionary character of Chartism towards a more realistic and more accommodating pragmatism, to, for example, the attempted achievement of more limited and piecemeal advances *within* the mainstream parties. On a more general level, and while many working-class radicals still wished to achieve the suffrage, political means and solutions increasingly lost their former hegemony in working class movements. Class consciousness did not suddenly expire. But it was often redirected into (and in some instances became more diluted over time within) less overtly political channels, such as co-operation, trade unionism, educational 'improvement' and temperance. For example, at Ashton-under-Lyne, 'perhaps the most radical and Chartist of all the factory towns', a group of workers formed a Bond of Brotherhood and a Truth Seekers' Class in the wake of the Chartist 'rising' of 1848. At nearby Failsworth a Chartist and member of the Failsworth Mechanics' Institution , Ben Brierley, observed that 'On the bursting up of the Chartist movement the branch association . . . threw aside its politics, and the members turned their attention to intellectual pursuits'.[6] At Oldham many Chartists turned to co-operation in 1848. And during the late 1840s numerous Chartist leaders throughout Lancashire and the West Riding of Yorkshire took the pledge. At Halifax, for example, Ben Wilson resolved in 1849 'not to taste of any intoxicating drink or smoke tobacco as long as I lived'.[7] It is to a study of the institutional expressions and fortunes of such 'turns' or new directions that we will now move.

We can usefully begin with a study of *the* success story of the post-Chartist period, the co-operative movement. Co-ops had, of course, existed before the 1840s. But a mixture of poor management, exaggerated ambition, too close an involvement with other movements, the provision of credit, and hostility from shop-keepers, merchants and those in established positions of power and authority had resulted in ephemeral successes and overall failure. While none of the Rochdale Principles of 1844 (democratic control, no credit, open membership, a fixed rate of interest, un-adulterated goods, the 'divi', political and religious neutrality, and support for education) was in itself new, they were combined and put into practical effect in such a way as to bring about a 'genuine turning point' in the history of consumer Co-operation.[8] John Cole informs us that at Rochdale itself the weavers and others (often with Chartist ties) who made up the original Pio-neers did not enjoy instant success:

> the Pioneers initially made slow progress. From . . . 28 members in 1844, the Society grew to 74 members in 1845 with only a further six added to the books in the following year. In 1847 there were 110 registered members, rising to 140 by the end of 1848.

However, by 1860,

> the membership was nearly 3,500, the financial stability of the store was guaranteed and the Pioneers were extending into other fields.[9]

Cole's conclusion, that 'Shops based on the Rochdale Principles proliferated, firstly in neighbouring towns, then throughout the North and nationwide', is incontrovertible. There were many instances of co-operative failure and disappearance, especially during periods of depression, and of uneven development. (In Lancashire itself, observes Walton, co-op growth was particularly marked in the cotton centres with their relatively good supply of well paid, regular work but 'stunted or at least delayed' in the casual and seasonal labour markets of inner Liverpool or Blackpool.[10]) Nevertheless, all writers on the subject agree that the overall picture amounted to one of outstanding progress. For example, the post-Owenite Co-operative Movement experienced rapid growth at mid-century. The success of the Rochdale Pioneers led to widespread imitation, and by 1850 there existed more than 200 co-operative societies run according to the Rochdale principle, the majority being in the north of England. It is difficult to provide precise figures for the pre-1870 years, but one estimate sets the number of consumer co-operatives in England and Wales in 1863 at 100,000 . . . a further sign of the overall vitality of the movement lay in the setting up of the Co-operative Wholesale Society in 1863. In 1867 the *Co-operator* enumerated 560 co-operative societies in England and Wales with a total membership of 173,600, 72 per cent . . . being concentrated in Lancashire and Yorkshire. By the end of 1872 industrial and provident societies in Britain had at least 301,157 members.[11]

Walton and Martin Purvis similarly demonstrate the centrality of the Lancashire cotton towns, along with neighbouring parts of the West Riding of Yorkshire, to the overall expansion of the movement. For example, by 1865 Purvis's 'North West', an amalgam of Lancashire and Cheshire, held just over one-third of the national co-op membership, a figure which would decline only slightly during the remainder of the century (to 28.4 per cent by 1901).[12] Between the early 1870s and the end of the century, 'the period of most rapid expansion', the recorded membership of all co-operative societies mushroomed, according to P.H.J.H. Gosden, from 403,010 in 1874 to 1,681,342 in 1900. By the latter date co-operation had attained truly national and international standing.[13]

Two other features of co-operative development merit our immediate attention. First, under the terms of the Industrial and Provident Societies Acts of 1852 and 1862 co-operative societies were recognised as 'virtually trading friendly societies', having powers of incorporation with limited liability and the power to invest capital in another society. As observed by Gosden, these two acts were crucial landmarks in the development of a legal framework conducive to the successful growth of co-operation. As was the case with friendly and building societies, co-ops were henceforth to have full legal protection in their property against fraud or theft, could sell goods to persons other than their own members, and had the benefit of corporate status (such as the power to hold property) and limited liability for members.

Further legislation in 1867, 1871, 1876 and 1893 generally extended and consolidated the vital gains made in the post-Chartist years. As Gosden concludes, 'The importance of providing a suitable legal framework within which the cooperative societies could operate had thus been fully appreciated by the time the Royal Commission made its inquiries in the early 1870s.'[14]

Second, as practical schools of self-help, industry, thrift and sobriety the co-ops increasingly attracted the attention and approval of prominent national leaders (See document 1) and large sections of the middle class. In Lancashire and Cheshire leaders of mid-century co-ops invariably attributed their collective-institutional and personal successes in the aftermath of Chartism to the cultivation of 'sound' personal habits. Many developed a strong attachment to temperance and education, opposed the 'distasteful' and 'frivolous' habits of the 'pothouse' masses, and were fiercely determined in their independence and 'manly endeavour'. Simultaneously they welcomed (as had the Chartists) genuine offers of friendship and help from the middle classes and saw co-operation (especially in the form of producer co-ops) as constituting the solution to the 'barbaric' and 'archaic' class conflicts of pre-1850 decades. As such, both their own characteristics and those of their self-helping institutions were warmly praised by prominent members of local communities. Co-ops were thus portrayed by many of their middle-class supporters as 'cultivators of the true capitalist values of self-help, competition and enlightened self-interest which served the wider public good'.[15] And growing ties between co-operation and the middle classes (especially the reforming and more progressive sections of the latter) were everywhere evident. At Ashton and Stalybridge, for example, noted, and in polite circles notorious, for their rough-hewn, frontier characteristics of drink, 'robustness' and acute class conflict, prominent employers were very keen in the post-Chartist years to cultivate links with local co-operative societies. Such employers frequently spoke at co-operative functions and praised the respectable, socially soothing and improving endeavours of the members. At the national level, notwithstanding the predominantly working-class character of the membership, middle-class reformers frequently occupied prominent positions within the leadership of the mid to late Victorian co-operative movement.[16]

Improved legislative protection and increased middle-class approval and involvement in the running of the more established societies, such as the Manchester Unity of Oddfellows and the Ancient Order of Foresters, were also prominent features of the mid-Victorian friendly societies. Laws enacted in 1850, 1855 and 1875 provided effective protection and, in the latter case, promoted the more efficient internal management of the societies' affairs and their reliability as insurers. Membership of the friendly societies had expanded rapidly during the 1830s and 1840s. The period between 1848 and the mid-1850s saw sluggish growth, but from the latter point up to the 1870s and beyond there was a further massive increase. 'In 1872,' notes Gosden,

> there were 34 societies described as affiliated orders which had more than 1,000 members each. Their total membership amounted to 1,282,275, of which about two-thirds was represented by the Manchester Unity of Oddfellows (426,663) and the Ancient Order of Foresters (388,872).

However, as Gosden further observes, the Royal Commission concluded in 1874 that, 'there were probably 4,000,000 members of friendly societies and about 8,000,000 persons interested in them as beneficiaries'.[17] In sum, from a numerical point of view the friendly societies constituted the most impressive example of collective self-help among workers, the 1,857,896 members in 1872 being set against 217,128 for trade unions and 300,157 for co-ops.

As implied in the previous sentence, the mid-Victorian trade union movement enjoyed fortunes more mixed than either the co-ops or the friendly societies.[18] Generally speaking, the third quarter of the century belonged to the new model unions in engineering, the building trades, shipbuilding, the metal trades in general and other craft, skilled and overwhelmingly male sectors of the economy. The period also saw the growth of trade unionism (of both the open and the closed membership types) in cotton and coal mining; and during the early to mid-1870s there emerged important, if largely ephemeral, examples of mass unionism in agriculture, the docks and elsewhere. But, as indicated earlier, in trade union terms the third quarter of the century belonged to the 'pukes' (to borrow Royden Harrison's term) who had largely sheltered from the storms of Chartism and mass industrial militancy during the 1830s and 1840s, and who emerged, during the

1860s, as the 'true statesmen' of labour, preaching (if by no means always practising) moderation, class (re) conciliation, and abidance by the rules of supply and demand. Notions of the male breadwinner, female domesticity and natural helplessness and inferiority *vis-à-vis* the male provider came with increasing frequency and ease to the lips of these 'pukes'; as did sectionalism and exclusivity in terms of trade unionism and wider issues of status and social intercourse.[19] Above all, trade unionism and industrial agitation lost much of their wide occupational embrace, their generosity of spirit, the informality and even spontaneity of the pre-1850 years. 'Incremental gradualism', by means of strict attention to organisational efficiency and strength and the pragmatic art of the possible, became the ruling trade union 'common sense'. (See document 2.)

On a far more positive note, it must, however, be remembered that trade unionism did register impressive advances in a climate of public opinion in which the unions, unlike the co-ops and the friendly societies, were frequently seen as wrongheadedly interfering with the rights of capital, the laws of the market and the truths of orthodox political economy. The astute tactical and strategic and public and private use by trade unionists of the discourses of moderation and manly independence, of opposition to militancy and uncivilised and wasteful class discord, and of the central importance of the self-help and friendly society aspects of trade unionism did bring important rewards. For example, following the Hornby *v.* Close decision of 1867, which deprived unions of their imagined legal status, and the 'Sheffield outrages', which saw the employment of terrorism against non-union saw grinders, trade unionists feared the worst from the Royal Commission set up to investigate events at Sheffield and the nature of trade unionism in general. However, as noted by John Belchem, in the event 'the unions emerged in a favourable light', the attention of the commission having being drawn successfully 'away from the violence of the old, local societies to a laudatory examination of the actuarial soundness and friendly society functions of the amalgamated unions'.[20] Indeed, the minority report of the commission served as a basis for the Liberals' Trade Union Act of 1871 which gave the unions 'legal status in law and protection of their funds'. In addition, as observed by Jonathan Spain, trade unions were deemed to be 'exempt from conviction under the law of conspiracy by reason of their merely being in "restraint of trade"'.[21] The confirmation of the legality of peaceful picketing under the terms of the Conservatives' Conspiracy and Protection of Property Act in 1875 (which crucially repealed the anti-picketing clauses of the Criminal Law Amendment Act of 1871) and the abolition, under the terms of the Employers and Work-men Act of 1875, of the unequal standing and treatment of em-ployers and workers (traditionally expressed in the master and servant legislation) further signalled the 'official' acceptance of trade unionism as representing a legitimate interest in the wider polity.

By such means had trade unionists come to enjoy freedoms, rights and immunities which were the envy of their counter-parts in the United States and Europe. The situation has been excellently, if somewhat exaggeratedly, reconstructed by Ross McKibbin in the following manner:

> By 1875 the necessary withdrawal of the state from bargaining was generally complete. The British unions were given a freedom of action unique in Europe and (as far as I know) in the world, unencumbered by law or opinion. In part Disraeli's 1875 legislation (actually, legislation drafted by the preceding Gladstone ministry) was simply an element in that corporate pluralism which was char-acteristic of the Liberal state; but the legislation not so much en-dowed the unions with rights as extended to them an almost archaic corporate immunity. The unions claimed and received the kind of associational privilege previously allowed to many upper- and middle-class institutions . . . Civil society thus promoted its own stability by subverting the coercive powers of employers.[22]

The growth of what McKibbin has termed, again in very percep-tive if somewhat inflated ways, the 'exclusion of the market' (i.e. relations, often of an antagonistic kind, between labour and capital) 'from "politics"' and 'a "politics" that permitted a viable class-neutral state' thus played a crucial part in the trade union movement's increasing enmeshment with and accommodation towards that very state and its foremost progressive representa-tive, the Gladstonian Liberal Party.

By way of contrast, relations with employers were generally more tense. As we shall observe in due course, large numbers of mid-Victorian employers remained extremely reluctant to coun-tenance, let alone recognise and negotiate with, trade unions, however moderate and conciliatory the latter might have become. Employers were above all concerned with the threat posed by trade unions, as third parties, to their right to absolute control within the workplace and over their businesses. Indeed, this control issue was present, directly or indirectly, in many of the high number of industrial conflicts, in both paternalist and non-paternalist enterprises, which characterised the mid-Victorian 'golden years'. On the other hand, we would be entirely wrong to suggest that nothing had changed since the Chartist period. In comparison with the latter, employers were generally far more prepared by the early 1870s, albeit more for pragmatic than ideological reasons, to come to terms with the existence of unions and especially skilled and craft new model unions. Furthermore, there did emerge a minority of 'new model' employers, such as A.J. Mundella, who supported trade union recognition, arbitration and conciliation and welcomed contacts with responsible union leaders. (See document 3.) Perhaps most significantly, overall trade union membership in Britain increased from approximately 250,000 in 1850 to about 500,000 in 1870 and thence to around the 1 million mark during the economic and trade union boom of the early 1870s. The onset of the great depression saw a reversion to the half-million mark by the mid-1870s. Furthermore, the period between the 1850s and the mid-1870s saw the establishment of trades councils in most large towns (to encourage co-ordinated action and mutual support among affiliated trades in a particular locality), and 1868 saw the formation of the TUC, which, by the early 1870s, had established itself as the effective national voice of the trade union movement.[23]

Co-ops, friendly societies and the trade unions constituted the most prominent examples of forms of working-class collective self-help which developed strongly in the mid-Victorian period. As indicated earlier, mutual improvement and temperance societies also flourished, especially in the wake of Chartist failure and defeat in 1848. Furthermore leading figures in these societies were of the unanimous opinion that members' chances of achieving success and advancement had improved markedly from the mid to late 1840s onwards.

It was thus an important feature of the mid-nineteenth-century educational and social landscape that beyond the various educational organisations and initiatives of the middle classes there existed a number of more informal educational endeavours undertaken by workers themselves. (It is also worth reminding ourselves that the tradition of indigenous radical working-class educational effort was well established by the Chartist period.[24]) J.F.C. Harrison informs us that mutual improvement usually involved small groups of workers meeting together to conduct essay readings and discussions. Instruction was given by the members themselves and was intended to promote proficiency in reading, writing and arithmetic. In some cases geography, history, languages and science subjects were also studied. Catering to a wide, if predominantly male, working-class membership (which went well beyond the boundaries of a labour aristocracy, however defined), mutual improvement societies also 'offered a valuable platform on which to practise public speaking'.[25]

That there occurred at mid-century a proliferation of such societies, whether in the cotton district of Lancashire and Cheshire, the woollen district of the West Riding of Yorkshire or in other centres of former Chartist strength, there can be no doubt. In 1849 and 1850, for example, a *Manchester Guardian* correspondent was greatly impressed with the autodidactic activities of manual workers in the Tonge and Royton districts of Lancashire. In the environs of Tonge

> weavers, bricklayers, labourers, silk weavers, foundrymen and others built up libraries, exchanged books and, attired in their Sunday best, gathered at each other's houses at weekends to discuss the great affairs of the day.

In Royton and its vicinity the correspondent was shown

> a temperance society, various book societies, a mutual improvement society, a youth seminary and a Chartist reading room. All these societies were run by manual workers at low rates of subscription.

At the Chartist reading room, 'a cold, comfortless place',

> thirty members met nightly to partake of mutual instruction in reading, writing and arithmetic, and to discuss current political matters. Occasionally the local butcher was hired to teach for a fee of $1\frac{1}{2}$d per week, but more often than not the members were left to

their own limited devices and the aid of an 'Irish scholar' ... a rather tidy-looking Irish tailor ... whiffing his pipe. He was the headmaster, I was given to understand.

The correspondent's conclusions were highly favourable:

> To myself one thing is evident and that is if the working population of this part of the country is not looked after, with a view to ... the acquirement of knowledge ... it will look after itself; nay, it is doing so. Their great cry, in short, is that of the dying Göthe [*sic*], Light! More light! More light![26]

The popular thirst for educational enlightenment extended, of course, beyond Royton and Tonge, to embrace large parts of the country. Equally widespread and worthy of genuine praise were the very real sacrifices made by workers in the attainment of education. The case of Robert Howard, a Lancashire textile worker, who emigrated to the United States, illustrates the sense of struggle and the level of unremitting determination involved. 'From the time when I was very young,' wrote Howard,

> I was fond of reading, and I remember many occasions when I have gone to my supper and taken my daily paper in my hands, and have slept there until about eleven o'clock. Then I have been determined to read it, and have put my lamp beside me when I went to bed, and have gone to sleep again with the paper in my hand, and lain there just as I put myself down, without stirring, until morning, the result of exhaustion.[27]

These notions of earnest endeavour, sacrifice and serious purpose in life – the avoidance, in Ben Brierley's words, of 'The too common frivolities of youth' – were also strongly present among working-class members and supporters of temperance societies. As was the case with education, popular attachment to the cause of temperance grew in importance during the mid-Victorian period, especially among working-class women who managed the purse strings of the family and had a keen eye towards, and a crucial role in the cultivation and maintenance of, its respectable image within the local community.[28] For a large number of workers support for the causes of education and temperance went hand in hand. Both causes conveyed common or similar meanings and messages of self-control, self-respect, dignity, independence, wholesome family life, partial insurance against poverty and abject dependence upon and deference towards one's superiors, the ability to control one's destiny and achieve individual and collective emancipation both as an empowered individual and as a member of wider collectivities of active and enlightened workers and/or people. What is of fundamental significance about such meanings and messages in the post-Chartist period is not the total disappearance of collectivist characteristics and their replacement by purely individualistic or bourgeois motivations, so much as the ways in which they became more privatised and status-conscious in character as a result of the greatly enhanced successes which attended the efforts of working-class practitioners of education and temperance.

The following examples will suffice briefly to illustrate the nature of these successes, as expressed in terms of upward social and occupational mobility and changed values. Reunions of the Ashton-under-Lyne Mutual Improvement Society and Bond of Brotherhood held during the 1850s clearly revealed the marked advances achieved by many members:

> One member, a former bookbinder, enjoyed great success in America in his new-found role of gold digger; the stonemason became an assistant surveyor in an English manufacturing town; one of the self-actor minders attained the position of overseer; and one of the warpers became a 'first-class' photographic artist in Stalybridge.

Education had resulted in improvement more than revolt. The members were keen to encourage the more widespread adoption of similar schemes:

> It is just such an institution as we desire to see working men creating throughout the town and country; for the Bond teaches that industry, supported by habits of frugality and self-denial, with a firm resolution to do what is right, are the grand elements of success in life . . . join your Mutual Bond of Brotherhood society . . . try to create among the people an earnest desire for intellectual improvement.[29]

By the 1860s many of the working men who attended the Royton Temperance Society in the 1840s had grown in status and local prominence. One had become a vicar, and others had risen to become cotton spinners, foremen, managers and schoolmasters. And in numerous other instances cultivation of the habits of self-help, education and temperance was seen as the key to the marked increase in the attainment of municipal office by working men during the mid-Victorian years.[30]

The successes achieved by working-class practitioners of education and temperance must be located within a broader context of greatly accelerated experiential advancement. As Christopher Godfrey has rightly observed, many former Chartist activists and their families suffered sorely from poverty and ill health as a result of the personal sacrifices, imprisonment and blacklisting involved in fighting for the cause.[31] But by the early 1870s protests against immiseration, persecution and outsider status had, at least on the part of male working-class leaders, become very rare. As indicated earlier, the confident, even triumphal, language of success, the achievement of a stake in society, of progress and of improvement had become dominant. Writing in the 1880s, Ben Wilson, veteran Halifax Chartist and co-operator, nicely recaptured this pronounced contrast in working-class fortunes:

> What a change since 1849! If, at the last meeting when we broke up our co-operative society in that year, someone had said that in less than twenty years there would be a co-operative society in Halifax with 6,000 members, a capital of £60,000, and having a turnover of £3,000 per week, there was not one that would have credited it.

Counting Wilson among their number, the former Chartists who held a reunion in Halifax in 1885 drew a marked distinction between their erstwhile poverty – having all been 'poor working men earning low wages' – with their present affluence – many having become 'men of business'.[32] (See document 4.) Similarly, evidence relating to 144 males active in a variety of leadership roles in mid-Victorian working-class organisations in the cotton districts of Lancashire and Cheshire clearly demonstrates the high level of upward occupational, political and social mobility achieved by these men. In addition to the movement of the craft and skilled into the middling ranks of society, the sample reveals the importance of success by means of bureaucratic advancement within labour movement institutions (especially the co-ops) and by the achievement of municipal office as councillors, justices of the peace, poor law guardians, aldermen, mayors or as members of school and hospital boards.[33] At the national level, and notwithstanding the fact that most upward mobility for workers at this time was of a very limited intra-class character, the skilled upper sections of the male working class, those with higher, more secure and more stable earnings, who took special pride in their respect-ability and who were prominent in leadership roles, enjoyed much better prospects or life chances than the non-skilled masses. From a sample of 10,835 marriage registers in ten English districts Andrew Miles has demonstrated that between 1839 and 1854 'An astonishing four-fifths of the sons of skilled working-class men followed in their fathers' footsteps, while seven out of every ten men from the unskilled working class failed to move out of it.[34] In so doing Miles has added specific strength to Hobsbawm's general observation that

> It is quite probable that, relatively speaking, the position of the skilled British artisan has never been higher than in the 1860s, nor his standard of living and access to education, culture and travel (by contemporary standards) so satisfactory, nor the gap between him and the small local manufacturers who employed him so narrow, nor that between him and the mass of 'labour' so wide.[35]

Finally, while mid-Victorian improvements in living standards for the mass of workers were relatively modest up to the 1860s, they were undoubtedly more substantial for those more regularly employed operatives and the labour-aristocratic skilled and craft workers who dominated the leadership positions and constituted much of the membership of the co-ops, trade unions and friendly, temperance and mutual improvement societies.[36]

The institutional and individual successes outlined above con-stituted the main sociological and economic roots of reformism. (The sources of working-class political and cultural accommoda-tion are explored in Chapters 4 and 5.) They also strongly under-pinned labour's new-found rhetoric of delight and satisfaction with its post-Chartist achievements, its growing moderation and its heightened, indeed 'Whiggish', confidence in its future. Such rhetoric was most marked in relation to the co-operative move-ment.[37] For example, in 1869 Ernest Jones, former independent-minded Chartist and a Liberal candidate for Manchester in the 1868 parliamentary elections, observed, in curiously modern, New Labour fashion, that co-operative successes had enabled members to become 'independent men, having a stake in the country as well as the richest lord who lives in the land'. The *Co-operator*, the official organ of the movement, maintained in 1861 that co-operation had resulted in 'thousands of men' enjoying that 'independence and contentedness of mind which is the happiest state the natural man can feel, having plenty of clothes and food, and something to spare for the needy', and that 'there is probably no country on the face of the globe where sober, industrious young men can so soon raise themselves to ease . . . and comfort, as in England'. Five years later J.C. Edwards, a leading co-operator, anticipated, with uncanny accuracy, massively extended influence for the movement:

> Co-operators are no longer poverty-stricken labourers, but creators of wealth and power, which will make itself felt and enable us to exercise our influence not only in the affairs of our own country, but perhaps in the affairs of the entire world.

Significantly, at the heart of co-operation's mid-century language of success and progress was an aversion to social levelling:

> Co-operation aimed to prosper, 'not by pulling down the rich – excepting those who are rich with ill-gotten gains – but by lifting up the poor'.

Official handbooks of the movement set great store by the fact that co-operators sought not to

> set class against class, but rather to build up and promote that sympathy and friendship, which is of such vital importance to the national welfare.

Workers were accordingly exhorted to rise without infringing the property rights of others.[38]

The marked linguistic contrast with the popular despair, dissatisfaction and outrage of the Chartist period was also much in evidence among mid-Victorian leaders of friendly societies and trade unions. For example, in keeping with their improved and solidly respectable standing and image, leaders of the friendly societies were keen to promote patriotism, of an increasingly 'loyal' kind, among their members. Thus:

> The Oddfellows . . . exhorted their members to join the Volunteer Force . . . [and] contributed generously to the Patriotic Fund in 1854 . . . in 1863 various lodges of the order celebrated the marriage

of the Prince of Wales. In Manchester meetings were often addressed by prominent volunteers, and the national anthem was sung with great gusto . . . The Foresters boasted of their loyalty to the throne, and counselled their members to be patriotic and peaceful citizens.[39]

Notwithstanding instances to the contrary, trade union leaders also looked back on the post-Chartist years with a good deal of satisfaction. The cultivation of an active practice of union impartiality, and of opposition to employer and worker excesses and hostilities, had helped to generate more of a family spirit in the workplace. This spirit had in turn been fed by a minority of enlightened employers, as manifested in their more widespread paternalism and union recognition. As a result employers were generally far less likely than in the pre-1850 decades to treat workers and their unions with supercilious contempt and to 'pitch their memorials into the fire'.[40]

However welcome and richly deserved, success did not, however, bestow unmixed blessings upon labouring men. It is perhaps in the very nature of successful self-helpers (whether of the collective or of the individual kind) within capitalism that they tend to equate failure, and especially failure in material terms, with character defects, and especially with 'a want of initiative, enterprise and endeavour', with a lack of self-help. In the mid-Victorian period successful co-operators and others by no means entirely lost sight of the structural causes of poverty and inequality. After all, many of them had subscribed fully to Chartism's systemic view of poverty. But success, by means of self-help, undeniably led to a loosening of class-based loyalties and understanding. As we shall see in some detail in Chapter 5, those 'steady respectables' involved in the labour movement did, to a much greater extent than during the 1830s and 1840s, come to view the poor, such as seasonal and irregular workers and many of the post-Famine immigrant Irish Catholics, as 'rough', as lacking in 'ideas', as 'vacant', as besotted by drink and, *ipso facto*, in dire need of a self-helping personality transplant. The *Co-operator* expressed this changed focus in the following way:

> The poverty of the great masses is not the result of want of means, of opportunties, or of laws excluding them from the attainment of wealth. Their poverty is a poverty of ideas in the first place. Ill

furnished minds and badly trained faculties can no more produce thrift and comfort than an undrained marshy wilderness. They have sunk where they are not because anybody oppresses them . . . but because they have no powers of self-guidance as motive powers within them, except those which children, savages and lower animals posssess.[41]

Limitations and qualifications

The underpinnings and growth of working-class reformism in the post-Chartist years have so far been presented as relatively straightforward, one-dimensional and linear processes. Indeed, the reader may be tempted at this stage to regard mid-Victorian co-operators, trade unionists and others as (albeit collective as well as individual) practitioners of the Thatcherite version of Victorian values – struggling with might and main against adverse circumstances, 'pulling themselves up by their own bootstraps', exuding smug satisfaction at their self-help achievements, insensitively exhorting the less fortunate to follow their lead, and finding a relatively secure and recognised niche in the market place. While there is some truth in this characterisation, matters as a whole and Victorian values in particular were far less simple and one-dimensional. It is now incumbent upon us to introduce the necessary limitations and qualifications into our narrative in order to bring us more closely into line with the overall historical record.

We must observe, in the first instance, that mid-Victorian co-ops, trade unions, friendly and mutual improvement societies and other collective working-class means of advancement, accommodation and success enjoyed only limited presence and appeal among the working class. As noted earlier, friendly societies were genuinely mass organisations, appealing to a broad cross-section of workers, skilled and non-skilled, urban and rural. But even in this case there existed important limitations and boundaries. There were clearly observable gradations in status and financial stability. Gosden demonstrates that the more prestigious affiliated orders, such as the Oddfellows and Foresters, were particularly popular among the better-paid workers.[42] And before the last quarter of the century the affiliated orders were much stronger in the urban than in the rural areas. As Alun Howkins has shown, many local rural societies or 'village clubs' were in fact founded not by workers themselves but by paternalistic members of the clergy (supported by equally paternalistic farmers and members of the gentry) to promote 'industry and morality' among the labouring people.[43] Furthermore, despite the existence of female Foresters, female Oddfellows and female Rechabites, most working-class women were not members of friendly societies. The growing popularity in working-class circles of notions of the male breadwinner and of female dependence further reinforced the idea that a woman's true place was in the home rather than at work. As such, the wives and daughters of skilled and/or regularly employed males benefited indirectly rather than directly from the partial insurance against sickness and unemployment provided by friendly society membership. However, much of the (extremely limited and patchy) evidence so far unearthed by historians of this period concerning working-class women's own 'actions, motivations and psychology' would suggest that, notwithstanding their generally outsider or inferior status, many working-class women identified more with the mutualistic concerns of their families and communities and female and male members of their class than with purely individualistic or cross-class feminist perspectives.[44]

As the main providers and purchasers of family needs, working-class women – and especially wives of the more regularly employed males – were far more active as members of consumer co-ops run along Rochdale lines. Recent research has demonstrated that the co-operative movement in general appealed to a relatively large group of workers who defined themselves as sober and respectable, rather than to a clearly demarcated labour aristocracy comprising the top 10-15 per cent of the working class.[45] Although respectability is a notoriously slippery concept, evading totally objective, unchanging and uniform definitions ('roughness' and 'respectability' were cultural constructs rooted in specific and changing chronologies and contexts and were centrally informed by the perceptions and habits of class, gender and ethnicity), and although there existed no absolute correlation between respectability and income or type of employment, nevertheless we can suggest that in the mid-Victorian years co-operators increasingly associated respectability with the more successful and regular workers and lack of respectability with failure, irregularity and the poor. Within this context Walton's observation is most apposite:

> Where co-op membership records have been examined locally, we find a mid-Victorian preponderance of skilled or otherwise relatively well-paid male workers in regular employment, along with substantial numbers of women whose social status is harder to establish.[46]

Certainly craft and skilled males and factory operatives were prominent as co-operative society leaders; and the 'no credit' rule, although relaxed informally in some communities, acted as a strong deterrent to the widespread involvement of the poor in co-operation. It was, furthermore, undoubtedly in areas of relatively regular and secure employment – in, for example, the cotton and woollen textile factory districts of Lancashire and Yorkshire, rather than in centres of casual and unpredictable work, such as parts of Liverpool and London – that mid-Victorian co-operation made its greatest gains. But of equal, if not greater, significance was the fact that the majority of co-op leaders had experienced acute, and in some cases chronic, poverty and insecurity during their lives (especially as children and young people), had often started work in distinctly non-labour-aristocratic occupations, had fought incessantly, by individual and collective means, to improve their lot, and 'had eagerly grasped those opportunities for personal and collective improvement which had been in marked evidence from the mid to late 1840s onwards'.[47] In sum, the concept of the labour aristocracy is too narrow and constricting adequately and accurately to represent the experience of our respectable co-operators. It should also be noted that much the same conclusion can be applied to the experience and values of working-class practictioners of temperance and educational improvement.[48]

Trade unionism in the post-Chartist period undoubtedly constituted far more of a minority, labour-aristocratic experience than that of the friendly societies or the co-ops. In 1850 the unions embraced only 250,000 out of a total working-class population of approximately 16.2 million: by 1870 the corresponding figures were 500,000 and 20.3 million. Throughout these years major occupational and social groups and sectors of the economy remained entirely devoid of or barely touched by trade unionism.[49]

For example, domestic and personal services employed 1.3 million, or 13 per cent of the occupied population in 1851, domestic service being the largest single employer of working-class women; but the almost total control exercised by employing families and their dependants over servants' lives, the often isolated and fragmented nature of the work situation, and the powerful conditioning factors of paternalism, deference and expectations, indeed frequently formal requirements, of proven 'ladylike' behaviour and attitudes on the part of aspiring servants effectively precluded the growth of formal trade unionism, if not informal bargaining and even reolotance on the part of ouch workers. Up to the 'revolt of the field' in the 1870s, which saw the successful, if ephemeral, organisation of 150,000 workers, mid-Victorian agriculture was likewise a generally unpropitious area for trade union growth. And we must remind ourselves of the important fact that 2.1 million people, or 22 per cent of the total work force, were employed in agriculture, forestry and fishing in 1851.

Manufacturing, mining and quarrying accounted for 37.1 per cent of the work force, or 3.6 million workers, in 1851. It was in these sectors that mid-century trade unionism would take strongest root – among a range of traditional skilled and craft workers in printing, bookbinding and the like, in cotton and coal, and among generally newer groups in engineering, shipbuilding, boilermaking and the metal trades in general. But even within these sectors there existed all manner of limitations and boundaries. In cotton and coal, for example, progress was far from easy and uniform. Those 'contrived aristocrats' (to employ Joseph White's apt phrase), the spinners, did recover from the serious financial and control setbacks of the 1830s and 1840s to recoup much of, and indeed strongly to enhance, their earning capacity, their workplace controls and their trade union bargaining powers by the early 1870s. However, in the face of mixtures of stiff, if uneven, employer opposition, competitive product markets, localised labour markets and divisions within the labour force trade union advances in weaving during the third quarter of the century were far more patchy. And in the card room, where low earnings and the absence of a craft tradition of organisation were most marked, trade unionism was generally weak and ephemeral. In truth the permanent mass organisation of cotton would await the amalgamations of the 1880s.[50] Similarly, coal mining's traditional reputation for strong trade unionism was a product far more of late nineteenth and early twentieth-century developments than of events which took place during the mid-Victorian years. There were attempts at organisation during the latter period. But divisions within the work force, the fragmentation of the industry, employer hostility, highly differentiated market conditions across and even within coalfields, and the dominance of the unions by the sectional and exclusive hewers all combined to produce those 'sudden upheavals and violent collapses' characteristic of mid-Victorian mining trade unionism.[51]

Within those industries, such as engineering and the building trades, in which the principles of new model trade unionism were most pronounced, and in established areas of craft organisation and control, such as printing, we must nevertheless be careful not to exaggerate the extent or the influence of trade unionism. The widespread and determined insistence of employers upon their right to manage and active opposition to 'excessive' craft privileges and controls; the labour market insecurities and competition which, as Trevor Lummis has reminded us, undoubtedly affected even the most skilled and supposedly aristocratic workers; and adverse technological effects upon worker skills and controls – all these factors placed serious limits upon trade union strength.[52] Furthermore, the very aristocratic attitudes of skilled workers in these industries meant that they had little or no inclination to include within their own organisations, or extend the principles of trade unionism to, the mass of non-skilled labour.

In such ways was mid-Victorian trade unionism concentrated mainly among craft and skilled males. The non-skilled, such as women jute workers and cotton weavers and Irish Catholic immigrants in cotton weaving and the building industry, did undoubtedly demonstrate a strong capacity for collective organisation and, where necessary, strike action – action which negates stereotypes of immigrant and female docility, submission and subordination.[53] But, as seen most clearly in cotton weaving, even in the 'mixed' occupations and unions, with a large (native-born) female and (predominantly female) immigrant component, men occupied overwhelmingly the positions of power and authority. In such ways did gender, patriarchy and ethnicity, as well as place in the labour market and the possession of skill, fundamentally inform the minority character of mid-Victorian trade unionism.

The social appeal of the institutions of working-class self-help thus extended well beyond the boundaries of a labour aristocracy and generally failed substantially to embrace the vast number of poorer, less regularly employed and less respectable workers. In similar ways, the benefits of greatly improved living standards, of upward social mobility and of success and advancement in general were far from uniformly bestowed and equally distributed. It is true that the third quarter of the century as a whole did see an advance in average real wages in the United Kingdom of approximately 36 per cent. But against this advance we must set a number of serious qualifications. First, real wages rose by only 5 per cent during the whole of the 1850s, and for the first eight years of that decade were actually below the 1850 level – effectively invalidating the claim that Chartism's decline from the late 1840s to the early 1850s can be attributed wholly or mainly to significant mass improvement. Second, the most substantial increase, of 28 per cent, took place very belatedly between 1863 and 1874.[54] Third, as shown by a number of recent studies and by the contemporary social investigations of Henry Mayhew in London and Hugh Shimmin in Liverpool, poverty and insecurity remained basic facts of life for the vast majority of labouring people. The unemployed and those in casual and seasonal work were hit hardest. And, as brilliantly demonstrated by Stedman Jones's study, *Outcast London*, there prevailed strong middle-class fears concerning the presence and potentially unchecked growth and 'contaminating' and 'degrading' effects upon respectable society of the chronic poor, or residuum.[55] But, as with respectability and roughness, there was a very thin dividing line between the states of sufficiency and poverty which many working-class people continually straddled or periodically traversed in their lifetime. Want and insecurity were accordingly by no means strangers to the families of respectable, regular and self-helping 'Rochdale man' and many supposedly aristocratic, if frequently insecure, workers.[56] Extremely poor environmental conditions also continued to blight the daily lives of the vast majority of workers during the 'golden years'.

Finally, in marked contrast to the high incidence of upward

social mobility enjoyed by our selected craft and skilled labour leaders, the great majority of the sons of the unskilled would follow in their fathers' occupational footsteps. However, as Savage and Miles have observed, differential intra-class patterns of mobility, revolving crucially around the axis of skill, must be set within what was in many ways the more significant context of the overwhelming presence and determining structural influence of class within the wider society. Thus between 1839 and 1914 nine out of every ten men in Miles's sample of almost 11,000 English marriage registers 'who were in a working-class occupation at the time of their marriage were themselves the sons of working-class men'. And, while working-class women were 'more likely to move to a different social class by marrying a husband of a different social standing than were men who relied on moving into a different type of job', nevertheless, 'prior to 1914 . . . the English working class was a very stable and mature structural entity. Its members' horizons, whether they looked backwards or forwards, were severely restricted.'[57]

Structural and ideological obstacles to unqualified notions of success, consensus and class harmony were not confined to the area of social structure. At the workplace, for example, the 'moral discourse' of desired harmony and reciprocity between employers and workers, and of the 'evils' of strikes and lock-outs, was often severely strained and periodically dissolved in the face of the harsh realities of economic division and conflict. (See document 5.) For example, and taking into account the emergence of a 'new-found spirit' on the part of increasingly paternalist employers and conciliatory union leaders, the cotton industry experienced persistent, and at times (in 1853–54, 1861, 1867 and 1869) extremely bitter and acute unrest throughout the mid-Victorian period. Most employers in cotton, paternalist and non-paternalist alike, remained adamant in their ideological opposition to unions, and especially non-skilled unionism in weaving and the cardroom. For their part, workers were determined, 'reasonably' if at times 'forcefully', to keep employers to their side of the moral-economic bargain. In 1853, for example, the operatives 'politely' and 'respectfully' requested the masters to honour their pledge, given at the time of a 10 per cent reduction in wages during the depression of 1847, to restore the cuts once prosperity returned to the industry. Notwithstanding buoyant trading conditions, the employers declined the request and so triggered off a wave of 'ten per cent' agitations throughout Lancashire and Cheshire which climaxed in the extremely bitter twenty-eight weeks' Preston lock-out of 1853–44. The lock-out, involving the importation of 'knobsticks', ended in defeat for workers in Preston and cuts in cotton operatives' wages throughout the cotton districts.

It is highly significant that during the struggles of 1853–54 'reasonable' and 'moderate' cotton operatives widely regarded the employers' action as totally unreasonable, and jettisoned words of harmony and reconciliation in favour of language of conflict reminiscent of that adopted by 'physical force' Chartists and the militant Plug Plot strikers of 1842. Thus the Preston masters were commonly seen as 'greedy tyrants', 'hypocrites', 'inhuman monsters', 'the most oppressive ... in the county'. According to Mortimer Grimshaw, one of the operatives' leaders, the *Manchester Guardian* was the masters' Bible, 'the *Examiner and Times* was their Testament ... Gold was their God, silver their Jesus Christ, and copper their Holy Ghost'.[58]

No further conflicts affecting the cotton district as whole took place took place between 1854 and the mid-1870s, but in a number of localities issues of union recognition and control in general, and of wages and conditions, continued regularly to embitter workplace relations in cotton. Contemporary press opinion well captured this state of affairs, eagerly congratulating employers and workers upon examples of new-found harmony yet generally despairing of any profound and enduring improvement in the industry's workplace relations. As the *Ashton Reporter* observed in 1869,

> Their distrust of each other dates many years back, and the growing intelligence, of which we ever and anon are reminded by warmhearted and enthusiastic masters and men, seems to leave them, on the whole, very much as it found them. During periods of cotton prosperity exciting speeches are delivered respecting the oneness and identity of their interests, but when a recurrence of bad trade takes place we see really nothing whatever significant of the altered relations or improved intelligence of those classes who were almost ready to embrace each other when times were good ... The actual appreciation of each other's interests, and the recognition of each other's rights, appear as far off as ever.[59]

We should modify the sentiments expressed in the *Reporter's* final sentence. But, taken as a whole, the quoted passage constitutes far more of an accurate summary of the state of industrial relations in cotton during the third quarter than does the influential picture of institutionalised calm drawn by Patrick Joyce.[60]

In a similar fashion the emergence of the new model Amalgamated Society of Engineers hardly signalled the onset of an era of industrial peace in the mid-Victorian engineering industry. Indeed, both nationally and in Lancashire, engineering constituted the industrial storm centre of the early 1850s when employer attempts to mechanise production more extensively, to increase the number of semi-skilled machine operatives and to introduce piecework and systematic overtime met with strong resistance from the skilled engineers. A period of acute industrial conflict during 1851 and 1852 climaxed in the lock-out of 1852 and defeat for the fledgling ASE. As a result of their victory, the engineeering employers won the formal right to 'place labourers on machines, to employ non-union labour, and to impose systematic overtime'. In many instances workers were also compelled to sign the document renouncing trade union membership. It is true that rapid export-led growth from the mid-1850s to the 1870s 'facilitated the re-emergence of strong craft regulations and controls within the workshop'. But such gains, along with the growing power of the ASE, were achieved far more through daily struggle and clear demonstrations of union power and durability and of skilled worker solidarity than as a result of shared discourses and values on the part of employers and workers. In other skilled sectors of the economy, such as the building and iron trades, major conflicts revolving around wages and hours were also in evidence.[61] In sum, the notion of mid-Victorian consensus, with respect to a balanced evaluation of the attitudes and actions of employers and workers, variously requires serious qualification and correction.

Beyond the workplace – in community life, in culture in general and in relation to politics and the law – class-based divisions and conflicts were by no means absent. For example, given their central emphasis upon the transforming powers of working-class independence, organisation and self-help, the co-ops, friendly societies and trade unions fit very uneasily into a picture of pervasive and internalised deference among the world's first major industrial proletariat. As with the Chartists, such instititutions welcomed genuine offers of friendship and relations of equality with reforming and progressive elements of all social strata. But any hint of middle and upper-class condescension, of being 'petted, pampered and patronized', was instantly to be rebuffed. In 1863 a section of the annual report of the Great and Little Bolton Co-operative Society read:

> Co-operation instills into the people a spirit of self-reliance – that is reliance on the power they themselves possess. It teaches the working classes to look to themselves for the amelioration of their condition, and no longer to be powerless at the feet of the so-called higher classes – the capitalists.[62]

Continued allegiance on the part of working-class leaders to the principles of independence, corporate (and in some instances class) pride and the proven benefits of collective organisation strongly suggest that there did not occur a wholesale process of capitulation to, or incorporation within, a purely individualistic set of values and ideas. As Robbie Gray has perceptively noted, class-based compromises in mid-Victorian society were frequently 'uneasy and double-edged, liable to break down and subject to constant renegotiation'.[63] Even in those areas of working-class experience, such as co-operation, where the imprint of success and reformism was particularly strong, the revolutionary desire to create a truly civilised and equitable moral social order were by no means extinguished. For example, in 1861 two leading co-operators, Pare and Travis, could still write:

> The reason why many of us are such ardent supporters of co-operation is because we believe the present system of society is altogether wrong . . . We see . . . a gulf existing between the present system – which we are compelled to denigrate as a system of unmitigated selfishness – and that system of social and political equality which we feel to be in accord with natural justice.

Similarly, a member of the Ashton-under-Lyne Co-operative Society drew attention to the transforming potential of co-operation:

> unless they took something else into account other than mere abstinence from intoxicating drink, and getting knowledge, and stores, and large dividends, the freedom of the working class . . . would not

be realised. He contended that no man would be free so long as he was called another man's property, whether as slave in the shape of goods and chattels, or as a paid or hired servant in the name of wages.[64]

Mid-Victorian popular resort to the language of class conflict and social revolt developed most strongly around those issues and incidents in which workers were treated as malcontents and undeserving outsiders and/or in which working-class independence of spirit and pride were especially prominent. Conflicts at work, demonstrations in favour of the extension of the franchise in 1866 and 1867, disagreements between working-class radicals and middle-class reformers concerning the relative merits of manhood versus household suffrage, and wider tensions between old Chartists, on the one hand, and, on the other, Liberals and Conservatives concerning equality of treatment, representation and involvement in political movements and institutions and dissatisfaction with class-biased aspects of the law (such as the particularly harsh treatment meted out to working-class debtors and the anti-picketing clauses of the Criminal Law Amendment Act) – these constituted some of the key moments of tension, even crisis, for mid-Victorian stability and class tolerance.[65] It was at such moments that respectable Rochdale man could be transformed into militant former Chartist, denouncing workers' lack of citizenship rights, and the tyrannies of landowners and capitalists, and advocating a threatening alliance between the respectable and poor sections of the working class to achieve 'due balance, protection and reward' for the 'labouring class' or classes.

Conclusion

In the final analysis we must nevertheless observe that such moments occurred less often and with less disruptive effects upon social stability during the third quarter than they had done in the Chartist years. On balance, the language and practices of working-class success, differentiation and accommodation to the existing order of things greatly overshadowed those of discontent, class solidarity and revolt. Furthermore, unlike the Chartist period, there occurred a marked loosening of the ties between workplace struggle and the political campaigns and allegiances of workers. During the 1850s and 1860s periods of industrial unrest did not, for the most part, lead to any widespread demand for the revival of Chartism or the creation of a new, independent working-class political movement. Rather, as we shall see in the next chapter, independent Chartism declined and popular accommodation to the established political system and the mainstream parties grew apace.

Notes

1 E.P. Thompson, 'The Peculiarities of the English', in his *The Poverty of Theory and Other Essays* (London, 1978), p. 71.

2 J. Walvin, *Victorian Values* (London, 1988), chapter 1.

3 J. Hinton, *Labour and Socialism: A History of the British Labour Movement 1867–1974* (Brighton, 1983), chapter 2.

4 M. Jenkins, *The General Strike of 1842* (London, 1980), p. 219.

5 Saville, quoted in N. Kirk, 'In Defence of Class', *International Review of Social History*, 32:1 (1987) 45–6. See also C. Godfrey, *Chartist Lives* (London, 1987).

6 B. Brierley, *Home Memories and Recollections of a Life* (Manchester, 1887), p. 49.

7 B. Wilson, *Struggles of an Old Chartist* (Halifax, 1887), p. 212, in D. Vincent (ed.), *Testaments of Radicalism: Memoirs of Working Class Politicians 1790–1885* (London, 1977).

8 J. Cole, *Conflict and Cooperation* (Littleborough, 1994), pp. 44–5.

9 *Ibid.*, pp. 46–7.

10 J.K. Walton, 'Co-operation in Lancashire 1844–1914', *North West Labour History*, 19 (1994–5) 119, 121–2.

11 N. Kirk, *The Growth of Working Class Reformism in Mid-Victorian England* (Beckenham, 1985), pp. 149–50.

12 Walton, 'Co operation in Lancashire', p. 118; M. Purvis, 'The Development of Co-operative Retailing in England and Wales 1851–1901: A Geographical Study', *Journal of Historical Geography*, 16 (1990) 314–31.

13 P.H.J.H. Gosden, *Self-help: Voluntary Associations in Nineteenth-century Britain* (London, 1973), p. 195.

14 *Ibid.*, pp. 194–5.

15 Kirk, *Reformism*, p. 146.

16 *Ibid.*, pp. 145–8; 199–200; P. Gurney, *Co operative Culture and the Politics of Consumption in England 1870–1930* (Manchester, 1996), chapter 6.

17 Gosden, *Self-help*, pp. 39–40, 74.

18 For such mixed fortunes see Kirk, *Reformism*, chapter 6.

19 S.O. Rose, 'Gender Antagonism and Class Conflict: Exclusionary Strategies of Male Trade Unionists in Nineteenth-century Britain', *Social*

History, 13:2 (1988) 191–208; K. McClelland, 'Some Thoughts on Masculinity and the "Representative Artisan" in Britain 1850–1880', *Gender and History*, 2:1 (1989) 164–77; E. Gordon, *Women and the Labour Movement in Scotland 1850–1914* (Oxford, 1991).

  20 J. Belchem, *Industrialization and the Working Class: The English Experience 1750–1900* (Aldershot, 1991), p. 181.

  21 J. Spain, 'Trade Unionists, Gladstonian Liberals and the Labour Law Reforms of 1875', in E.F. Biagini and A.J. Reid (eds), *Currents of Radicalism: Popular Radicalism, Organised Labour and Party Politics in Britain 1850–1914* (Cambridge, 1991), p. 111.

  22 R. McKibbin, 'Why was there no Marxism in Great Britain?' in his *The Ideologies of Class: Social Relations in Britain 1880–1950* (Oxford, 1991), p. 28.

  23 N. Kirk, *Labour and Society in Britain and the USA*, II, *Challenge and Accommodation 1850–1939* (Aldershot, 1994), pp. 62–3, 67–80.

  24 See, for example, P.A. Pickering, *Chartism and the Chartists in Manchester and Salford* (London, 1995), pp. 130–5.

  25 J.F.C. Harrison, *Learning and Living: A Study in the History of the English Adult Education Movement* (Toronto, 1961).

  26 Kirk, *Reformism*, pp. 208–10.

  27 *Ibid.*, p. 210.

  28 D. Thompson, 'Women and Nineteenth-century Radical Politics: A Lost Dimension', in her *Outsiders: Class, Gender and Nation* (London, 1993), pp. 99–100.

  29 Kirk, *Reformism*, p. 224.

  30 *Ibid.*, pp. 225–6.

  31 Godfrey, *Chartist Lives*; C. Godfrey, 'The Chartist Prisoners 1839–41', *International Review of Social History*, 23 (1979) 189–236.

  32 Wilson, *Struggles*, pp. 229, 242.

  33 Kirk, *Reformism*, pp. 134–48.

  34 M. Savage and A. Miles, *The Remaking of the British Working Class 1840–1940* (London, 1994), p. 34.

  35 E.J. Hobsbawm, 'Trends in the British Labour Movement since 1850', in his *Labouring Men* (London, 1974), p. 324.

  36 J. Benson, *The Working Class in Britain 1850–1939* (London, 1989), chapter 2.

  37 Kirk, *Reformism*, pp. 148–52; M. Hewitt, *The Emergence of Stability in the Industrial City: Manchester 1832–67* (Aldershot, 1996), pp. 204–5, 228.

  38 Kirk, *Reformism*, pp. 151–2, 157–8.

  39 *Ibid.*, p. 160.

  40 *Ibid.*, pp. 286–7.

  41 *Ibid.*, p. 228.

42 P.H.J.H. Gosden, *The Friendly Societies in England 1815–1875* (Manchester, 1961), pp. 75–93.

43 A. Howkins, *Reshaping Rural England: A Social History 1850–1925* (London, 1992), pp. 80–1, 291; D. Neave, *Mutual Aid in the Victorian Countryside* (Hull, 1991).

44 E. Roberts, *Women's Work 1840–1940* (London, 1988), pp. 14–17, 25, chapter 4; D.A. Galbi, 'Through Eyes in the Storm: Aspects of the Personal History of Women Workers in the Industrial Revolution', *Social History*, 21:2 (1996) 142–59.

45 Kirk, *Reformism*, pp. 199–200; Walton, 'Co-operation in Lancashire'.

46 Walton, 'Co-operation in Lancashire', p. 122.

47 Kirk, *Reformism*, p. 135.

48 *Ibid.*, pp. 189–98, 201–2; Hewitt, *Emergence of Stability*, pp. 176–8.

49 N. Kirk, *Labour and Society in Britain and the USA*, I, *Capitalism, Custom and Protest 1780–1850* (Aldershot, 1994), pp. 164–9.

50 Kirk, *Challenge and Accommodation*, pp. 70–3, 98–105.

51 *Ibid.*, pp. 74–5; J. Benson, *British Coalminers in the Nineteenth Century: A Social History* (London, 1989), pp. 189–213.

52 T. Lummis, *The Labour Aristocracy 1851–1914* (Aldershot, 1994), chapter 6; E.H. Hunt, *British Labour History 1815–1914* (London, 1985), chapter 8.

53 Gordon, *Women and the Labour Movement*, chapter 4.

54 Kirk, *Reformism*, pp. 99–103; R.A. Church, *The Great Victorian Boom* (London, 1975); Benson, *Working Class*, pp. 52–6.

55 G.S. Jones, *Outcast London: A Study in the Relationship between Classes in Victorian Society* (Harmondsworth, 1976), Part III.

56 Kirk, *Reformism*, pp. 103–8; Lummis, *Labour Aristocracy*, pp. x, 91–6, conclusion.

57 Savage and Miles, *Remaking*, pp. 32–3.

58 Kirk, *Reformism*, pp. 250–1.

59 *Ashton Reporter*, 20 March 1869.

60 P. Joyce, *Work, Society and Politics: The Culture of the Factory in Later Victorian England* (Brighton, 1980), pp. 64–82.

61 Kirk, *Reformism*, pp. 246; P. Joyce, *Visions of the People* (Cambridge, 1991), chapter 5.

62 Kirk, *Reformism*, pp. 212–13.

63 See Gray's comments in *Society for the Study of Labour History Bulletin*, 40 (1980) 7.

64 Kirk, *Reformism*, pp. 166–7.

65 See, for example, P. Johnson, 'Class Law in Victorian England', *Past and Present*, 141 (1993) 147–69;

4

Politics: independence and accommodation

Chartism was a national political movement of the predominantly working-class people which, between the late 1830s and
1848, had at its core the guiding principle of *political independence*.
During the 1830s hard political, economic, social and cultural
experiences had led to the conclusion that neither the propertied
classes nor the Whig and Tory parties were to be entrusted with
the emancipation of the people. Thus, whereas the Tories were
regarded by the Chartists as the the traditional, if open, enemy of
progress and reform, the Whigs, following the betrayal of 1832,
their enactment of the 'blatant class legislation' of the 1830s and
their persecution and imprisonment, as establishment forces of
law and order, of Chartists in 1838 and 1839, were increasingly
cast in the role of 'a treacherous, deceitful bad lot'.[1]

There were, of course, local and regional variations upon, and
important exceptions to, the guiding theme of political independence. Chartism was not a uniform, undifferentiated movement
articulating blanket oppposition to other political and social
groups. For example, within their overall class-based way of
viewing politics and society, the Chartists drew a distinction between 'honourable' shopkeepers and small masters (who shared
producerist and moral-economic interests with the labouring people) and 'dishonourable' master manufacturers whose structured
practices of buying cheap and selling dear and enforcing per-
petual 'wage slavery' were perceived to be fundamentally at odds
with the interests and actions of workers.[2] Furthermore, in some
instances, as in parts of London and Scotland, and even in towns

in the predominantly independent-minded and class-conscious cotton district of Lancashire and Cheshire, there did emerge links and alliances between the Chartists and reforming Liberals whose advanced views were not generally in accord with those of mainstream Whiggery.[3] There also developed, albeit less extensively and intensively, ties between Chartists and radical Tories.[4]

Notwithstanding such variations and exceptions, and even taking into account differences among the Chartist leaders concerning the advisability or otherwise of an alliance with the middle-class reformers, our insistence upon the central importance of political independence to mainstream Chartism must be retained as being in accord with the balance of the evidence. For example, the vast majority of the middle classes retained their fear of Chartism as constituting a violent threat to property and the social order and dismissed its supporters as uncivilised, wrongheaded, extreme and even animalistic. And, as Dorothy Thompson has reminded us, even those radicals among the middle classes who supported the principle of manhood suffrage 'never made common cause with the Chartists for more than a fleeting moment', were very reluctant to treat the Chartists and the Chartist movement as meriting equality of respect and treatment with themselves and their own movements, and were generally regarded as traitors to their class.[5] Furthermore, common radical linguistic commitment to words such as 'the people', 'democracy' and 'reform' should not blind us to the different, indeed conflicting, class-based meanings which were often attached to such words. Thus,

> Chartists' notions of collective control at the workplace, of equality of membership of political organisations, of the accountability of office holders, of manhood suffrage, of participatory local democracy and mutuality and co-operation were often at odds with the beliefs of 'democratic' middle-class radicals in hierarchy, authority and power (especially in the workplace), in their own cultural and social superiority and in their support for more limited political reforms and popular political involvement (as seen in their advocacy of household suffrage and triennial parliaments, and their strong desires to retain control of the levers of political power).[6]

In truth, the *dominant* discourse within *national* Chartism during the late late 1830s and for much of the 1840s – as articulated by the movement's most prominent and successful leader, Feargus O'Connor, in opposition to William Lovett and other advocates of a cross-class radical alliance – rested upon the belief that ultimately neither the Liberal reformers nor the Tory radicals went far enough fully to satisfy Chartist demands for root-and-branch political change and economic and social justice. Accordingly the Chartist 'people' were exhorted by O'Connor to rely first and foremost upon their own efforts in order to secure their salvation. Those alliances which the Chartists developed with Liberals and Tories were thus frequently formed around specific electoral and other issues, were often contingent and ephemeral, and issued primarily from a desire to maximise the tactical and strategic advantage of Chartism rather than from any principled commitment to the mainstream parties. As Robert Sykes has perceptively observed,

> Towards the middle class in general, and the established political parties, the radical attitude to political co-operation remained essentially instrumental and opportunistic. Exactly the same radicals who had supported the Whig Reform Bill were quite prepared to back the Tory Sadler . . . for he was committed to another desirable reform, the ten hours bill. They were not being inconsistent, but were continuing the familiar radical view that the established Whig and Tory parties were both objectionable factions opposed to the interests of the people. Thus the only real issue was how the party battle could be exploited for radical gain, either by achieving some worthwhile reform, or by promoting the political instability which would weaken the whole political system.[7]

It was by no means accidental that Chartism's emphasis upon the maintenance of an independent political stance received its strongest support, from both leaders and followers, during the movement's early phase, 1838–42. It was during these years that Chartism constituted a truly hegemonic force in many working-class communities, bringing together, under the umbrella of the Six Points, the various strands of popular radicalism which had developed in earlier years, and offering the vision of a more democratic and egalitarian society. Symptomatic of Chartism's dominance was the fact that in many of the cotton centres in Lancashire and Cheshire both the Anti-Corn Law League and the Conservatives failed in their attempts to develop, in this early period, strong operative associations of their own which would successfully challenge the local organisational and community-based strengths of the Chartists.[8]

Following Parliament's rejection of the second Chartist petition in 1842 and the defeat of the general strike there was, however, growing evidence of change. Most significantly, a formerly united movement began to fracture into the different ways of trade unionism, co-operation, and educational and other forms of self-improvement. Furthermore, within Chartism strategies which challenged the independent position of O'Connor did, for a time at least, gain some momentum. At the same time it is important to record the overall failure of such challenges in the years up to 1848. Similarly, the mid-1840s 'turns' to trade unionism and/or co-operation often did not signal the abandonment of a principled commitment to the Six Points but rather, within the context of Parliament's rejection of the second Chartist petition and the seeming inability of the movement to make much overall progress towards the achievement of its goals, pragmatic attempts to try other means of advancement.

What was, however, changing most significantly in this middle period, 1843–47, was that Chartism as a movement, complete with its central ideological emphasis upon the primacy of the Six Points – upon the belief that significant and lasting economic and social improvement for the people must necessarily await the enactment of the charter – was losing some of its former strength among and immediate relevance to sections of the working class. Co-operation and skilled trade unionism were gradually, if very haltingly and unevenly, perceived to bring tangible benefits and rewards to sections of the working class. The achievement of manhood suffrage increasingly did not appear to be the *sine qua non* of 'improvement'; as such, the primacy of politics to the emancipation of the people was, in effect, being questioned. Furthermore, the partial retreats of the 1840s state and governments from the class legislation of the 1830s and outright repression of radical movements gave sustenance, as claimed by Stedman Jones, to the view that more was to be gained from cross-class alliances and pressure-group politics than from a militantly independent stance.

Up to and including 1848, however, we must be careful not to exaggerate the extent and depth of Chartism's decline. In 1848 Chartism demonstrated a revived and strongly independent presence. From a national perspective the regenerated movement did not match its impressive strength of the early period. But it did manifest a strong influence in London, its new-found heartland, in Liverpool (where Irish involvement was particularly marked) and in more established centres in parts of Yorkshire and Lancashire. Furthermore, as we shall see in more detail below, the period of late Chartism, 1848–58, saw the continuation of a robust tradition of independent, Chartist-inspired radicalism in a number of places throughout the country. This late and even post-Chartist radicalism often found itself either at odds or in 'negotiated tension' with Liberalism. As such, and contrary to the claims of the liberal revisionists (see the introduction), mid-century radicalism cannot unproblematically be subsumed under the heading of 'popular Liberalism'.[9]

The existence of such independent-radical continuities could not, however, disguise two major breaks in mid-Victorian popular politics: the growth of popular Liberalism and Conservatism; and the overall decline of Chartism. In the post-1848 context of defeat, declining support and mounting divisions within Chartism O'Connor himself was forced to reconsider his position, initially favouring and then opposing a middle-class alliance.[10] Ernest Jones, O'Connor's rival, and a fierce advocate of 'the charter and something more', subsequently gained control of the movement. For the greater part of the 1850s and well into the 1860s Jones remained suspicious of an alliance with middle-class Liberals and made strenuous efforts to steer Chartism, the Manchester Manhood Suffrage League and the Reform League in an independent political direction. Notwithstanding continued suspicion on both sides, Jones was, however, adopted as a candidate by the Liberal Party in the 1868 general election. As Tony Taylor observes, Jones's candidature symbolised the wider and 'final absorption of radical energies into Liberalism'.[11] Indeed, the third quarter as a whole saw the movement of Chartism into Liberalism and the adoption of Liberal radicalism as the 'official' creed of the British labour movement. (See document 6.) However, the 1868 elections revealed, to shocked Liberals and radicals, substantial working-class (as opposed to significant labour movement) support for the 'No Popery' Conservative Party, especially in former Chartist strongholds in the cotton towns of Lancashire and Cheshire. From being widely regarded as something of a joke in the 1840s, Conservatism had developed a strong popular base which it would retain for much of the second half of the nineteenth century and beyond. It is to an examination of mid-Victorian popular Liberalism, followed by attention to popular Conservatism, that we now turn.

Popular liberalism

Both 'old' and 'new' proponents of political continuity have maintained that the movement from Chartism into mid-Victorian Liberalism took place relatively smoothly, harmoniously and more or less inevitably. For example, writing in the early 1970s, Brian Harrison drew attention to those respectable values, attitudes and leisure patterns which drew together Chartist radicals, such as Robert Lowery and William Lovett, and middle-class Liberals such as Bright and Cobden. Both groups shared:

> a distaste for mobs, and a repudiation of the whole complex of behaviour associated with race courses, fairs, wakes, brothels, beerhouses and brutal sports. He [the respectable artisan] was more likely than his inferiors to vote Liberal, if only because his work situation frequently fostered individualism, self-education and social ambition. If he drank at all he drank soberly, without neglecting his wife and family; he often took his recreation with them and believed that the family should keep to itself. He was probably interested in religious matters – often a chapelgoer or a secularist. He was strongly attracted by the ideology of thrift, with its stress on individualism, self-respect, personal, moral and physical effort, and prudence.[12]

As recently emphasised by a prominent 'new' advocate of continuity, Patrick Joyce, shared, indeed agonising, concern with and commitment to independence, earnest and moral purpose in life, the fate of humankind as a whole, as opposed to the sectional and selfish interests of social class, the righteous and productive as opposed to the sinful and parasitical/wasteful of *all* social strata, and duties and sense of community as well as rights and unfettered individualism must be added to Harrison's checklist.[13]

As indicated in the introduction, Joyce is, alongside James Vernon, Eugenio Biagini, Alastair Reid, Jon Lawrence and Gareth Stedman Jones, one of the liberal revisionists whose recent writings have done so much to make the case in favour of the enduring, inter-class-based nature of political radicalism in modern England, as against the class-based, discontinuous three-stage model of Edward Thompson and Eric Hobsbawm. The reader will recall that, according to the revisionists, the distinguishing politico-economic characteristics of nineteenth-century radicalism resided in its belief in the political (i.e. non-class-based) as opposed to economic nature of oppression and exchange, and in its opposition to the forces of Old Corruption (the 'taxeating' state and parasitical landed aristocrats, placemen, sinecurists and speculators) rather than in opposition to capitalist manufacturers. Indeed, in his active managerial and wealth-creating (as opposed to his exchange-based or middleman) role the capitalist entrepreneur is claimed to have shared the same 'producerist' outlook as the employee. But sources of cross-class radical political unity are claimed by all the revisionists to have gone beyond economics to embrace a totalising social and moral purpose and vision. Thus Biagini and Reid:

> the central demands of progressive popular politics remained largely those of radical liberalism well into the twentieth century: for open government and the rule of law, for freedom from intervention both at home and abroad, and for individual liberty and community-centred democracy . . . in a vision of the ideal citizen-patriot who would be independent of both government pressure and excessive party loyalty, and who would therefore be able to decide on political and social issues in a conscientious and public-spirited way . . . in general radicalism was characterised by a broad emphasis on pragmatism, in its acceptance both of constitutional methods and of the already existing aspirations of the people.

Radicalism, furthermore, had a pedigree dating back to the sixteenth century:

> The resilience of these attitudes through a range of different political contexts can be understoood in terms of their very deep historical roots, which can be traced back through the eighteenth-century 'country' opposition and the seventeenth-century 'Puritan Revolution', to the impact of Renaissance humanism, above all in the form of the Calvinist project for the Reformation of the Church.[14]

Thus united in their general emphasis upon the continuous and largely inter-class nature of the radical tradition, the liberal revisionists as a whole tend, somewhat predictably, to ignore or play down the independent and class-conscious features of Chartism and to exaggerate aspects of continuity between Chartism and Liberalism.[15] As a result, the various tensions which frequently characterised relations between Chartist radicals and Liberals remain mainly unexplored. In such ways are the protracted, negotiated and far from untroubled aspects of the movement from Chartism into Gladstonian Liberalism largely missing from the accounts presented by Joyce, Vernon, Lawrence, Reid and Biagini.

It is, however, important to note at this point Gareth Stedman Jones's partially dissenting voice, from within the liberal revision ist camp, in relation to the specific issue of radical continuity during the 1830s and 1840s. In his two influential essays entitled 'The Language of Chartism' (1982) and 'Rethinking Chartism' (1983) Stedman Jones propounded a thesis of (what may be termed) modified or qualified radicalism during these two decades. According to Stedman Jones, the events of the 1830s – opposition to the New Poor Law, workplace conflict, growing concern with 'white slavery' in the factories, mounting opposition to employer tyranny and 'capitalist oppression', the increased levels of unemployment and the uniform intransigence and hostility of the system to popular demands – did seriously test and stretch the traditional radical perspective and language of Old Corruption. 'Undoubtedly there was a shift of emphasis and imagery in the Chartist period,' observed Stedman Jones: radicalism had become, by the early 1840s, more exclusively working-class in character, Chartism had largely divorced itself from the middle-class reformers, and, at least in the north of England, the factory owners had been identified as the principal enemies of the workers, the 'main tyrants'. Nevertheless, continued the author, this shift constituted a temporary adjustment to the specific experiences of the 1830s rather than a fundamental change, or discontinuity, in the basic tenets and character of radicalism. It would thus be wrong, argued Stedman Jones, to suggest that 'the radical analysis that lay behind the Charter was in the course of displacement by a different and more class-conscious mode of thought'. The Chartists

remained convinced of 'the political origin and determination of oppression'; that the 'monopolisation of the land' [which had 'made them "landless" wage slaves in the first place'] continued to be seen as 'the prime cause of the misery of the worker', with the monopolisation of money and machinery as secondary derivatives; and that 'the depth and extent of antagonism' towards the 'steamlords' should not be allowed to obscure the fact . . . that the Chartists did *not* develop a theory of capitalist exploitation in production, and especially *not* 'a class-based theory of exploitation of a social democratic or Marxist kind'.[16]

Finally, the mellowed character of state and government policies during the 1840s – as a response to the 'vehemence of opposition' to the previous decade's class legislation – was primarily responsible for the decline of Chartism and the development of popular Liberalism.

In its attentiveness to the important links between, on the one hand, the radical ideas and language of the 1830s and 1840s and, on the other, (predominantly) political events and experiences, Stedman Jones's thesis has far more to recommend it than the largely absolute and inadequately contextualised, idealist notions of mid-Victorian radical continuity and consensus presented by the other liberal revisionists. At the same time, however, Stedman Jones's attention to the necessary contextualisation of ideas and language is partial and ultimately unconvincing. Thus, while in Stedman Jones's essays on Chartism ideas and languages are engaged with political events and processes, they are not fully engaged with material factors. We may suggest that in his commendable aversion to economic reductionism – which treats ideas and values as passive reflections of an underlying economic base – Stedman Jones has bent his methodological stick too far in the opposite, idealist direction. In effect Stedman Jones treats language and politics as largely self-referential and autonomous. As such they are inadequately related to their material and cultural pressures and limits.

In terms of our immediate discussion, three major practical weaknesses issue from Stedman Jones's inadequately contextualised 'primacy of politics' approach. First, the full extent and depth of (largely non-socialist forms of) class consciousness among the Chartists – of shared ideas, values and interests and opposition to other social and political groups – is undervalued. As a number of historians have shown, the class consciousness of the Chartists – which grew out of a wide range of discrete and yet interrelated political, economic, social and cultural experiences – was directed not only at the political target of Old Corruption but also increasingly at the structured economic, social, ideological and cultural oppression which was seen to be practised by employers and large sections of the middle class.[17]

Second, as observed in Chapter 2, Stedman Jones gives insufficient weight to the extent to which the 1840s state continued to employ coercive measures towards popular movements alongside its more conciliatory and accommodating measures. Thus the level of class consciousness is understated while at the same time the softened visage of the state is exaggerated.

Third, given the high levels of class and coercion which characterised the 1840s, Stedman Jones underestimates the full extent of the changes, or discontinuities, which were necessary to ensure the passage from Chartism to Liberalism. We can, by way of example, briefly turn the reader's attention to two such necessary discontinuities: the retreat from the sharp and wide-ranging, class-based social critique and transforming social vision offered by Chartism; and the greatly softened tone and substance of post-1847 middle-class Liberalism. We will address these subjects in turn.

Notwithstanding largely shared commitments to respectability and Nonconformity, middle-class mid-Victorian Liberals would undoubtedly have baulked at forming effective alliances with working-class radicals who continued *centrally* to articulate the Chartist language of outsider status, of wage slavery, capitalist tyranny and physical force, and who displayed continued determination to 'arrest the emergent force of industrial capitalism' and fundamentally to transform society in democratic, co-operative, human/moral and equitable ways.[18] We have indicated in previous chapters that by no means all aspects of Chartism's militant language and its apparently revolutionary (at least in the eyes of many of the propertied classes) alternative social programme were jettisoned during the mid-Victorian 'golden years'; and that the continued expression of such language and aims could still excite middle-class fears of popular disaffection and radical, even revolutionary, intent. Nevertheless, we have also indicated that, on balance, the more uncompromising strands of Chartism's many languages and the movement's 'totalising' critique and vision retreated during the 1850s and 1860s before the triumphant advance of the labour movement's concern with accommodation, moderation and social harmony, piecemeal gradualism and 'success'. In sum, reformism achieved ascendancy and greatly facilitated cross-class alliances, especially with progressive Liberals.

At the same time the threat posed by Chartism and the visibly exposed position of property had effected something of a change of heart on the part of the state and the propertied classes. There were indeed, as suggested by John Foster for Oldham, accelerated general attempts on the part of both Liberals and Tories (especially from the introduction of the Ten Hours Act, in 1847, onwards) more effectively to accommodate 'the working-class interest'. In terms of middle-class Liberals, this attempted accommodation manifested itself in a variety of ways. Of particular note were the following developments: Liberal employers' involvement in the 'new paternalism' (Joyce); a softening of the tenets of orthodox political economy; increased support for selected examples of working-class self-help; the promotion of measures to improve education and public health; prominence in the various mid-Victorian inter-class campaigns for general municipal improvement and the more active cultivation of civic pride (by means, for example, of the provision of parks and libraries and improved roads and supplies of water and gas); the growing acceptance of factory legislation and other selected forms of state intervention; generally increased, albeit chequered, toleration of trade unionism; and active support for a further extension of the franchise.[19]

The changed attitudes and practices of leading Liberals in the former Chartist strongholds of Ashton, Stalybridge and Bradford precisely illustrate in dramatic, if somewhat extreme, form some of the general changes listed above. For example, Hugh Mason, a wealthy cotton manufacturer and future mayor of Ashton, was notorious for his attachment to purse-proud 'intransigent Whig dogma' during the 1830s and the 1840s. Mason's opposition to Chartism, trade unionism and factory reform, his rigid adherence to the impersonal 'truths' and 'laws' of orthodox political economy, and his prescription of restraint and self-help as the 'true cures' for popular ills won him precious few friends among Ashton's workers. Yet the profound shocks of Chartism and industrial conflict, combined with general mid-Victorian prosperity and the accumulation of substantial personal wealth from his cotton-spinning business, induced a remarkable transformation on Mason's part. In 1859 he admitted that the Ten Hours campaign 'had been nobly fought, and fairly won'. By the 1860s his harsh political economy of the 1840s had been tempered by humanitarian concern:

> He was not indifferent to the teachings of political economy, but he should be very sorry if the rigid and abstract rules of political economy alone prevailed in his workshops. It would be impossible for him to buy the labour of his workpeople, and for the workpeople to sell him that labour, the same as an ordinary commodity over the counter of a shopkeeper. He felt a deep interest in the welfare of his workpeople . . . The bond which united them was not the cold bond of buyer and seller.

During the Cotton Famine Mason variously took issue with the miserly attitudes of some of the local millowners, attempted to keep his mills running full-time between 1861 and 1865, distributed free food and clothing to the unemployed operatives, fought to secure increased scales of relief, wrote off rent arrears and held concerts in his works to raise money for the local relief fund. Further acts of generosity followed the Cotton Famine:

> In 1865 he volunteered an advance of ten per cent . . . in 1868 new reading rooms and baths were opened at the mills; and in 1870 he both supported the Saturday half holiday, and chaired a meeting of the local miners' association at which he argued for better inspection of the mines and the eight-hour day for miners.

Mason's sharply changed appreciation of the duties and responsibilities of capital, expressed in the idiom of religious 'calling', his new-found role as a leading progressive and paternalistic employer, and his increasingly articulated wish to advance the interests of the whole people or community, rather than those of the sectionalised class or party, did much to enhance the popular appeal of Liberalism in the Ashton area. Furthermore, several local Liberal employers followed suit. And operatives responded to the actions of these new model employers with genuine warmth and gratitude.[20]

The town of Bradford, in the West Riding of Yorkshire, likewise experienced a remarkable change at mid-century in the character of local Liberalism. Theodore Koditschek's important study of class formation and social relations in Bradford informs us that by 1848,

> it became clear that the class struggle of the previous decade . . . had actually opened people's eyes to the necessity of compromise and had thus begun to lay the foundations for a new and enduring era of relative social peace.[21]

In response to the strength of Chartism, economic crisis, acute and bitter class conflict, and urban blight, Bradford's ruling Liberal elite softened significantly their traditional and hard-headed allegiance to self-interested, deregulated, entrepreneurial capitalism and offered social peace and stakeholding by means of a new-found commitment to a programme of urban and political reform, built around a 'progressive alliance of "the people" '. As in many other places there had been evidence of the beginnings of Lberalism's radical change of course in Bradford in the immediate post-Plug Plot years. But it was from the late 1840s onwards that the inter-class structure of popular Liberalism and the creation of a viable urban industrial society under bourgeois rule were firmly established. During the 1850s an Improvement Act was passed (largely in response to the cholera epidemic of 1849), many adult male, skilled workers received the municipal franchise, the private waterworks company was municipalised and Liberal commitments were made to street and public health improvement. In the following two decades, observes Koditschek,

> corporate activism quickened as building codes were tightened, downtown street improvements were co-ordinated, the gas service was brought under public ownership and a subterranean system of arterial sewerage was finally laid.[22]

By such accommodating means was a strong basis for liberal consensus created in formerly crisis-ridden Bradford.

Equally important, if often less sharp and pronounced, changes in the character and direction of mid-Victorian liberalism have been observed in studies of Bolton, Rochdale, Oldham, Manchester, Edinburgh and Kentish London.[23] But of equal significance has been the emphasis, highlighted rather than 'invented' in recent and current studies (despite claims to the contrary), upon the continued tensions and points of negotiation, renegotiation and contestation which accompanied the successful passage from

Chartist radicalism to Liberalism. As John Breuilly, Gottfried Niedhart and Anthony Taylor have observed in relation to 'the consensus which is supposed to underlie the emergence of popular liberalism' by the end of the 1860s, 'too much has been made of a convergence of values . . . Instead one could see the construction of a broad and popular liberalism as a matter of difficult and tough negotiation between distinct interests.'[24]

Brief references to mid-century political and social developments in selected urban areas can serve to illustrate some of the obstacles to the smooth and consensual development of popular Liberalism. Of paramount importance in this context was the continued existence of an independent and robust radical tradition into the 1850s and 1860s which often constituted a strong countervailing point of allegiance to that of Liberalism. Anthony Taylor, for example, has convincingly shown that in London, where the scope and space for an alternative, radical form of politics were not successfully closed down by the mainstream parties, independent working-class radicalism maintained a strong presence and appeal throughout the mid-Victorian period. By way of contrast, claims Taylor, the ability of Manchester's Cobdenite Liberals to exert a hegemonic influence upon the city's political and social affairs (centrally around programmatic and organisational concern with cheap and efficient civic government, free trade, civil and religious liberties, temperance, and the rights of oppressed nationalities), combined with the appeal of social-radical and anti-Catholic Tories, had effectively marginalised local Chartism's political influence by the early 1850s.[25]

Nevertheless, as Taylor is also keen to point out,[26] even in Manchester, largely under the inspiration and leadership of Ernest Jones, Chartism refused either to expire or to merge unobtrusively and smoothly into Liberalism. Indeed, as noted earlier, apart from his short-lived attempted tactical accommodation with the middle-class reformers in 1857 and 1858, Jones was fiercely determined to steer both Manchester and national Chartism and its political successors in the 1860s in an independent direction. Above all, Jones remained suspicious of the proposal for household, as opposed to manhood, suffrage put forward by John Bright and the middle-class reform movement in general. And this suspicion, which was a strong feature of late Chartism on a national scale, often did not issue solely or even mainly, as claimed by the liberal revisionists, from tactical differences *within* a supposedly harmonious cross-class 'radical community' concerning the degree of suffrage extension realistically to be extracted from a Parliament dominated by conservative landed interests. Rather the central issue revolved, at least for Jones and like-minded radical Chartists, around the *class-based power implications* of the various suffrage proposals being made. Thus, whereas Bright's and Gladstone's support for household suffrage was equated, by Jones, with the further growth of middle-class power, only the enactment of universal manhood suffrage would enable the working class to exert its full influence upon, and eventually to achieve its 'due recognition, respect and reward' from, society. In 1859 Jones thus described Bright's proposal for 'household suffrage clogged with the ratebook' as 'a suffrage for the middle classes – and exclusion for the great masses of the people'. Seven years later he resigned his position as vice-president of the Reform League in opposition to the League leaders' support for Gladstone's and Russell's Bill for limited franchise reform. As the following extracts from a letter written by Jones make clear, his criticisms of the Bill were explicitly class-based in character.

It is nothing but a war of classes, between aristocracy and money, and whichever gains, whichever is the victor, the working man will gain nothing by the victory . . .

If the monied interest can so far alter the basis of representation as to create a preponderance . . . in its favour, the problem is solved, and you have middle-class Government (that is, class Government in its most hideous and revolting form) in England.

Lord Russell's bill is planned to secure this result. *It is a bill to diminish the power of the working classes and establish middle-class ascendancy* . . . Working men! Your enemies (aye, 'enemies', that is the word) hardly conceal from you their object. They recommend this bill because it enfranchises so few working men and so many of the middle class. It is a bill to culminate class government – the Government of the middle class – and you are tamely and blindly lending yourselves to its support!

. . . the working men are once more being deluded as they were in 1832, but with this difference. The bill of 1832 did not go as far to deprive them of their chance; *the bill of 1866 does* – at least by constitutional means – for it completes the Government of the middle class.[27]

It is, of course, the case that following the introduction of household suffrage in 1867, under the terms of the Second Reform Act, Jones did lower his ambitions somewhat and pragmatically accept the fact that, in the absence of mass support for independent political organisation and further franchise extension, the future of popular radicalism lay *within* the Liberal party. At the general election of the following year he was accepted as a candidate by the United Liberal Party of Manchester with a view to increasing Liberalism's appeal to the newly enfranchised sections of the working class. This acceptance did not, however, signify the sudden or complete termination of tensions and conflicts between Jones and mainstream Liberalism. As Taylor has argued, it would appear that members of the committee of the United Liberal Party regarded their adoption of Jones as a Liberal candidate as a marriage of convenience rather than a welcome, if belated embrace of a natural yet wayward Liberal. Jones's defence of the Fenian martyrs in Manchester, his commitment to the cause of female suffrage, his strong support for trade unionism, his threatening, anti-middle class rhetoric, his 'physical force' Chartist past, and his imprisonment in 1848 (ironically at the hands of his 1868 campaign manager, Sir Elkanah Armitage, wealthy millowner and elder statesman of Manchester Liberalism) were factors which continued to engender suspicion, indeed hatred of Jones among most middle-class Liberals. In his support, between 1866 and 1868, for reform of the land laws, educational improvement and the disestablishment of the Irish Church, and in his admiration for Gladstone, Jones did attempt to reconcile Chartism and Liberalism. And many of the Liberal luminaries of Manchester did turn out for his funeral in 1869. But this symbolic demonstration of Liberal unity could by no means erase the memory of Ernest Jones, 'agitator and Chartist'; nor would it effectively prevent the future occurrence of tensions and conflicts within Manchester Liberalism.[28]

In Manchester during the 1850s and 1860s – indeed, in many other places throughout the country – questions concerning the full and equal recognition, treatment and representation of the popular or 'labour' interest at the polls also continued to generate tensions and conflicts between Chartist radicals and mainstream Liberals. In 1859 and 1865, for example, Abel Heywood radical publisher, Chartist, Manchester city councillor and a political ally

of Ernest Jones in the Manchester Manhood Suffrage Association
– stood unsuccessfully for election to Parliament for Manchester
as an 'advanced Liberal'. In 1858 Heywood had joined Jones in
advocating an alliance with the middle-class reformers. In the
following year the Manchester Manhood Suffrage Association
nominated Heywood as an 'advanced' or 'Chartist' parliamentary
candidate likely to appeal to both working and middle-class elec-
tors (Heywood having proven links with middle-class reformers).
However, Heywood's candidature was rebuffed by the Liberals,
and eventually a compromise Liberal candidate, Milner Gibson,
was chosen. Heywood chose to mount a separate campaign.
He gained almost all the votes of the working men on the
roll but came an unsuccessful third. While Taylor has claimed
that Heywood's candidature presented 'merely the illusion of
independence whilst in reality working in tandem with the
Cobdenites' electoral machinery', nevertheless the truth of the
matter would seem to lie closer to Pickering's view that 'However
much some middle-class reformers were prepared to co-operate
with working-class radicals, they were not yet ready to send a
Chartist to Westminster.' In 1865 Heywood, supported by Jones,
was again nominated as a manhood suffrage candidate but once
more failed to gain either the endorsement of the middle-class
reformers (they were divided on the issue) or election to Parliament. Declaring that 'the working classes did not receive enough
representation in the House of Commons', Heywood ascribed his
defeat to 'snobbishness', to the defeat of 'fustian' by 'broadcloth':
it was that feeling which would not allow a man to represent the
city unless he wore broadcloth . . . unless he occupied some great
warehouse here'.[29] Similar accusations by mainstream Liberal organisations, or Whig cliques, against the proposed candidatures
of those with 'advanced' views, especially if the latter presented
themselves as working men's or people's advocates, were to be
heard in many places beyond Manchester.[30] Once again, largely
class-based issues – relating to equality of respect, consideration
and treatment – underlay what may appear at first sight to
have been questions solely or mainly of political tactics and
expediency.

Particularly marked in London, and represented by Jones and
his colleagues in Manchester, the continued tradition of independent popular radicalism – complete with its often tense rela-

tions with Liberalism – nevertheless often manifested itself strongly (as with Chartism) in the manufacturing towns surrounding the cities. For example, David Gadian has recently claimed, in direct opposition to the revisionism of Michael Winstanley, that class-based tensions between radicalism and liberalism (revolving around the issues of trade unionism, factory legislation and the poor law) persisted in Oldham into the 1850s. In making this claim Gadian is adding current support to Kate Tiller's past contention (concerning late Chartism in Halifax) that 'the political passage of Chartism into popular Liberalism was never an easy, passive, untroubled or complete process'.[31] In her work on Halifax Tiller has shown that Chartism, relatively strong in the town in 1848, continued to exert an independent political presence and appeal, especially to textile craftsmen and small manufacturers and tradespeople, throughout most of the 1850s. Chartist candidates (as in the other Yorkshire centres of Leeds, Bradford and Sheffield) contested municipal elections in Halifax with a fair degree of success, and in 1847 and 1852 Ernest Jones stood unsuccessfully as a parliamentary candidate. Significantly, following the 1852 contest Jones concentrated his heaviest critical fire upon the successful middle-class radical Liberal candidate, Francis Crossley, millowner, 'Manchester reformer', free-trader and one of those 'hypocrites and traitors' who 'make of political liberalism a cloak under which to carry on social tyrannies unquestioned'. Furthermore, the ideas and policies of Halifax Chartism 'continued to be independently articulated after 1858, later putting considerable pressure on "established" Liberalism, and later still rediscovered in Labourism'.

In successful opposition to the conventional wisdom (associated most closely with the pioneering work of John Vincent and elaborated upon most recently by Joyce[32]), John Cole[33] has clearly demonstrated that the radical flame in mid-Victorian Rochdale was kept alive much more by the democratic and progressive ideas and actions of Thomas Livsey, a small master and the 'true' 'champion of the local working class', and his group of Chartist radicals than by the professed 'standard bearer of the people', John Bright, and his fellow Liberals. There had been points of agreement in the past between working-class radicals and middle-class reformers, most prominently around their common opposition to the levy of a Church rate. But the strikes of 1842, the demand for manhood rather than household suffrage, the issue of 'physical force' methods, and attitudes towards trade unionism, factory legislation and political economy in general had served to effect a growing division between Rochdale's Chartists and Liberals of the Bright stamp. As at the national level, there also existed differences in tone and style. Livsey and his supporters 'spoke the dialect and were the product of a wilder, more boisterous age than austere Nonconformists like Bright' who 'did a good stroke of business on Good Samaritan, Temperance and Missionary platforms'.

Divisions of style and policy were carried through into the 1850s, to reveal themselves most prominently in Bright's continued opposition to trade unionism and manhood suffrage, and in the famous victories won by Livsey and his allies in favour of a more extensive local franchise and democratic form of town government than was desired by Bright and many other Liberal millowners. As Cole suggests, Livsey and his group sought 'to impose the Charter at local level' as against employer attempts to establish middle-class political as well as economic power. Indeed, for much of the 1850s Livsey's group was in control of the town council. Livsey's death in 1864 accelerated popular movement into and accommodation with local Liberalism. But, as Cole concludes, up to the mid-1860s this movement had been extremely limited. Thus:

> local middle-class attempts at proselytisation met with very little success throughout our period. The working classes retained a remarkable independence of spirit, selecting those planks of reformism which suited their purpose and rejecting those which they considered to be irrelevant or actively detrimental to their interests.

Finally, we can revisit fruitfully our initial examples of Ashton, Stalybridge and Bradford further to indicate the contradictions and tensions which often characterised even mellowed forms of mid-Victorian Liberalism. As we shall see in more detail below, Tories, and especially Tory radicals such as Rayner Stephens, continued to attract considerable popular support in Ashton and Stalybridge for their condemnations of the 'tyranny', 'hypocrisy', 'intolerance' and 'inhuman' doctrines of the ruling elite of Nonconformist Liberal manufacturers. Stephens, for example, was loud in his criticisms of the continued opposition of leading Manchester School paternalist and non-paternalist Liberal employers to factory legislation and trade unionism, their simultaneous support for 'freedom' and wage slavery, their attempted absolute control (often masquerading as paternalist concern) over their operatives' lives both inside and outside work, their fierce intolerance of drink and non-'improving', robust patterns of working-class culture, and, in manifest opposition to their carefully constructed public declarations of a change of heart, their effective treatment of workers less as human beings than as impersonal items of cost, as objects. Furthermore, as shown by Janet Toole, during the industrial conflicts of the early 1860s and the ensuing Cotton Famine independent working-class opposition to, respectively, liberal 'wage slavery' and reactionary chattel slavery (the latter as practised in the American south) was extensively voiced in Ashton and Stalybridge.[34] In Bradford, as in many mid-Victorian urban centres, continued adherence to the principles of 'economy' and individualism placed serious limits upon the extent to which new-found Liberal commitments to urban and social reform by means of municipal intervention and initiative would be translated into practice. In Bradford practical improvements in public health provision and in general environmental conditions thus fell a long way short of the rhetorical promise of unlimited advance and progress. As Koditschek has concluded,

> Bradford Liberals' commitment in principle to a program of positive urban reform was not matched by any concrete sense of how this might be embodied in practical measures that were neither so costly as to be rejected by the ratepayers or so restrictive of competitive individualism as to be incompatible with the general precepts of the entrepreneurial ideal.[35]

In turning, finally, away from our urban case studies to a consideration of the attitudes of radicals and Liberals towards more general policy issues, a similar picture of a complex and changing mixture of points of agreement, accommodation, negotiation, difference, tension and conflict – emerges from the evidence. For example, Margot Finn's recent work has highlighted both the shared support of Chartists and middle-class reformers for Continental nationalist movements between 1848 and 1858 and the considerable differences (most prominently around the issues of intervention versus non-intervention in foreign affairs, and *laissez-faire* versus state intervention in socio-economic matters and the promotion of radical social change) which continued to divide them.[36] It is Finn's further contention that, in the context of the nationalist movements of the 1860s (especially in Poland and Italy), middle-class reformers 'began to develop a more pragmatic liberalism in collaboration with radical working men'.[37] Modification of the principles of *laissez-faire* and voluntarism, a more sympathetic approach to issues of state intervention and trade union recognition and legal protection, overlaps in personnel and ideology between the Reform Union (1864) and the Reform League (1865), combined working and middle-class agitation for reform in 1866 and 1867 and support for disestablishment of the Church in Ireland, and some middle-class radical support for the causes of republicanism and land reform in the early 1870s, have thus been cited by Finn as evidence of the mid- as opposed to (the conventionally dated) late Victorian emergence of 'New Liberalism'.

There are important elements of truth in Finn's contention. As noted earlier, we cannot doubt the very significant facts of 'liberalisation' across and within classes and political organisations and the merger of popular radicalism and Gladstonian Liberalism. However, as David Nicholls has persuasively argued, Finn's case is overstated. The commitment of middle-class radicals to social democratic politics was 'limited and ephemeral and not . . . sufficient to regard this period as marking the inauguration of a New Liberalism'. Similarly, many elements of the old Liberalism, centrally embracing liberal individualism, were temporarily put aside during the late 1860s and early 1870s period of enhanced working-class political and industrial agitation and pressure, rather than permanently abandoned. As Nicholls concludes, Liberalism in the 1870s embraced a variety of attitudes and positions which rose and fell in absolute and relative importance more in accordance with 'strategic and episodic responses to moments of conflict and crisis in capital–labour relations' than with any linear intellectual progression from individualism to collectivism. And fluctuating moments of class-based tension and harmony constituted essential features of a Liberal alliance which was negotiated, constructed and renegotiated rather than 'given' in any absolute, final sense.[38]

Popular conservatism

Just as the evidence concerning mid-Victorian popular Liberalism lends itself to the case for 'discontinuity' more than to that for continuity, so it does, in far more pronounced and unambiguous a fashion, in relation to the development of mid-Victorian popular Conservatism. As noted in the introduction, and *pace* the claims of David Walsh,[39] Conservatism generally failed to put down strong working-class organisational roots in the 1830s and 1840s. The Operative Conservative Associations established during these decades frequently contained far more middle-class members than workers. Similarly, the ideological appeal of Toryism to 'the people' was very limited, especially in those urban areas where Chartism was strong. The Conservative Party was thus widely associated far more with the defence of property and inequality and with opposition to the causes of political reform and the advancement of religious and civil liberties than with social radicalism. Indeed, beyond its heartland in the West Riding of Yorkshire, Tory radicalism – complete with its support for factory legislation and other forms of paternalist state regulation and for working-class collective defences, such as trade unionism, against unrestrained market forces – was weak. For example, in several Lancashire cotton centres, including Preston, Bolton, Blackburn, Bury and Rochdale, Conservatives were prominent members of the 'millocracy'. In many cases they actively opposed factory reform and any form of working-class threat to the absolute rule of property.[40] As noted earlier, the Chartists did at times form alliances with the Tories. But these were temporary and tactical rather than principled in character.

From the mid-1840s there was growing, if uneven and qualified, evidence to suggest that Conservatism was both increasingly appreciative of popular support and prepared to modify its policies accordingly. The threat posed by Chartism to the *status quo* and a desire to compete with the power and popularity of the Anti-Corn Law League underpinned, in large measure, significant and greatly enlarged Conservative support for factory legislation in the form of the Ten Hours Bill. In some towns, such as Oldham, former Chartist radicals who were strongly opposed to liberal individualism and *laissez-faire* did find the anti-Manchester School views of mid-Victorian Conservatism far more congenial than the 'condescending' and 'self-righteous' improving message of Liberalism.[41] And at the national level Robert Peel did make a genuine and very determined effort, by reducing taxes on consumption and the repeal of the corn laws, to present Conservatism as representing the national interest rather than purely sectional concerns.[42] Simultaneously, however, neither the extent, speed nor popular influence of such changes should be exaggerated. Notwithstanding our extremely limited knowledge of 1850s and early 1860s popular Conservatism (which presents a marked contrast to the historiographical attention lavished upon popular Liberalism in the same period), we do know that well into the mid-Victorian years (and beyond) many Conservatives retained their dread of 'social levelling' and 'mobocracy'. Furthermore, as the reader will already be aware, the vast majority of organised labour's mid-Victorian leaders pledged their support to radicalism and Liberalism rather than Conservatism. While these leaders equated radicalism and Liberalism with 'the ideals of enlightenment, toleration, progress and reason', they continued to identify Toryism with 'ignorance, reaction, intolerance and an appeal to the "baser instincts" of rowdyism, bellicosity and hedonism'. The notions of independence, self-respect and corporate, even class pride – so dear to the hearts of labour activists – were believed to be incompatible with the very idea of Conservatism. Thus

> A political party which represented aristocratic privilege and monopoly (the 'privileges of Wellington boots and the humble and reverent submission of clogs') and which, despite its actions in 1867, had a strong tradition of opposition to the franchise, was hardly to the liking of labour leaders who prided themselves upon their progressive views and their sturdy independence which 'fears no influence and obeys no master but the dictates of its own reason'.[43]

We can also detect, during the 1850s and 1860s, considerable anxiety in Conservative circles, and smugness on the part of the Liberals, concerning the party's supposed failure effectively to reach not only organised labour's committed activists but also significant numbers of the wider working class and especially those workers living and working in impersonal urban, as opposed to close rural communities who were believed to be naturally beyond the sway of tradition and influence. The growing reassertion – indeed, significant spread and development – of paternalism among predominantly wealthy Conservative as well as Liberal employers, combined with Conservatism's defence of Church and Queen against 'aggressive Popery', the party's established dominance in many rural communities and among selected groups of 'instrumental' workers (such as coal miners locked, in certain locations, into the 'paternalism–deference equilibrium'[44]) acted to mitigate Tory anxieties. However, in truth, it appeared to many within the party that the 'popular cause' had effectively been won by the radicals and Liberals. For example, during the mid-Victorian period of Liberal ascendancy in the cotton district of Lancashire and Cheshire many Conservatives 'often bemoaned their failure to enlist active and widespread popular support'. In Stockport lack of support forced the disbandment in 1856 of the Tradesmen's and Operatives' Conservative Association, while at neighbouring Ashton and Dukinfield the Conservatives confessed to having little organised and effective popular presence before the unexpected upheavals wrought by the general election of 1868. Even in the more auspicious climate of that year – when Conservatives were to make full political capital out of the No Popery issue – a Conservative working man was still held by the Liberals of Ashton to be 'the strangest creature imaginable'.[45]

There is, nevertheless, no doubt that, especially in Lancashire, Conservatism's popular appeal and electoral record underwent a dramatic and generally sustained improvement from the mid to late 1860s onwards. Given the paucity and patchiness of the evidence available for the pre-1868 years, it is difficult to set a precise date upon this transformation in Conservatism's fortunes. But we do know that in many of the Lancashire cotton towns outbreaks of anti-Irish Catholic feeling (for example, in Stockport in 1852 and Oldham in 1861) had already been accompanied by intensely passionate appeals to the 'people' by Conservatives and, in some cases, Orangemen to rally round the established Church in defence of English liberties – against the alleged desires of the papacy to establish universal Catholic domination (with the Irish immigrants as 'papal puppets'), to make Queen Victoria a papist, to transform England (through the unwitting agency of the poverty-stricken immigrants) into 'a great workhouse' and 'to persecute and prosecute every Protestant . . . to set up the inquisition in our land'.[46] The extent to which the Tories had derived both sizeable and lasting popular support from such urgent appeals and dire warnings is difficult to measure. It was certainly the case that in parts of Lancashire, such as Liverpool and Wigan, and western Scotland powerful ethnic antagonisms and allegiances remained at the very core of working-class life for most, if not all, of the nineteenth century and contributed greatly to the strong and intimately related popular appeal of Conservatism and Orangeism. By way of contrast, in the north-east of England anti-Catholic disturbances and the ethnic foundations of popular Toryism were far less pronounced.[47] In the cotton towns matters were, at least in the 1850s and early 1860s, quite complex and uneven. In some towns, such as Bolton, it appears to have been the case that Conservatism's enhanced appeal of the 1850s and its newly created 'mass following' of the ensuing decade owed less to the political fall-out of ethnic conflict (although Tories and churchmen did attempt to exploit anti-Irish Catholic feeling in the post-Famine years) than to its 'endorsement of traditional forms of leisure and amusement in the face of Bolton's increasingly visible temperance movement'.[48] In those centres which had witnessed serious and repeated anti-Irish Catholic disturbances during the 1850s, such as Stockport and Ashton, the various Protestant 'defence' associations, closely allied with the forces of local Conservatism, registered important increases in their popularity among cotton operatives and other workers. There were also ominous signs of revived Orangeism. In 1857, for example, Ashton's most prominent Orangemen, Booth Mason (brother of the leading Liberal, Hugh), contested the general election on the platform of No Popery and support for manhood suffrage. Mason received the show of hands at the hustings but was defeated at the poll. In many of the cotton towns the Orange Order, equipped with an explosive ideological cocktail of anti-republicanism, anti-Catholicism and frequent support for trade unionism and factory legislation, made important popular gains between the mid-1850s and mid-1860s. Furthermore, there developed very close links between Orangeism, Conservatism and the various Protestant associations. Tragically, Chartism, a potent force for internationalism and working-class unity, capable of challenging and overturning religious and cultural prejudices among workers, no longer enjoyed mass support. Leading figures in the labour movement and the Liberal Party did continue to voice their opposition to chauvinism and bigotry, but to limited effect. Notwithstanding variations in the presence, and the ebbs and flows, of ethnic divisions and conflicts in the mid-Victorian cotton district, there is little doubt that by the mid-1860s strong ethno-cultural foundations had been laid for the growth of popular Conservatism.[49]

Matters came to a head in 1868. Anti-Fenianism (during 1866 and 1867) combined with economic distress (during the winter of 1867), Gladstone's plans for the disestablishment of the Irish Church (which figured prominently in the general election of 1868) and the ubiquitous presence and anti-Catholic demagogy of William Murphy and other fanatical members of the Protestant Electoral Union conspired to produce ugly, and in centres such as Ashton and Stalybridge chronic, anti-Catholic riots in 1868 both in Lancashire and well beyond. The emotive and extreme tone of the general election, which turned crucially upon the Conservative and Orange slogan of 'No Popery', was reflected in a Conservative election placard at Stalybridge. 'THE QUEEN OR THE POPE,' read the placard issued in favour of Sibebottom, the Conservative candidate,

> which will you have to reign over you – Will you suffer Mr Gladstone to destroy the supremacy of your sovereign and substitute the supremacy of the POPE? SIDEBOTTOM CALLS to 'English freemen' to assert their rights.[50]

In the event Gladstone survived such inflammatory propaganda to guide the Liberals into office. However, in the cotton district, and often within urban areas of former Chartist strength, mid-Victorian Liberal electoral ascendancy was effectively overturned. As John Walton has observed, 'In the 1865 general election, Lancashire's twenty-eight seats had been evenly divided; three years later . . . the Conservatives won twenty-four to the Liberals' twelve.'

Furthermore, notes Walton, the 'remarkable reversal of fortunes' in 1868 was no mere flash in the pan. Thus:

The Conservatives held on to most of their gains in 1874, and the Liberals' recovery of lost ground in 1880 was only temporary. Under the wider county franchise of 1884, and the ensuing redistribution which increased the number of Lancashire seats to fifty-eight, the Conservatives won thirty-eight seats in 1885, including five out of six in Manchester, and they continued to dominate the county's electoral map until the Liberal landslide of 1906.[51]

As contemporaries fully realised, the elections of 1868 and beyond revealed 'the hitherto unsuspected strength of working-class Conservatism'. Under the household suffrage provision of the Second Reform Act, the electorate in the cotton town constituencies was increased 'fivefold or sixfold', thus giving working-class voters 'a clear predominance in the manufacturing towns'. Furthermore, it was these newly enfranchised working-class men who exerted a significant influence upon Tory electoral successes in 1868. For example,

> At Manchester approximately 7,000 workers voted Tory, and at Ashton, Milner Gibson, the defeated Liberal candidate, claimed that the working-class vote had proved decisive at the election. Sidebottom, the popular millowner and successful Conservative candidate at Stalybridge, claimed that he was not the nominee of 'some half-dozen gentlemen in broadcloth ... but the working people of the district'. Sidebottom had been 'brought out' by some 2,000 workers.

Henceforth, many former strongholds of Chartism in the cotton district, such as Stalybridge and its neighbourhood and Hulme and New Cross in Manchester, would be known – to the end of the century and even beyond – more for their 'clog Toryism' (a combination of old-fashioned paternalism, ethno-chauvinism and Orangeism) than for their class-conscious transforming radicalism.[52] Finally, it is important to note that the strong growth of popular urban Toryism in the cotton district was part of a national trend which saw, between 1868 and the 1890s, 'a serious decline for urban Liberalism' and a 'lurch towards Conservatism' in 'important urban, manufacturing communities'.[53]

A key factor in the remarkable transformation of the fortunes of Conservatism among workers has already been identified. The adoption of the slogan No Popery usefully served the interests of Conservative politicians and Orangemen in a variety of ways.

First, it enabled them to be seen as both traditional and radical Protestant heroes, prepared to defend and fight for those religious, political and social rights of the 'freeborn Englishman' – liberty of individual conscience and 'rational' choice, parliamentary government, the rule of law and limited monarchical power – which had been won during the Reformation and the seventeenth century against the 'evil', 'dark' and 'tyrannical' powers of the papacy, the forces of the Counter-Reformation and either openly pro- or crypto-Catholic monarchs and their supporters. Thus the Pope's restoration of the Catholic hierarchy in 1850 met with a storm of (predominantly middle-class) Protestant opposition on the grounds that it signalled an immediate threat to such hard-won rights and freedoms, and aimed officially to strengthen and geographically to extend the influence of papal power and authority and the 'irrational superstitions' of the Roman Catholic religion. Restoration simultaneously confirmed in the minds of, and alerted many Protestants in England to, the papacy's enduring plans for universal domination, its close identification with political and religious autocracy and mumbo-jumbo, the 'mindless uniformity' demanded of its flock and its supposed antipathy to parliamentary values and government. In a similar fashion Gladstone's proposed disestablishment of the Irish Church would later be portrayed by many Conservatives (in a manner to be perfected by twentieth-century Cold War domino theorists) as craven capitulation to the despotic global designs of the papacy, to alien domination. Furthermore, demagogues such as Murphy deliberately added sexual fears and threats to those of religion, politics and culture by 'disclosing', often to purely female gatherings, the 'hidden desires' and 'awful acts' of the Catholic priesthood.[54]

Second, traditionally radical, if also sometimes inflammatory, prurient and thinly substantiated, aspects of the No Popery propaganda were, however, greatly overshadowed by racist and reactionary usages, directed specifically against the post-Famine Irish Catholic immigrants. Notwithstanding the dissociation of some prominent Conservatives from the excesses of Murphyism and Orangeism, and the considerable efforts made by the Catholic Church to render its constituents more acceptable to the host population (by means, for example, of frequent protestations of loyalty to the people and institutions of their adopted country, and of the more widespread promotion of respectable habits, values and institutions), there is no doubt that Conservatives and Churchmen regularly adopted the most negative stereotypes of the Catholic immigrants and their religious leaders. As our preceding narrative has suggested, the immigrants were thus often portrayed as the ignorant, unthinking dupes and puppets of their scheming masters and subversive of the living and moral standards of the host working class, while the priesthood was variously seen as autocratic, irrational, indecent and hypocritical in its beliefs and behaviour.

In sum, and taking due account of important variations in the incidence, extent and duration of anti-Catholic disturbances in mid-Victorian Britain, the visceral politics of No Popery, chauvinism and racism furnished important bases of popular support for the Conservative Party. As the Liberal *Ashton Reporter* declared in 1868, workers voted Conservative because they believed Protestant warnings that 'we were on the verge of Popery, and unless measures were taken to arrest its progress, the Pope of Rome would be King of England'.[55] (See document 7.)

At the same time, however, we must cast our explanatory net wider and deeper in order to present a suitably complete and balanced view of the development of popular Conservatism. Even in 1868 a minority of Tories were sceptical of or opposed to the aggressive anti-Catholicism of their party. (And we must remember that there was a strong tradition of indigenous and wealthy Roman Catholicism in Lancashire.) Similarly, by no means all those labouring people in the cotton district who moved from Chartism to Conservatism did so necessarily, primarily or exclusively on grounds of opposition to Irish Catholic immigrants and their religion. Some who retained their Chartist commitment to internationalism, working-class unity and religious and cultural diversity, toleration and liberty were seemingly influenced far more by the softened, more accommodating and extended social-radical features of mid-Victorian Conservatism than its 1868 battle-cry of No Popery. It is, for example, interesting to note the continued and strong appeal within the district of Ashton and Stalybridge, itself the very epicentre of anti-Catholic rioting, of the personality and social radicalism of Joseph Rayner Stephens.[56] A supporter of Conservatism and a committed churchman and monarchist (still, in the 1860s, advocating alliances based upon 'The Altar, the Throne and the Cottage' and 'The Aristocracy and the People'), Stephens nevertheless voiced his strong opposition to anti-Irish Catholic actions and sentiments. As implied earlier in this chapter, Stephens's continued popular appeal was rooted in his criticisms of the harsh, parsimonious and hypocritical Manchester School economic doctrines of many local Liberal employers (especially during the Cotton Famine) and in his enduring support for factory legislation, trade unionism and the Englishman's right to 'the mug that cheers' against the temperance and teetotal sentiments of local Liberalism. Furthermore, and not withstanding Liberalism's softened mid-Victorian image and practice, Stephens's brand of social radicalism found ready support and echoes among Conservatives in Lancashire, Yorkshire and indeed nationally. For example, widespread reference was made by Tory candidates at the 1868 general election to John Bright's opposition to the Ten Hours Bill and, to say the least, his continued ambiguity towards the principles and practices of trade unionism. In Manchester the leading Conservative W.R. Callendar worked with the Tory leaders of the Manchester and Salford Trades Council, W.H. Wood and S.C. Nicholson, to promote wider public acceptance of trade unionism. In the West Riding of Yorkshire, especially in Huddersfield, Bradford and Keighley, the Tory radical cause remained strong. And in Ashton and Stalybridge local Conservatives 'mounted fierce and unrelenting attacks upon Liberal "dictatorship"'. For example, those in Hugh Mason's extensive works who succumbed to the temptations of beer, tobacco and 'general frivolity' were, according to 'local knowledge', strongly in danger of losing their jobs and their rented homes in Mason's 'Oxford Colony'. As Patrick Joyce has concluded,

> If the Tory politician was tarred with the brush of reaction, the Liberal was tarred with that of social and economic *laissez-faire*. No matter how much the rigours of political economy had been moderated, something of the charge stuck, and the Tories did their best to see that it stuck.[57]

The development of a distinct Conservative style, tone and culture also helped to enhance the party's popular appeal. For example, while the practices of paternalism – of 'trips and treats' and attempted employer influence over the entire way of life and political allegiance of the factory neighbourhood – were followed by Tory and Liberal employers alike, nevertheless the former often addressed and sought to cultivate different working-class habits and customs from those of the latter. Above all, Tory paternalists and politicians empathised far more with the robust, outgoing, relaxed and commonsensical forms of working-class life than their more improving and earnest Liberal counterparts. Thus,

> Whether in Blackburn, Stalybridge or Wolverhampton the Tories prided themselves upon their broad, relaxed, informal, tolerant, robust and patriotic appeal to 'the people' . . . Much like the Liberals, the Tories consciously attempted to create a political culture rooted in the notion of 'community'. But whereas the Liberals sought 'community' in the the earnest, temperate, self-improvers of all social strata, the Tories were far more tolerant of the 'weaknesses' of the people. The 'respectable' working man – who nevertheless liked sports, including 'manly' blood sports, betting, drinking . . . and was sociable and easy-going, who was a 'natural' defender of Church and State . . . who identified a close affinity between himself and his family and the propertied rulers of society, who disliked the self-righteous, morally intense and priggish among Liberal working men, and who had a strong sense of 'place' as embodied in local and national pride – constituted the target of Tory propaganda. Conservatism thus situated itself within the culture of 'conviviality and bonhomie', of 'beer, bacca, billiards and Britannia' rather than within the straitjacketed Liberal domain of 'moral exhortation' and the 'improving tract'.[58]

To argue in this manner is not to ignore the presence among Conservatives of eminently respectable, earnest and 'improving' types, or to suggest the very incompatibility of Liberalism, drink and boisterous behaviour. It is, however, to indicate patterns of cultural preference and predominant attachments, much in the manner of pointing to the close, as opposed to invariable, connections between Conservatism and Anglicanism and Liberalism and Nonconformity. Joyce's perception is most apposite:

> There were many 'improvement'-conscious Tory employers and 'improving' Tory working men, but Toryism in general, rather more than Liberalism, was adaptable, and capable of appealing to all

social and cultural levels, the godly and the godless, the 'abstinent' and the indulgent. The Tory voice often spoke of things the chapel knew not, in the accents of indiscipline and unrespectability.[59]

Brief attention to the style, tone and place of Conservatism in the north Lancashire weaving town of Blackburn can serve to illustrate the general points made above. In 1867 Blackburn was described as 'a thoroughgoing Tory community'. The town was dominated by Conservative employers, especially the Hornby family in cotton, who provide a nice contrast to Hugh Mason, our depicted exemplar of changes in mid-Victorian Liberalism.[60] Like Mason, the Hornbys underwent something of a transformation at mid-century. Shot at during the strikes of 1842, William Henry Hornby, the employer of well in excess of 1,000 cotton operatives, had on several occasions been the butt of radical anger and frustration. However, by the late 1840s Hornby had become a firm defender of the Ten Hours Act. Between the mid-1850s and the beginning of the twentieth century Tory political, social and cultural hegemony prevailed in Blackburn. And the Hornby family - with their mixture of social radicalism, paternalism and appeal to the John Bull-like qualities of the people - played a vital role in the establishment and consolidation of that hegemony. In 1853, for example,

> William Hornby treated members of the Operative Conservative Association to a trip to Blackpool and a ball and banquet on their return. In his speech at the banquet Hornby 'congratulated them on their continued existence and on the recent success of the town's working class . . . in gaining an increase of ten per cent'. He further defended the legitimacy of trades unionism, and denounced the 'tyrannical masters' . . .

As Geoffrey Trodd has splendidly demonstrated, the 'common sense' of 'flamboyant Hornbyism/Toryism' was rooted far less in any commitment to a formal and precise political programme than in strong identification with 'common' and 'natural' ways of seeing and being, with the very routines and values of daily life. A permissive attitude was adopted to popular pastimes, and the key institutions of the community - the pubs, friendly and burial societies, football teams and parts of the trade union movement - were profoundly influenced by a partisan Tory presence. The active cultivation of a sense of place - of established, enduring and valued personal and local relationships and connections – and of service to the community were vital ingredients in the succcess of Blackburn Conservatism. Harry Hornby 'gave generously' to football clubs, church schools and boys' clubs. Members of the family as a whole were strongly populist, abiding by the common touch and instinct rather than aloof intellect, theory or intentions of 'getting on'. Thus

> W.H. Hornby had once been a steeplechaser and Harry Hornby's brother, the cricketer A.N. Hornby, was known as 'a bit of a card' and 'The Boss', rode to hounds, had been a member of Blackburn Rovers for a time and taken on boxers in fairground booths. John Rutherford, 'owd Jack', kept a prizewinning racehorse and liked to end his speeches by drawing a union jack from his pocket like a conjuror and waving it at the audience.

Abundant references to the blessings of empire and monarchy and negative references to foreigners (including both those predominantly non-whites beyond the British Isles and Liberal, Labour and socialist 'improvers', unversed in and alien to 'local ways') completed this populist portrait.

Blackburn's Tories' attempts to portray themselves as the true representatives of the community, the nation and the working man and his family (women being seen as supportive and secondary figures) and to brand the Liberals as puritanical killjoys were to be repeated, albeit to varying degrees and within distinct local and regional contexts, in many communities throughout the country. At the national level, the linkage of a robust and predominantly anti-intellectual and masculine cultural appeal to traditionalism, paternalism, No Popery, social radicalism and (following Disraeli's 'leap in the dark' in 1867) Tory democracy rendered Conservatism a potent, and far from unnatural or deviant, political force among workers. By the late 1860s radicals and Liberals had to face the uncomfortable fact that the Conservative Party had become a serious threat to their assumed right to represent the 'popular mind'. Those Chartist veterans possessed of even longer political memories could rue a more fundamental discontinuity: the mass, independent working-class politics of the 1830s and 1840s had more or less disappeared from sight. Working-class political fragmentation, along the lines of progressive Liberalism and populist and radical Toryism, had become the order of the day.

Notes

1 N. Kirk, *The Growth of Working Class Reformism in Mid-Victorian England* (Beckenham, 1985), pp. 63–4.

2 N. Kirk, 'The Continuing Relevance and Engagements of Class', *Labour History Review*, 60:3 (1995) 9.

3 See, for example, M. Winstanley, 'Oldham Radicalism and the Origins of Popular Liberalism 1830–52', *Historical Journal*, 36:3 (1993) 619–43; P.F. Taylor, *Popular Politics in Early Industrial Britain: Bolton 1825–1850* (Keele, 1995), chapter 4 and conclusion; G. Crossick, *An Artisan Elite in Victorian Society: Kentish London 1840–1880* (London, 1988); B. Harrison and P. Hollis (eds), *Robert Lowery: Radical and Chartist* (London, 1979); B. Harrison and P. Hollis, 'Chartism, Liberalism and the Life of Robert Lowery', *English Historical Review*, 82 (1967) 503–35.

4 R.A. Sykes, 'Popular Politics and Trade Unionism in South-east Lancashire 1829–1842' (Ph.D. thesis, University of Manchester, 1982), pp. 455–68.

5 D. Thompson, *The Chartists* (Aldershot, 1986), p. 237.

6 Kirk, 'Continuing Relevance', 10.

7 Sykes, 'Popular Politics', pp. 453–4.

8 *Ibid.*, chapter 10.

9 J. Breuilly, G. Niedhart and A. Taylor (eds), *The Era of the Reform League: English Labour and Radical Politics 1857–1872* (Mannheim, 1995), general introduction; Edward Royle's review of John Belchem's *Popular Radicalism in Nineteenth-century Britain*, *Labour History Review*, 61:3 (1996) 346–8.

10 A.D. Taylor, 'Modes of Political Expression and Working-class Radicalism 1848–74: The London and Manchester Examples' (Ph.D. thesis, University of Manchester, 1992), pp. 70–2.

11 *Ibid.*, p. 541.

12 B. Harrison, *Drink and the Victorians: The Temperance Question in England 1815–1872* (Pittsburgh, 1971), p. 25.

13 P. Joyce, *Democratic Subjects* (Cambridge, 1994).

14 E.F. Biagini and A.J. Reid (eds), *Currents of Radicalism* (Cambridge, 1991), pp. 5–6; E.F. Biagini, *Liberty, Retrenchment and Reform: Popular Liberalism in the Age of Gladstone 1860–1880* (Cambridge, 1992).

15 This is particularly evident in Joyce's very thin treatment of class-conscious Chartism in Lancashire and Cheshire and of conflict with

Liberalism. See N. Kirk, 'Setting the Standard: Dorothy Thompson, the Discipline of History and the Study of Chartism', in O. Ashton, R. Fyson and S. Roberts (eds), *The Duty of Discontent: Essays for Dorothy Thompson* (London, 1995), p. 30, n. 35.

16　N. Kirk, 'In Defence of Class', *International Review of Social History*, 32:1 (1987) 8–9; G.S. Jones, 'The Language of Chartism', in J. Epstein and D. Thompson (eds), *The Chartist Experience: Studies in Working-class Radicalism and Culture 1830–1860* (London, 1982), pp. 13, 20, 30–1, 34. See also Miles Taylor, *The Decline of British Radicalism 1847–1860* (Oxford, 1995), for the notion of a decline in *independent* radicalism and the latter's growing incorporation into the two-party system by the late 1850s, especially pp. 6, 338.

17　See, for example, D. Thompson, *Outsiders: Class, Gender and Nation* (London, 1993), pp. 21–37; Kirk, 'In Defence of Class', 37–43.

18　For the aims of Chartism see Kirk, 'In Defence of Class', 35–7; G.S. Jones, 'Class Struggle and the Industrial Revolution', in his *Languages of Class* (Cambridge, 1983), pp. 58–9, 73.

19　J. Foster, *Class Struggle and the Industrial Revolution* (London, 1974), pp. 186–94, chapter 7.

20　Kirk, *Reformism*, p. 294.

21　T. Koditschek, *Class Formation and Urban Industrial Society: Bradford 1750–1850* (Cambridge, 1990), p. 565, chapter 18; T. Koditschek, 'The Dynamics of Class Formation in Nineteenth-century Bradford', in A.L. Beier, D. Cannadine and J.M. Rosenheim (eds), *The First Modern Society: Essays in English History in Honour of Lawrence Stone* (Cambridge, 1989), p. 511.

22　Koditschek, 'Dynamics', p. 545.

23　Winstanley, 'Oldham Radicalism'; Taylor, *Popular Politics*; Foster, *Class Struggle*; Crossick, *Artisan Elite*; R.Q. Gray, *The Labour Aristocracy in Victorian Edinburgh* (Oxford, 1976); J. Vincent, *The Formation of the British Liberal Party 1857–1868* (London, 1972); A.D. Taylor, 'Ernest Jones, his Later Career and the Structure of Manchester Politics, 1861–1869' M.A. thesis, University of Birmingham, 1984); D. Gadian, 'Radicalism and Liberalism in Oldham: A Study of Conflict, Continuity and Change in Popular Politics 1830–52', *Social History*, 21:3 (1996) 268.

24　Breuilly *et al.*, *Era of the Reform League*, p. 70; J. Vickers, 'Pressure Group Politics, Class and Popular Liberalism: The Campaign for Parliamentary Reform in the North West 1864–1868' (Ph.D. thesis, Manchester Metropolitan University, 1997), p. 43.

25　Taylor, 'Modes of Political Expression'.

26　Taylor, 'Ernest Jones'; Breuilly *et al.*, *Era of the Reform League*, pp. 16–22, 115–16, 120.

27　Breuilly *et al.*, *Era of the Reform League*, pp. 41, 115–16, 167–8.

28 P.A. Pickering, *Chartism and the Chartists in Manchester and Salford* (London, 1995), pp. 173–5; Taylor, 'Ernest Jones', pp. 86–90.

29 Taylor, 'Modes of Political Expression', pp. 397, 417–18; Pickering, *Chartism and the Chartists*, pp. 181–2.

30 N. Kirk, *Labour and Society in Britain and the USA*, II, *Challenge and Accommodation 1850–1939* (Aldershot, 1994), p. 188.

31 Gadian, 'Radicalism and Liberalism'; Winstanley, 'Oldham Radicalism'; K. Tiller, 'Late Chartism: Halifax 1847–58', in J.A. Epstein and D. Thompson (eds), *The Chartist Experience* (London, 1982).

32 Vincent, *Formation of the Liberal Party*, pp. 145–6; P. Joyce, *Democratic Subjects* (Cambridge, 1994), Part II.

33 J. Cole, *Rochdale Revisited: A Town and its People*, II (Littleborough, 1990), pp. 37–44; J. Cole, 'Chartism in Rochdale' (unpublished MS, Manchester Polytechnic, 1986); Kirk, *Challenge and Accommodation*, pp. 185–6.

34 J. Toole, 'Workers and Slaves: Class Relations in South Lancashire in the Time of the Cotton Famine', *Labour History Review* (forthcoming).

35 Koditschek, *Class Formation*, p. 537.

36 M. Finn, *After Chartism: Class and Nation in English Radical Politics 1848–1874* (Cambridge, 1993); Breuilly *et al.*, *Era of the Reform League*, pp. 68–70.

37 D. Nicholls, 'The New Liberalism – after Chartism?', *Social History*, 21:3 (1996) 330.

38 *Ibid.*, J. Belchem, *Popular Radicalism in Nineteenth-century Britain* (London, 1996), chapter 6.

39 D. Walsh, 'Operative Conservatism in Lancashire 1833–1846' (Occasional Paper 11, Department of Politics and Contemporary History, University of Salford, 1987).

40 Vincent, *Formation of the Liberal Party*; Taylor, *Popular Politics*, pp. 66–70, 120–5; P. Joyce, *Work, Society and Politics: The Culture of the Factory in Later Victorian England* (Brighton, 1980), chapter 1.

41 Gadian, 'Radicalism and Liberalism', 279.

42 Sykes, 'Popular Politics', p. 467; Jones, *Languages of Class*, pp. 176–7.

43 Kirk, *Reformism*, p. 161.

44 E.P. Thompson, *Customs in Common* (London, 1991), p. 71. It should be noted that Thompson's usage referred to eighteenth-century relations between 'patricians and plebs'.

45 Kirk, *Reformism*, pp. 335, 347.

46 *Ibid.*, pp. 316–17.

47 P.J. Waller, *Democracy and Sectarianism: A Political and Social History of Liverpool 1868–1939* (Liverpool, 1981); F. Neal, *Sectarian Violence: The Liverpool Experience 1819–1914* (Manchester, 1988); F. Neal, 'English–Irish Conflict in the North-east of England', in P. Buckland and J.

Belchem (eds), *The Irish in British Labour History* (Conference Proceedings in Irish Studies, 1, University of Liverpool, March 1992); A. Campbell, 'Honourable Men and Degraded Slaves: A Comparative Study of Trade Unionism in Two Lanarkshire Mining Communities, *c.* 1830–1874', in R. Harrison (ed.), *Independent Collier: The Coal Miner as Archetypal Proletarian Reconsidered* (Hassocks, 1978), pp. 82–97; R. Swift and S. Gilley (eds), *The Irish in Britain 1815–1939* (London, 1989).

48   Taylor, *Popular Politics*, pp. 120–6, 223.

49   Kirk, *Reformism*, pp. 316, 318–20, 337–8; D. Thompson, 'Ireland and the Irish in English Radicalism before 1850' in her *Outsiders*.

50   Kirk, *Reformism*, p. 340.

51   J.K. Walton, *Lancashire: A Social History 1558–1939* (Manchester, 1987), p. 258.

52   Kirk, *Reformism*, p. 336: Pickering, *Chartism and the Chartists*, p. 183.

53   J. Lawrence, 'Popular Politics and the Limitations of Party: Wolverhampton 1867–1900', in Biagini and Reid, *Currents of Radicalism*, p. 66.

54   For similar 'disclosures' see *Awful Disclosures of Maria Monk* (London, 1836).

55   *Ashton Reporter*, 28 November 1868.

56   Toole, 'Workers and Slaves'; Kirk, *Reformism*, pp. 189–90.

57   Joyce, *Work Society and Politics*, p. 323.

58   Kirk, *Challenge and Accommodation*, pp. 194–5.

59   Joyce, *Work Society and Polities*, p. 187.

60   For Conservatism in Blackburn see G. Trodd, 'Political Change and the Working Class in Blackburn and Burnley, 1880–1914' (Ph.D. thesis, University of Lancaster, 1978); Joyce, *Work, Society and Politics*, pp. 187–91, 215–17; Kirk, *Challenge and Accommodation*, pp. 195–7.

5

Divided cultures

Substantive and methodological issues

Attention was drawn in the previous chapter to the widespread assumption among contemporaries of the centrality of culture – employed in its broad sense to mean a way of life – to politics. Thus, whereas both of the mainstream parties set out to cast their socio-cultural net as wide and deep as conventional 'respectable' and gender-based norms would allow, nevertheless we have observed that conscious processes of socio-cultural preference, marginalisation, exclusion and stereotyping were strongly at work. The vast majority of mainstream politicians saw women as properly belonging to the private sphere of the home and as naturally outside the public world of politics. Similarly, and notwithstanding party utilisation of their services upon selected occasions (such as during elections riots and the exertion of the political 'screw'), neither party generally wished to publicise support drawn from non-respectable, poor or 'rough' working-class elements, the 'rags and tatters' of mid-Victorian society (poverty and 'roughness' being frequently, if mistakenly, seen as natural companions). On a more positive note we have observed that many Liberals prided themselves upon their supposed appeal to the sober, respectable, improving, earnest and industrious among the working and other classes. Similarly positive Tory messages to the 'robustly respectable and patriotic' have been noted. Chartism had, of course, addressed itself broadly to the unenfranchised 'people', most of whom were believed to be generally respectable,

independent-minded and radical, but even in this case preferences and limitations had been in evidence. For example, and
taking due account of the continued existence of independent
female radical and democratic associations, women's involvement in Chartism had been predominantly supportive and familial in character. And within mainstream Chartism's wide appeal –
to the 'fustian jackets and unshorn chins' as well as the 'superior
artisans' – we can detect on the part of many leaders special
affection for the more 'temperate, intelligent and industrious'
among the labouring people.[1]

The purpose of this chapter is to investigate the nature, validity
and correspondence or otherwise of these cultural types and representations – especially the key notions of 'respectability' and
'roughness' – to the social structure and lived experiences and
values of the mid-Victorian working class. However, before em-
barking upon this investigation we should alert the reader to
some of the many methodological and substantive dangers and
obstacles involved in such an exercise.

Above all, perhaps, it can be argued that cultures carry within
them such an abundance of shifting appeals, meanings and functions as to defy precise historical definition and evaluation and
sociological categorisation. For example, many historians have
concretely demonstrated the wide appeal and complex, fluid and
contradictory features of nineteenth-century respectability and its
many-sided meanings and effects.[2] The criterion of respectability
was, for example, employed by many of those in positions of
power and authority, such as middle-class charity organisation
officials and poor law guardians, in purportedly natural or
commonsensical yet in reality highly charged subjective and ideological ways, to differentiate between, and to attempt to control
and to reward or punish the deserving and the undeserving sections of the working class. At the same time notions of respectability could issue from within, and be an integral part of, the daily
routines of workers' lives. The meanings and intended functions
of these two notions of respectability, as issuing either from above
or from below, often showed significant and conflicting class-
based differences. Different inter-class usages could also be accompanied by multiple, and at times conflicting intra-class habits
and values. Within the Victorian working class, for example, respectability could be seen variously as a badge of individual,

family and community status, a mark of distinction and respect at work, a source of class pride, or a contradictory jumble of all these significations and more besides. To complicate matters even further, the same individual could adopt a variety of roles and attitudes, at times respectable and at other times distinctly less so. Thus Peter Bailey has drawn our attention to the fact that some socially constructed roles – appearances in court and interviews with those in positions of power and influence – demanded *instrumental* respectability on the part of the summoned. However, public shows of respectability and even profound religiosity could be combined with cruelty and bullying in the home and the general adoption of the double standard in attitudes towards sex. And as acutely observed in the 1860s by Thomas Wright, the journeyman engineer, inevitable bouts of unemployment and short-time working could rapidly undermine the respectable standing, both at work and in the home, of even the most prosperous mid-Victorian artisan.[3]

There also exist major problems concerning the partial and fragmentary nature of the evidence available to the historian. For example, some voices and opinions are represented far more heavily than others in the documentary record. Thus, while Victorian women played the key role in the cultivation of respectability within the home, nevertheless their values, norms and aspirations in life are much harder to recapture than those of men. Whereas the former were expected to lead private and largely unrecorded lives, the latter, especially if middle and upper-class, were encouraged to put pen to paper and to mould respectable public opinion. Similarly, many of the voices and the habits and customs of the labouring poor and the 'residuum' (the Victorian equivalent of late twentieth-century Britain's 'underclass') are largely silent and opaque, or come to us indirectly and often in fragments from the works of Victorian novelists and social investigators. However skilful, dedicated, open-minded and possessed of empathy some of the authors of these works may have been (the name of Henry Mayhew, author of *London Labour and the London Poor* immediately springs to mind), the majority all too easily and readily 'saw' and judged the poor far less in terms of rigorous attention to the 'facts of the matter' than in accordance with their preconceived middle-class notions of, and prescriptions for, right and proper behaviour. Writers and public spokesmen from within, or on the fringes of, the post-Chartist working class also increasingly wore their self-help notions of success and advancement upon their sleeve. As we shall see below, while by no means entirely forgetting or neglecting to mention the structural causes of poverty, these writers and spokesmen were also tending by the 1860s to make instant, insufficiently substantiated assertions concerning the close connections between non-respectability and the poor. As seen in the writings of Thomas Wright and Henry Mayhew, there were modifications of and exceptions to the general rule. Mayhew's conversations with the London poor also allow us important, if indirect and rare, access to that invaluable aid of the late nineteenth and twentieth-century historian, oral history.

While recognising the importance of such methodological and substantive difficulties, we should not regard them as insuperable. All students of history are faced with the problems of complexity, subjectivity and bias, of the limitations and imperfections of the evidence, of the nature of the correspondence, if any, between representations of the world and the world itself, of how to evaluate different views or representations of reality, of how to 'work through' and arrive at a balanced assessment of the creative tensions thrown up by complex, multi-faceted and contradictory historical processes and phenomena, and, in the most general sense, of how to justify the status or epistemological credentials of historical knowledge. The historian usually responds to such difficulties and challenges by resort to the tried and trusted practices of the craft or 'rules of method' briefly referred to in the introduction. As indicated, such practices may be seen to reside in the unending and open-minded dialogue between concept and evidence, theory and fact. This dialogue involves constant attention to the strengths and weaknesses of the evidence (to be duly read and assessed for points of bias, silences, limitations and so on); to the engagement of different and conflicting pieces of evidence; to the necessary *contextualisation* of cultural typologies and representations (which reveal their dominant, subordinate and residual and changing characteristics and meanings only when set in their full societal context over a period of time); to the need to decode some kinds of evidence (for example, in the absence or partial presence of 'historical voices', to look for clues to people's values and norms in their patterns of behaviour); to the nature of the assumptions, procedures and views carried to the evidence by both historians and their subjects; and to close scrutiny of the consistency, rigour and appropriate nature of the concepts and theories brought into dialogue with the empirical material. Finally, it is by reference to the criteria of sound evidence and rigorous theory that the historian's work is judged to be adequate or true (in the sense of being provisionally true until supplanted by more convincing paradigms of knowledge and concentrations of evidence).[4] The adoption of such rules of method enable us more effectively to tackle the methodological and substantive difficulties identified above.

Respectability: nature, appeal and meanings

Both the Chartists and the vast majority of those involved in the mid-Victorian labour movement prided themselves upon their respectability. Notwithstanding its subjective, relative and multi-faceted characteristics and the practical difficulties involved in its total and enduring acquisition, respectability did convey to those active in working-class movements a distinct and clear set of desirable norms, values and actions. Through the agencies of the co-op, the friendly society, the trade union, the adult education class, and their chapels and other religious organisations, male workers were exhorted to acquire and cultivate, to the best of their ability and means, a demanding range and depth of respectable virtues. These virtues centrally embraced industry, thrift, sobriety, discipline, restraint, honesty, modesty, courtesy, 'correct manners' and general abidance by the precepts of honourable and manly behaviour – involving a strong sense of moral and, increasingly among mid Victorian labour activists, religious (especially Nonconformist) duty to one's family and humankind in general; self-respect and self reliance, combined with personal and collective independence, initiative and advancement; mutuality (both in the workplace and outside it); good workmanship; strong allegiance to the collective institutions of the trade, community and class; a positive evaluation of the pleasures and responsibilities of hearth and home, as opposed to the 'loose frivolities' and potentially ruinous consequences of a life associated with excessive drinking, gambling and sexual 'enthusiasm' and the allurements of the gin palace, beerhouse, gambling den and other forms of 'low life'; and a thirst for learning (the slogan 'Knowledge is power' being commonplace among working-class radicals).[5]

Respectable working-class women were generally expected, once married, to become home-centred and ideally to give up paid employment. As Dorothy Thompson has observed, 'The Chartists often repeated their demand that there should be no female labour except in the hearth and the schoolroom. In general they regarded women's work outside the home as a burden, certainly for married women.'[6] Many Chartists had, in practice, modified their expectations, if not formal demands, in the light of the continued necessity and practice of paid female employment, the relatively fluid division of labour which had traditionally prevailed among numerous labouring families, and their movement's strong commitment to a shared, if unequal, relationship between the sexes.

Among the spokesmen and constituents of mid-Victorian working-class movements the Chartist notion of the 'proper' sexual division of labour was applied more strictly. Notwithstanding the accelerated feminisation of domestic service and the continued employment of large numbers of women, including married women, in textiles, in a range of largely depressed crafts and trades (albeit as a proportionately smaller part of the full-time work force) and in a variety of low-paid tasks (such as sewing and taking in washing) in the home, and the partial involvement of women workers in trade unionism, notions of a 'woman's place', firmly situated in the domestic sphere, and of the 'family wage', based *solely* rather than, as often in the past, *mainly* upon the income of the male breadwinner, took strong root in organised and wider working-class circles. Significantly, these notions were widely articulated, and quickly assumed the status of natural common sense, not only in the male-dominated areas of the waterfront, the coal mines and in the 'superior' reaches of craft and skilled production, but also in sectors, such as cotton textiles, in which paid women workers were present in large numbers.[7]

As in the Chartist period, emphasis continued to be laid by labour's spokesmen upon the positive moral and economic benefits to be derived from the accelerated movement of women into the home. For example, women were to be given the chance to escape from the grime, drudgery, 'unhealthy influences' and oppression and exploitation of the world of social production. It was also claimed that the reduction in the supply of female labour would increase the scarcity value and hence the price of male labour, at least in those labour markets where women had 'unnaturally' been compelled both to compete against, and supplant in work, their menfolk. Significantly, in both the Chartist and in the post-Chartist periods, such views were expressed by working-class women as well as working-class men. For example, as Carol Morgan has recently shown, women supporters of the Ten Hours Bill welcomed the opportunity presented by the reduced hours of paid work to spend more time with their children, to improve their state of health, better to attend to their household duties and to make their homes cleaner, tidier and more welcoming.[8]

However, against such positive attractions of a home-based life must be set a number of negative influences. Prominent among the latter was the continued, and in some instances increased, burden of the double shift for women – the state of affairs whereby unpaid housework was combined for most working-class women with generally low-paid work in order to secure the survival and advancement of the family. Furthermore, both the mid Victorian census takers and ideologues of the 'male bread-winner' norm greatly, and cruelly, underestimated and masked the true extent of continued paid work for women (especially if undertaken in the home by married women). In so doing they were, whether by accident or design, instrumental in the creation of an ideological smokescreen for the continued utilisation by employers of women as a supplementary and, as a corollary, cheap source of labour seeking 'pin money'. The growing offical identification of the world of work with social production and the home with consumption and leisure similarly helped to camouflage the existence, true extent and unremitting nature of women's work within the home. It could thus be convincingly argued that, irrespective of intentions and subjective assessments, the objective function of a growing number of mid-Victorian working-class women was freely and cheaply to service the needs of, respectively, the family and capital.[9] Growing and increasingly pervasive proclamations and assumptions of male superiority and power and female inferiority and subordination, of the 'natural' state of patriarchy, strengthen our overall conclusion that most working-class women lost far more than they gained in the mid-Victorian transition to 'true domesticity' and 'place'.

The deification of the home – as a vital source of marital and familial strength and contentment, and the preservation of social order and social stability – was a cardinal feature of organised labour's mid-century ideology. As the *Co-operator* declared in July 1865,

> The home of the workman – where love dwells, in which there is mutual confidence and mutual help between husband and wife, and loving care for the children – ought to be the nest of peace. The limitation of means of the working man is more than counterbalanced by the absence of brooding care, of ambitious views, of anxieties of the exposure of accumulated wealth to a thousand channels, which the rich man always feels.

In reality, the kind of mutuality advocated by the *Co-operator* largely confined women to the home in a dependent, service-based capacity and allowed them into the public sphere on selected occasions, mainly as secondary, supporting figures and helpers to males – as, for example, wives and sweethearts at co-op social and cultural functions or the makers of tea and refreshments at 'serious' meetings. Within their domestic place female working-class aspirants to respectability were expected and increasingly exhorted, by both their 'betters' and their menfolk, actively and unceasingly to develop the skills of housework and household management. The 1850s and 1860s thus saw a proliferation of classes for women in household management and related subjects. During the Cotton Famine the Central Relief Committee established sewing schools throughout the cotton district of Lancashire and Cheshire for unemployed female cotton operatives: by February 1863 over 40,000 women were receiving instruction. Designed to inculcate 'greater domestic management skills', some of the schools also taught basic literacy. Personally supervised by middle-class 'ladies', the 'girl' students were advised that, 'the lessons of cleanliness, order and thrift', which had been 'impressed upon their minds', would 'bear abundant fruit in the increased comfort of their homes and their own moral improvement for many years to come'.[10] Lectures upon the themes of 'Woman as Housebuilder' and 'The Model Wife' became both widespread and popular. The model wife would avoid 'wasting the day away' in 'idle gossip' and 'cheap reading' in order 'properly' to attend to the needs of her husband. The *Oddfellows' Magazine* counselled unremitting industry, foresight and planning:

> Always remember that it is possible to have a decent meal and decent abode, with even scanty resources, by the addition of a little prudent forethought, but quite impossible where the wife sits down to read the 'Ladies Journal', or gossips with her neighbours over the palings, while the beds are unmade, and the breakfast things are unwashed.[11]

Thomas Wright mantained that 'thousands of working men are driven by lazy, slovenly, mismanaging wives to courses which ultimately result in their becoming drunkards and disreputable members of society'. In addition to having male drunkenness and disreputable behaviour laid at their doorstep, home-based working-class women were also often called upon to express due gratitude and affection to their male protectors and foragers. William Marcroft, a prominent self-helping figure in the mid-century Oldham co-operative movement, and a 'model husband', unashamedly opined that

> Home is the heaven gained in female life. There she makes a world as she wills it; order, cleanliness, regularity and comfort are the four points of her compass. The husband is the altar of her worship, and to guide her children to do right is the pleasure of her life.[12]

(See also document 8.)

Given the extremely limited audibility of mid-Victorian working women's voices, it is exceedingly difficult satisfactorily to measure their reactions to the notions of 'place' and male superiority embraced by Marcroft. We should certainly beware of treating women purely and simply as passive victims of patriarchal structures. As argued by Jane Lewis and others, women possessed agency, and handled, modified and even changed their structured conditions of existence in important and varied ways. For example, the findings of Lewis herself, of Pat Thane, Carl Chinn, Elizabeth Roberts, Joanna Bourke and of Ellen Ross for the late nineteenth and early twentieth centuries have suggested, to varying degrees, that many working-class men and women did continue to practise mutuality, that women did take a pride in, and derive much satisfaction from, their 'jobs' of housework and looking after the children, did not feel unduly dependent upon their menfolk, did see wage-earning as a burden and did manage to carve out, within the considerable constraints of family, children and men, free time and space for themselves.[13]

However, on balance, and notwithstanding the work of Carol Morgan referred to earlier, far more negative conclusions must be drawn for the mid-Victorian years. Even taking into account the distinct probability that, in practice, economic adversity, the needs of the family and genuine attraction, affection and respect induced more equality and feelings of mutuality between mid-Victorian working men and women than stark notions of a woman's place and absolute patriarchy would permit, there does nevertheless remain a strong sense of loss as compared with the Chartist period. As Dorothy Thompson has persuasively written,

> The fact of the withdrawal from public activity by the women of the working class is incontrovertible . . . A change seems to have occurred in women's expectations and in their idea of their place in society. In the light of the hideous stories of unskilled child care and the overworking of women and children in the factory areas . . . the positive gains from the increasing tendency for married women with children to stay at home and care for their children do not need to be stressed. But in return for these gains, working-class women seem to have accepted an image of themselves which involved both home-centredness and inferiority . . . The Victorian sentimentalization of the home and the family, in which all important decisions were taken by its head, the father, and accepted with docility and obedience by the inferior members, became all-pervasive, and affected all classes. The gains of the Chartist period, in awareness and in self-confidence, the moves towards a more equal and cooperative kind of political activity by both men and women, were lost in the years just before the middle of the century.[14]

It is still possible in the mid-Victorian decades occasionally to encounter dissenting female voices. In 1851, for example, a meeting of radical women in Sheffield adopted a petition which called for the enfranchisement of women. And a section of a remarkable article written by Alice Wilson (See the last part of document 9) for the *Co-operator* in 1868 read: 'The very fact of a woman depend-ing upon a man for her daily bread gives him a power over her ... and in all but the very best natures, the man is thereby rendered egotistical, conceited and unjust.' Wilson went on to advocate 'the mechanisation of household chores and the establishment of co-operative communities in which men and women would enjoy equality'.[15] Such utopian thinking had, however, little purchase upon an increasingly patriarchal and 'realistic' labour movement. Simultaneously, that very same labour movement was instrumental publicly in creating inflated expectations of female respectability which greatly underestimated both the magnitude of the work-based demands made upon women and the severe limits placed upon their 'free time'. In all probability the unending pursuit, rather than the full attainment, of true respectability remained the daily lot of the majority of working-class women in the post-Chartist years.

In seeking to interpret and evaluate the 'respectability' of our working-class subjects, we can usefully develop answers in the process of critical engagement with three mainly distinct and conflicting approaches which have dominated the historiography of respectability.[16] First, historians such as John Foster have emphasised the essentially middle-class or 'bourgeois' character of respectability, and its successful utilisation as a method of social control from the late 1840s onwards. Focusing upon the rise and decline of a form of 'revolutionary consciousness' among Oldham's workers, Foster explained its decline mainly in terms of the conscious creation by Oldham's employers of an elite of authority-wielding workers – a labour aristocracy who were exposed to, and readily adopted, the improvement-oriented respectability of the bourgeoisie. In practising (in their mid-century co-ops, adult education and temperance societies) social assimilation the labour aristocracy of cotton spinners, engineers and others simultaneously turned their backs upon the non-respectable (i.e. non-improving and non-abstinent) masses. This supposed process involved 'the ritualistic assimilation of bourgeois values, an acceptance of bourgeois class attitudes, and above all the equation of social evil and the working class'. Yet, according to Foster, these self-same labour aristocrats also 'actively disseminated the culture of their employers', and acted as the system's 'messenger boys and interpreters in the labour community'. In sum, the contention is that respectability played an important, if secondary, role in the overall stabilisation of class relations in mid-century Oldham, in the cultural fragmentation of the local working class and in the embourgeoisement of the working-class elite who controlled the key institutions of working-class self-help. Significantly, William Marcroft was a prominent figure in these self-helping endeavours.

Advanced in 1974 in his stimulating and provocative book *Class Struggle and the Industrial Revolution*, Foster's thesis rightly drew attention to the ways in which respectability could be, and often was, used by employers and their allies to 'entice and entrap' post-Chartist workers into a highly competitive, individualistic and divisive bourgeois cultural system. Far less convincing, however, were Foster's narrow equation of respectability with bourgeois values and a bourgeois-minded labour aristocracy, and his claims that the cultural process of class control and the consolidation of bourgeois hegemony 'proceeded so rapidly, in such a simple, straightforward manner, and with minimal conflict'. We will now turn to address these important issues.

There is no doubt that middle-class versions of respectability existed in Oldham and elsewhere, and that accelerated moves were made at mid-century – as part of conscious attempts at social stabilisation and assimilation – more actively to spread the virtues of middle-class culture to the 'provident' and 'industrious' sections of the working class. But what Foster effectively ignores is the fact that respectability was far from one-dimensional in character, meaning and function. Precious little attention is paid in *Class Struggle and the Industrial Revolution* to those kinds of respectability which existed prior to mid-century (among, for example, Chartists and earlier radicals); which issued primarily from within working-class and labour movement experience and, as such, owed little or nothing to imitation of the middle classes and their cultural endeavours; and which, far from carrying messages of social assimilation and embourgeoisement, conveyed strong impressions of class pride and independence and even struggle, conflict and transforming social and political goals. It is, of course, these varieties of internally generated working-class respectability which constitute our main subject matter.

Working-class respectability – in the form of daily, indeed life-long, resort to industry, thrift and sobriety – constituted, in general, both a practical safeguard against recurrent threats of insecurity, poverty and unemployment and an aid to the attainment of personal and collective respect and dignity, rather than a means of individual escape from the working class. Most of the respectable endeavours of working-class women were precisely of this kind. Women sought, above all, to make ends meet by a variety of often self-sacrificing devices (such as going without in order to feed the children and male members of the family), to contribute to the collective unity, harmony and survival of that most important of working-class institutions, the family, and, by doing their utmost to keep a keen, tidy and welcoming home, to deter family members from extra-familial temptations which could lead, all too quickly, into a descent into the gutter and the outcast world of the residuum. In both the Chartist and the mid-Victorian periods, and notwithstanding the 'successes' and 'advances' achieved by a section of the working class during the latter (see Chapter 3), insecurity remained *the* major economic feature of working-class life; and the practice of 'respectable' habits remained the main way in which the daily battle against such insecurity was fought. We have also observed (again in Chapter 3) that much of the advancement secured was of a collective institutional rather than purely individual kind, and was attributed to unremitting cultivation of the habits of solidarity and mutuality (in the trade unions, co-ops and suchlike) and to personal and collective independence of mind and spirit rather than unlimited personal ambition and competition. For the mass of workers, it typically constituted desired advancement *within* rather than *out of* the working class.

The political and social ends towards which respectability was geared by the majority of Chartists also do not fit Foster's picture of incorporation into the bourgeois world and rejection of the 'failed masses'. Thus, while the temperate, proud and independent Chartists did not wish to be associated with the excessive drinking, introverted, fatalistic and deferential attitudes and 'prevailing low songs, low comic humour and vulgar mirth' characteristic of parts of the working-class world, they most definitely did not turn their backs upon and see the poor and poverty primarily as the result of moral failure and personality defects. Rather, exclusion from the political system and increasingly 'dishonourable' and systemic process of economic and social exploitation and oppression constituted the true causes of poverty. The poor were accordingly exhorted, as part of the excluded and oppressed 'people', to join the Chartist cause. During the Chartist years economic, political, social and cultural divisions and conflicts between large sections of the working and middle classes were often simply too acute to permit the development of a viable and durable alliance between 'respectable' Chartists and 'respectable' middle-class reformers.

Foster is right to alert us to important changes from the late 1840s onwards. Increasingly, as we shall observe in more detail below, the respectability espoused by self-helping working-class institutions became more private and status-conscious in character, did help to build cross-class alliances and promote social stability and accommodation to the social order, and did tend to lead to a divorce from non-respectable elements. Nevertheless, it is highly questionable whether even this tamed mid-Victorian form of working-class respectability can, so readily and uniformly, be described as bourgeois. We have seen in previous chapters that our respectable mid-Victorian political radicals, trade unionists and co-operators still placed a premium upon collective, as opposed to individual, self-help, prided themselves, above all else perhaps, upon their fierce independence and autonomy – which were fundamentally at odds with deference and *conscious* and open imitation of the manners of the *bourgeoisie* – still retained strong commitments to genuine (as opposed to hierarchical, property-driven notions of) democratic practice, fairness and labour's 'due acknowledgement and reward', still, at various points in time, and over a range of issues, came into conflict with members of the respectable middle classes and could still, on necessary occasions, articulate class pride and combativity. Class consciousness and idealism were diluted during the post-Chartist era, but they did not suddenly expire. In the 1860s the Oddfellows could still condemn those institutions in which

> the worker's imagination is oppressed by the spectral parson and the spectral capitalist morally patting him on the head, and bidding him, like the virtuous artisan he is, to attend church regularly and avoid the trade union.

Finally, while there is evidence to suggest the existence of significant, and in all probability growing, structural and cultural divisions between the skilled and non-skilled in the mid-Victorian period, and while respectable habits and values were undoubtedly pronounced among the upper sections of the working class, neverthless we may conclude that respectability appealed to a numerically much larger and occupationally far more varied group of workers than Foster's labour aristocrats. Simultaneously, 'rough' and 'improvident' behaviour was by no means the sole preserve of the 'dangerous classes'. We will substantiate these claims in turn.

Attention has been drawn, in the work of Roger Penn and of Mike Savage and Andrew Miles, to the important fact that 'the axis of skill' was vitally important in explaining income and other *economic* differentials among workers in this period. Unlike Penn, Savage and Miles maintain that this axis was also *socially* of 'central importance in separating the skilled working class from semi- and unskilled workers'.[17] Such separation manifested itself in differential patterns of occupational choice and mobility (see Chapter 3) and, increasingly, in housing and residential preferences. While recognising that respectability was 'not the preserve of the skilled workers or the labour aristocracy', Michael Thompson nevertheless suggests that in mid-Victorian Britain as a whole

> the artisan elite, with its higher incomes, superior skills, and greater independence, had clear aspirations to houses and homes of a style and dignity befitting their status and a tendency to congregate together in their own neighbourhoods.[18]

Such aspirations and patterns of behaviour were certainly to be found among sections of the skilled in a variety of urban locations. Thus

> Some of the skilled workers of Manchester ... demonstrated a strong desire to distance themselves physically from the less fortunate and gregarious street life of the central city areas. In the 1860s co-operative and friendly societies began to construct 'model cottages' away from the inner-city slum areas; and by the 1870s many of the newer properties in Ardwick, Hulme and Chorlton were inhabited by the better paid manual workers and lower middle-class elements ... Both Kentish London and Edinburgh saw the growth of specifically artisan housing areas, increased residential segregation and the adoption of an increasingly privatised life-style on the part of the skilled elite. Doubtless many shared the views of two 'model co-operators' in Edinburgh, who, having removed

themselves from the slums to 'a very pleasant part' of the city, were extremely reluctant to return to 'those dingy hovels' and to 'associate in any degree . . . with the people one sees there'.[19]

The general growth of bye-law housing in the main urban centres from the 1860s onwards, which 'sorted out and standardized house types', reinforced these differential patterns of housing. But whether the key division, in terms of the housing and living patterns of the mid-Victorian British working class as a whole, lay between, on the one hand, a labour aristocratic or artisan elite, comprising Hobsbawm's top 10–15 per cent of workers and inclusive of Foster's 'authority wielders', and the rest or, on the other hand, between a much larger group of the more regularly employed and better-paid workers and those occupationally varied yet increasingly casualised groups concentrated in, and unlikely to be able to move out from, the poorer slum areas is still, *pace* Thompson, very much open to debate. There is, for example, considerable evidence from social investigations carried out in the 1860s to suggest that, although the poor and the very poor were increasingly concentrated in certain parts or quarters of Manchester, nevertheless 'many working-class communities in the city contained a wide mix of occupations, with unskilled and skilled living side-by-side in the same streets'. In terms of the national picture, we urgently require far more extensive research into the census enumerators' books and a range of qualitative sources in order authoritatively to describe working-class dwelling patterns and more confidently to assess and order the wide range of factors – such as status, occupation, level of skill and earnings, the nature and location of employment, access to transport facilities, proximity to work, and kinship and neighbourhood ties – which influenced patterns of residence.[20]

Evidence drawn largely from contemporary sources may be cited in support of the argument that the division between the mid-Victorian skilled and non-skilled was not only structural but also cultural in character. Of particular relevance in this context was the close, and in some cases exclusive, association made by many contemporary writers and social investigators between respectability and the skilled or the upper sections of the working class. For example, in separating working men into 'at least three

leading sections', Thomas Wright drew a sharp distinction between, on the one hand, the 'refinement' and 'taste for reading',
and 'sober, industrious, prudent, and independent mode of life'
which characterised, respectively, the educated working man and
the intelligent artisan and, on the other hand, the 'large amount
of ignorance, drunkenness, venality and violence' to be found
among 'the poorer sections of the working classes'.[21] Henry
Mayhew argued that 'where the greatest want generally is, there
we shall find the greatest occasional excess'. Hugh Shimmin, in
his investigations of low life in mid-Victorian Liverpool, contrasted the 'dirty, ragged, miserable-looking men, women and
children' of the slums who patronised the grog shop with the
'very neatly and comfortably dressed' houseproud women and
the 'honourable and independent' position of the men who were
members of Liverpool Co-operative Provident Society. (See document 10.) Finally, although lacking the formal, apprenticeship-
based requirements of skilled status (and, as such, highlighting
the partly *socially constructed* nature of 'skill'), the cotton spinners
epitomised, at least in the opinion of Allen Clarke, the view that
respectability, skill and superior position in the workplace and
community went hand in hand. Clarke tells us that in the boom
years of the early 1870s

> The spinners or minders were the working aristocracy of Lanca-
> shire; they strutted in the shoes of importance, and talked with the
> voice of superiority . . . No spinner with any self-respect in his stom-
> ach would drink beer in the taproom with a common labourer; he
> must have his ale clad in shining glass, not paltry pot, and enjoy it
> in the company of his own class, or at least with engineers, and
> other artisans of the elevated grade, who had the time o' day and
> night told to them by gold watches with conspicuous chains to
> match.[22]

It was such contemporary evidence that greatly influenced
Thompson's conclusion that

> The distinction between slum and non-slum was a social as well as
> a physical distinction, and the corresponding, but somewhat wider,
> difference between the disreputable – who might be feckless, bad
> managers, or big drinkers, and not simply the very poor – and the
> respectable was the major line of division within the working class.
> Respectable working-class families, who paid their rents regularly

and took pride in their homes, did not wish to be associated with or live alongside families which abused their homes, defaulted on their rents, and flitted ceaselessly from one despairing landlord to another. Here was a powerful force separating one kind of working-class community from another . . .[23]

While agreeing with Thompson's primary emphasis upon the increasingly divisive role of respectability among mid-Victorian workers, we must nevertheless attach equal significance to his qualifying statement that 'Respectability . . . spread through much wider and more numerous echelons of the working class' than the skilled or labour aristocracy. Indeed, it is the wide social appeal of respectability which exposes a central weakness in Foster's thesis. As already indicated, the vast majority of the Chartists and their supporters prided themselves upon their high standards of morality, decency and self-respect, industry, thrift, sobriety, intelligence and independence, and on their reasonable attitudes and behaviour. Furthermore, and notwithstanding the patchiness of the extant occupational data, we can now reasonably conclude that the 'respectable' self-help institutions of the mid-Victorian working class – the co-ops, friendly societies, trade unions, educational improvement societies, the chapels and other religious organisations and the like – did have a much larger and wider occupational and cultural appeal – to a substantial and broad range of respectable urban and rural workers – than Foster's labour-aristocratic interpretation would suggest.[24]

When we move to a consideration of the appeal of respectability among working-class communities, a very similar picture emerges. As we are only too well aware in terms of late twentieth-century British experience, preoccupation with defining socio-economic groups and explaining social stratification in terms of moral and personal characteristics and stereotypes – such as 'respectable' and, *ipso facto*, 'deserving' and 'virtuous' skilled workers versus 'improvident', 'feckless' and 'undeserving' casual labourers and so forth – carries innumerable dangers and weaknesses. Above all, perhaps, the *structural*, as opposed to the *moral*, determinants of socio-economic position and status, of the economic roots of poverty and riches, of exploitation and class rule, are either partially or totally hidden. In that sense, the process of moral stereotyping is inherently ideological in character (acting as a defence of, and justification for, the *status quo*) and, as such, does not give us a full or 'true' view of social experience and structure. Furthermore, such a process flattens and schematises, and therefore does scant justice to, the complexity and richness of people's communities and their own experience, behaviour and consciousness. For example, in the accounts of many mid-nineteenth-century social investigators, such as those of Shimmin and the Charity Organisation Society, large sections of the casual poor, and most especially those in chronic poverty, the residuum or 'the dangerous class', are simply written off as 'lacking in character' and therefore undeserving. The 'solution' is accordingly defined far more in terms of personal and moral reform, and especially the cultivation of self-helping, respectable habits, than in terms of radical economic, social and political change (such as regulation of the deregulated market among the sweated trades of the metropolis). As Gareth Stedman Jones has written in relation to contemporary attitudes towards London's 'still unregenerate poor' – 'those who had turned their back on progress, or had been rejected by it' – during the mid-Victorian 'boom' years,

> The problem was not structural but moral. The evil to be combated was not poverty but pauperism: pauperism with its attendant vices, drunkenness, improvidence, mendicancy, bad language, filthy habits, gambling, low amusements, and ignorance.[25]

Given this dominant concern with negative, moralistic and ideological stereotyping, it is indeed remarkable that Mayhew displayed such strong and independent presence of mind, such an unwavering social-scientific commitment to uncovering the true facts of the matter, and such a 'sensitivity to the sub-cultures of the poor'. As Eileen Yeo has observed, Mayhew's greatest achievement, within the mid-Victorian *bourgeois* world of self-help and individualism, was 'to see poverty in the round' – as 'the product of an economic system, with devastating moral and social consequences and yet varied cultural manifestations'.[26] His keen and nuanced appreciation of the full importance of 'respectable' traditions among artisan trades reduced to chronic insecurity, casual labour and poverty by market forces was clearly evident in his inquiry into the Spitalfields silk-weaving trade. For example,

The weavers were, formerly, almost the only botanists in the metropolis, and their love of flowers to this day is a strongly marked characteristic of this class. Some years back, we are told, they passed their leisure hours, and generally the whole family dined on Sundays, at the little gardens in the environs of London . . . Not very long ago there was an Entomological Society, and they were among the most diligent entomologists, in the kingdom . . . There was at one time a Floricultural Society, an Historical Society, and a Mathematical Society, all maintained by the operative silk-weavers . . . Such *were* the Spitalfields weavers at the beginning of the present century; possessing tastes and following pursuits the refinement and intelligence of which would be an honour and a grace to the artisan even of the present day . . .

Unfortunately, concluded Mayhew, 'the weaver of our own time . . . though still far above the ordinary artisan, both in refinement and intellect, falls far short of the weaver of former years'.[27] Insufficient and irregular wages and an unending struggle for economic survival had now come to dominate the weavers' lives.

Within this metropolitan context of casualised labour markets and the mushrooming of 'dishonourable' employer practices (remorseless cost-cutting and profit maximisation at the expense of the work force), the number of difficulties facing the attainment of erstwhile artisan comforts and 'honourable' status and, more generally, routinised and respectable habits had grown substantially. The chronic uncertainty and irregulaity of life and income had become incompatible with 'regularity of habits'. Yet, in the midst of such adversity, Mayhew recognised the daily battles of the poor to make ends meet by means of industry, thrift and sobriety. Such respectable habits were seen to vary greatly among individuals and occupations, but of their plentiful existence there was no doubt. Although unlike any that he had seen in the same trade, the home of a destitute waistcoat maker poignantly reflected the widespread concern with respectability

all was scrupulously clean and neat. The old brass fender was as bright as gold, and worn with continued rubbing. The grate, in which there was barely a handful of coals, had been newly black-leaded, and there was not a cinder littering the hearth. Indeed, everything in the place evinced the greatest order and cleanliness.

The occupant, a woman whose 'neatness was partly the effect of habits acquired in domestic service, and partly the result of a struggle to hide her extreme poverty from the world', was 'in want of common necessaries to keep my strength and life together'. A man making soldiers' trousers told a similar story of irregular work and financial impoverishment, combined with fierce independence and pride. His home contained

> more comforts about it than I had been led to expect. He lived in a back room built over a yard. It was nicely carpeted, and on one side, to my astonishment, stood a grand piano. There were several pictures hanging from the walls, and a glass full of dahlias on the mantelpiece.

But most of these comforts were not owned by the man. Furthermore, the low prices paid for his work, and five weeks without work 'of any consequence', had induced the feeling within the trade that 'We had better go to bed and starve at once'. Notwithstanding such adversity, 'The general class of people . . . *won't* apply for relief – their pride won't let them . . . they have a dread of becoming troublesome'. The man was, according to his landlord, 'punctual in the payment of his rent, and, indeed, a most sober, industrious, and exemplary person'.[28]

Among the large number of workers employed throughout the country in more regular, if non-aristocratic and in many cases non-skilled, occupations there is likewise plentiful evidence of respectability. In 1849, for example, the *Morning Chronicle* published not only the findings of its London-based correspondent, Henry Mayhew, but also those of Angus Bethune Reach, the correspondent appointed to report on the state of the working classes in Manchester and the surrounding textile districts. Reach was immediately impressed with the 'improving' endeavours of the operatives of Manchester following the passage of the Ten Hours Bill:

> I have personally conversed with at least two dozen young men and women who have learned to read and write since the passing of the . . . Bill. Night schools for adults are now common; most of these have libraries attached to them. The men and boys learn reading, writing and cyphering; and the women and girls, in addition to these branches of education, are taught plain, and are in many instances teaching themselves fancy, needlework.

Respectability was a prominent feature of the lives of the city's work force:

> Saturday is generally the great weekly epoch of cleansing and set-
> ting things to right in the houses of the Manchester workpeople . . .
> The mills knock off work at about two or half after two o'clock, and
> if you visit the class of streets which I have been attempting to
> describe an hour or so thereafter, you will marvel and rejoice at the
> universality of the purification which is going forward. Children are
> staggering under pails and buckets of water . . . Glance in at the
> open portals, and you will witness a grand simultaneous system of
> scouring. The women, of course, are the principal operators – they
> are cleaning their windows, hearthstoning their lintels, scrubbing
> their furniture with might and main. The *pater familias*, however,
> does not always shirk his portion of the toil. Only last Saturday I
> came upon two or three lords of the creation usefully employed in
> blackleading their stoves.

Reach was pleased to conclude that, 'amid all the grime and dinginess' of Manchester's factory areas, 'there is no lack of homely comforts, good health, and good spirits'.[29]

The investigations of the Manchester Statistical Society and the Manchester and Salford Education Aid Society in the 1860s confirmed Reach's earlier conclusions. Respectability continued to inhabit the streets of all grades of workers in Manchester and Salford. In Ancoats, one of Manchester's main factory districts,

> Pavements have been duly cleaned, doorsteps edged with the inevi-
> table line of white, and passages rendered brilliant with 'elbow
> grease'.

Similar pictures prevailed in mid-Victorian urban and rural areas throughout the country.[30]

Finally, just as respectability was not the sole property of any particular group or stratum within the working class, neither were 'irregular' and non-respectable customs confined to those in the slums. As argued by Thompson, the uneven spread among workers of respectable views favouring sexual restraint and, increasingly, smaller family size owed far less to occupational distinctions than to 'differences in the timing and degree of exposure to industrialization' and the uneven development of consumer/commodity consciousness. Furthermore, casual and insecure patterns of employment among seamen, dockers, building tradesmen and even 'aristocratic' printers – some of whom earned high wages – were sometimes productive of 'irregular' and 'improvident' patterns of behaviour. Similarly, manifestly dangerous working conditions among miners, sailors and fishermen were often not conducive to the development of abstemious habits and long-term planning. Heavy drinking, the upholding of Saint Monday, and domestic violence directed at women continued to be prominent among artisans in unmechanised, small workshop trades in the mid-Victorian years.[31] In sum, the vast weight of evidence does not support Foster's picture of a sharp division between a respectable labour aristocracy and a non-respectable mass.

The second historiographical approach – as reflected in the writings of Brian Harrison, Thomas Laqueur and, in a more qualified manner, Michael Thompson – interprets respectability as the more or less spontaneous development of common values which transcended class lines and generated social order, stability and harmony. Harrison's emphasis – upon the way in which cross-class commitment to a range of respectable values promoted the wide appeal of Liberalism – has been noted in Chapter 4. Laqueur has claimed that the values promoted by the Sunday schools – 'honesty, orderliness, punctuality, hard work and refinement of manners and morals' – appealed to the respectable of all classes, and that the most fundamental divisions in early nineteenth-century England were not among social classes but 'between the idle and non-idle classes, between the rough and respectable, between the religious and non-religious'. Thompson sees the widespread appeal of respectability as crucial to the development of social order in mid-Victorian Britain, but argues that the internalised and diversified nature of that respectability, within and across social classes, meant that 'it had not turned out to be the cohesive force which its middle-class and evangelical proponents had imagined' and that 'an orderly and well-defined society . . . was not an inherently stable one'.[32]

The great strengths of this second approach reside in its identification of the growing ties between working-class and middle-class 'respectables' in the post-Chartist years, and the important contribution which the development of common or similar values made to social order and stability. At the same time, however, Laqueur and Harrison do not pay sufficient attention to two key issues: the capacity of respectability to generate cultural and ideological conflict as well as consensus; and the precise contextualisation of respectability in terms of time and place, change over time, and the material and other aspects of social being. (Thompson does more effectively explore the links between social life and respectability.) In effect, we are presented, in the works of these two historians, with a Parsonian view of society in which social order is derived essentially from the development of common values: the coercive and structural roots of social order are largely ignored. Given its partial, somewhat static and idealist characteristics, this second approach to respectability lacks overall conviction.

It is the third approach – exemplified by the work of Geoffrey Crossick and Robbie Gray[33] – which carries the most weight, especially in relation to the kinds of internally generated working-class and labour movement respectability described in this chapter. Crossick and Gray have highlighted the complex and multi-faceted character of respectability, its diverse and changing meanings and functions, and its capacity to generate class pride and independence as well as individual status, conflict as well as co-operation. Yet, in the midst of its complex articulations and effects, Crossick and Gray have convincingly pointed to the increasingly *divisive* role which respectability played among workers in, respectively, mid-Victorian Kentish London and Edinburgh – as manifested especially in the divorce of a skilled elite from the rest. Indeed, it is to a consideration of the divisive aspects of post-Chartist respectabilty – yet respectability divested of exclusive links with a labour aristocracy – that we shall move in the concluding part of this chapter.

During the 1850s and 1860s working-class 'respectables' did indeed seek increasingly to distance and dissociate themselves from those workers perceived to be non-respectable. Notwithstanding its broad appeal within the working class, respectability was increasingly associated by labour movement activists and spokesmen with the successful, better-paid and more regularly employed sections of the class (rather than being confined to a small elite of either craft/skilled or authority-wielding labour aristocrats) and lack of respectability with failure and the poor. As seen in the political rhetoric of Ernest Jones and some other leaders, the structural underpinnings of poverty were not completely forgotten. However, as compared with the Chartist years, we can detect an important shift of emphasis within working-class movements – away from ambitious attempts to transform structures and towards a growing concern with personal reform and those self-helping, respectable measures which, it was claimed, had underpinned the individual successes of workers and labour leaders and the collective advance of their institutions during the post-Chartist period. The non-respectable elements were accordingly exhorted, first and foremost, to help themselves. Those who were deemed not to have responded to such exhortations were increasingly judged to be the victims less of exploitation and oppression than of individual character defects. Moreover, much in the manner of the respectable middle classes, self-helping workers in successful co-ops, and friendly and educational societies were increasingly appalled by, and recoiled from, the enduring excesses, ignorance, and fecklessness of the 'lower depths'. A leader of the Stockport co-op declared,

> Look through the principal streets of our large towns and there you will see them standing in groups. Listen to the ribaldry of the language. See them pouring out of the gin shops and public houses . . . if we have any respect for our class, any hope for our race, we shall hail with joy any step, however humble, that may be taken to bridge over that gulf that lies between the more intelligent and ignorant portions of our class.

Other co-op members contrasted their steady, sober and industrious habits with those of their enemies, 'the swinish multitude'.[34]

In truth the non-respectable poor had become a source of embarrassment, and in some cases of hatred, to successful working class 'respectables'. Furthermore, as practised by the latter, respectability had become more private in character and aim, and more a badge of status, than during the Chartist period. In their strong advocacy of 'personal reformation' as the key to individual and collective working-class advancement, working-class 'respectables' had come to adopt some of the individualistic assumptions and values of their middle-class counterparts. Given this changed context, it is hardly surprising that inter-class cultural, social and political links and alliances between such 'respectables' became far more pronounced and extensive during the post-Chartist years. In such ways, and notwithstanding its continued association with class pride and collective advancement, did mid-Victorian working-class respectability promote cultural accommodation to the social order and its system of values and ideas.

Four specific aspects of these processes of intra-working-class cultural division and accommodation merit special note. First, our demonstration in favour of the wide and deep appeal of respectability carries with it the strong implication that – in opposition to the claim of Hobsbawm – there probably did not exist a clinical cultural division between mid-Victorian labour-aristocratic elites and the mass of respectable, regularly employed workers. The key importance of gender, family and household matters to the notion of respectability also suggest that Hobsbawm's framework of reference is too narrowly concentrated upon male workers and the world of social production. For example, *pace* the general findings of Miles, Penn's specific research into marriage patterns among workers in Rochdale does not support the notion of a division between the skilled and the rest. Rather, Penn's overall conclusion is in favour of 'massive amounts of working-class endogamy' between 1856 and 1964.[35]

Second, mid-Victorian notions of respectability and roughness possessed an ethnic/religious, as well as a status-based, dimension. More precisely, and notwithstanding the respectable, self-helping endeavours of the Catholic Church and growing links between the Liberal Party and sections of the immigrant community, the vast majority of the post-Famine Irish Catholic immigrants were branded as non-respectable or rough – as, for example, lacking the self-discipline, restraint and modesty of the Methodists, as clinging to their pre-industrial, 'irregular', 'loose' and 'wild and unruly' ways. Such negative ethnic stereotyping, combined with the predominantly low socio-economic standing of the immigrants, played a significant part in the dominant host view of the Irish Catholics as unwelcome outsiders or aliens. Furthermore, as we saw in Chapter 4, a climate was created in which poisonous racist views could mushroom.

Third, in so far as it included notions of a woman's place and the male breadwinner, and notwithstanding continued examples of mutuality between the sexes, respectability did highlight and harden gender-based differences and divisions within the mid-Victorian working class. As such, it severely limited, as observed by Dorothy Thompson, the scope for equality, co-operation and class-based action on the part of men and women. What was gained in male power and status was lost in the assumed dependence and inferiority of women.

Finally, we should take careful note of Michael Thompson's conclusion that respectability was increasingly articulated and practised in highly specific and diverse ways by a wide range of social groups and sub-groups.[36] The context in which respectability was expressed by such groupings within the working class became increasingly localised and fragmented in character. Senses of cultural and social place or belonging, and popular patterns of associational life became largely divorced from transforming political aims and movements. Chartism had been able to link the local with the national (institutionally, politically *and* culturally) and to offer 'the people' as a whole a radical, indeed hegemonic, alternative to political exclusion and social, economic and cultural oppression.[37] With the demise of Chartism this link – at least in a radical, hegemonic form – largely disappeared. Some – especially the poorer – working-class respectable groups became more introverted and fatalistic, more 'peculiarly English' in their attachment to mainly depoliticised local 'places' and cultures. Others attached themselves to the political cultures of the Liberals or the Conservatives. Simultaneously, the cultural pull of paternalist employers grew in importance. And, as we have seen, those active and involved in working-class movements increasingly harnessed their respectability to more gradual, limited, private and status-conscious goals (for piecemeal advancement, the space and freedom in which to operate and advance and official recognition) than in the Chartist period.

In such ways did culture serve variously as a source of accommodation, differentiation and division among workers during the mid-Victorian years. As we shall observe in Part II, attempts firmly to establish the appeal of class-based radical and revolutionary theory and politics among workers in the late Victorian and Edwardian periods were seriously limited by the divisive, localised, defensive, apolitical, partisan and reformist legacies bequeathed by the mid-Victorian working-class past.[38]

Notes

1 See, for example, *Life and Struggles of William Lovett in his Pursuit of Bread, Knowledge and Freedom* (London, 1876). For women see D. Thompson, *The Chartists* (Aldershot, 1986), chapter 7; A. Clark, *The Struggle for the Breeches: Gender and the Making of the British Working Class* (London, 1995).

2 F.M.L. Thompson, *The Rise of Respectable Society: A Social History of Victorian Britain 1830–1900* (London, 1988); E. Ross, ' "Not the Sort that would Sit on the Doorstep": Respectability in pre-World War I London Neighborhoods', *International Labor and Working Class History*, 27 (1985) 39–59; P. Bailey, ' "Will the real Bill Banks please stand up?" Towards a Role Analysis of mid-Victorian Working-class Respectability', *Journal of Social History*, 12 (1978–79) 336–65.

3 T. Wright, *The Great Unwashed* (London, 1868), pp. 246–92.

4 N. Kirk, ' "Traditional" Working-class Culture and "the Rise of Labour": Some Preliminary Questions and Observations', *Social History*, 16:2 (1991) 203–16; J.K. Walton, 'Doing Comparative Social History: North-West England and the Basque Country from the 1830s to the 1930s' (Inaugural Lecture, Lancaster University, 12 June 1996).

5 N. Kirk, *The Growth of Working Class Reformism in Mid-Victorian England* (Beckenham, 1985), pp. 207–20; H. McLeod, *Religion and the Working Class in Nineteenth-century Britain* (London, 1984), pp. 34–5, 61–2.

6 D. Thompson, *The Chartists* (Aldershot, 1986), p. 148.

7 S.O. Rose, *Limited Livelihoods: Gender and Class in Nineteenth-century England* (Berkeley, Cal., 1992), chapter 6, conclusion; E. Gordon, *Women and the Labour Movement in Scotland 1850–1914* (Oxford, 1991); J. Benson, *The Working Class in Britain 1850–1939* (London, 1989), pp. 11–12, 23–6; E. Roberts, *Women's Work 1840–1940* (London, 1988), especially chapters 1 and 2.

8 C. Morgan, 'The Domestic Image and Factory Culture: The Cotton District in mid-Nineteenth-century England', *International Labor and Working Class History*, 49 (1996) 26 ff.

9 C. Stansell, 'The Origins of the Sweatshop: Women and Early Industrialization in New York City', in M.H. Frisch and D.J. Walkowitz (eds), *Working Class America* (London, 1983), p. 95.

10 C. Evans, 'Unemployment and the Making of the Feminine during the Lancashire Cotton Famine', in P. Hudson and W.R. Lee (eds), *Women's Work and the Family Economy in Historical Perspective* (Manchester, 1990), pp. 248–70.

11 Kirk, *Reformism*, p. 218.

12 *Ibid.*, p. 219.

13 J. Lewis, *Women in England 1870–1950* (Brighton, 1984), introduction; P. Thane, 'The Women of the British Labour Party and Feminism 1906–1945', in H. Smith (ed.), *British Feminism in the Twentieth Century* (Aldershot, 1990); C. Chinn, *They Worked all their Lives: Women of the Urban Poor in England 1880–1939* (Manchester, 1988); Roberts, *Women's Work*, pp. 57–8; J. Bourke, *Working Class Cultures in Britain 1890 1960: Gender, Class and Ethnicity* (London, 1994); E. Ross, *Love and Toil: Motherhood in Outcast London 1870–1918* (Oxford, 1993).

14 D. Thompson, *Outsiders: Class, Gender and Nation* (London, 1993), pp. 99–100.

15 Kirk, *Reformism*, p. 220; J. Schwarzkopf, *Women in the Chartist Movement* (London, 1991), chapter 8.

16 For these approaches see Kirk, *Reformism*, pp. 176 82.

17 M. Savage and A. Miles, *The Remaking of the British Working Class 1840–1940* (London, 1994), p. 34; R. Penn, *Skilled Workers in the Class Structure* (Cambridge, 1985), pp. 182, 186–7, chapter 13.

18 Thompson, *Rise of Respectable Society*, pp. 181–2.

19 Kirk, *Reformism*, pp. 226–7.

20 *Ibid.*, pp. 229–30, 239–40 n. 232.

21 Wright, *Great Unwashed*, pp. 6–22.

22 E.P. Thompson and E. Yeo (eds), *The Unknown Mayhew* (Harmondsworth, 1973), p. 94; J.K. Walton and A. Wilcox (eds), *Low Life and Moral Improvement in Mid-Victorian England: Liverpool through the Journalism of Hugh Shimmin* (Leicester, 1991), p. 42, chapter 32; Kirk, *Reformism*, p. 226.

23 Thompson, *Rise of Respectable Society*, p. 181.

24 Kirk, *Reformism*, pp. 189–207; A. Howkins, *Reshaping Rural England: A Social History 1850–1925* (London, 1992), chapter 3.

25 G.S. Jones, *Outcast London* (Harmondsworth, 1976), p. 11.

26 Thompson and Yeo, *Unknown Mayhew*, pp. 100–9.

27 *Ibid.*, p. 124.

28 *Ibid.*, pp. 147–9, 157–63.

29 C. Aspin (ed.), *Manchester and the Textile Districts in 1849* (Helmshore, 1972), pp. 7–8.

30 Kirk, *Reformism*, p. 230; Howkins, *Reshaping Rural England*, especially chapters 3 and 7.

31 Thompson, *Rise of Respectable Society*, pp. 71–80; Kirk, *Reformism*, p. 227; T. Lummis, *The Labour Aristocracy 1851–1914* (Aldershot, 1994), chapter 6; A. Clark, *The Struggle for the Breeches* (London, 1995).

32 B. Harrison, *Drink and the Victorians* (Pittsburgh, 1971), pp. 388, 395–9; T.W. Laqueur, *Religion and Respectability: Sunday Schools and Working-class Culture 1780–1850* (New Haven, 1976), pp. 189, 194–7, 214–18, 239; Thompson, *Rise of Respectable Society*, pp. 360–1; Kirk, *Reformism*, pp. 178–80.

33 G. Crossick, 'The Labour Aristocracy and its Values: A Study of Mid-Victorian Kentish London', *Victorian Studies*, 19:3 (1976) 301–28; R.Q. Gray, 'Styles of Life, the "Labour Aristocracy" and Class Relations in Later Nineteenth-century Edinburgh', *International Review of Social History*, 18 (1973) 428–52.

34 Kirk, *Reformism*, pp. 227–9; M. Hewitt, *The Emergence of Stability in the Industrial City: Manchester 1832–67* (Aldershot, 1996), pp. 204–5.

35 Penn, *Skilled Workers*, chapters 12 and 13.

36 Thompson, *Rise of Respectable Society*, pp. 360–1.

37 On the relevance of spatial networks and senses of 'place' to class and political mobilisation see the stimulating piece by Michael Savage ('Space, Networks and Class Formation') in N. Kirk (ed.), *Social Class and Marxism: Defences and Challenges* (Aldershot, 1996), pp. 58–86.

38 R. McKibbin, 'Why was there no Marxism in Great Britain?', in his *The Ideologies of Class: Social Relations in Britain 1880–1950* (Oxford, 1991).

Part II

The emergence of mass labour and a mass working class 1870s–1920

6

Overview: class, continuity and change

As Ross McKibbin has observed, by the end of the nineteenth century Britain had become 'unquestionably a working-class nation'.[1] In 1901 'about 85 per cent of the total working population were employed by others, and about 75 per cent as manual workers'. As early as 1851 over 16 million of the total population of almost 21 million could be categorised as working-class (that is, engaged in, or dependent upon, manual labour). Between 1851 and 1921 this working class doubled in size and, as John Benson informs us, 'remained constant at between 75 and 80 per cent' of the total population.[2]

The massive army of manual workers was increasingly concentrated in urban areas (by 1911 thirty six cities of over 100,000 people contained 44 per cent of Britain's inhabitants, as compared with, respectively, ten cities and 25 per cent in 1851), and in non-agricultural occupations. As shown in Table 1, in 1851 Britain was already heavily industrialised, with 42.9 per cent of its work force employed in manufacturing, mining and building. Between 1851 and 1931 there was an increase from 42.9 per cent to 45.3 per cent (representing an absolute rise of 5.4 million workers) in these combined areas, while during the same period the percentage employed in agriculture, forestry and fishing fell from 21.7 to 6.0 per cent (a loss of 800,000 workers). The most pronounced shift away from agriculture in the post-1851 period was not towards manufacturing proper but to the tertiary sector of the economy (trade and transport, administration and service, especially white-collar, occupations). For example, between 1861 and 1911

143

Table 1   *The occupational structure of the work force, 1851–1931*

Year	No. (million)	% workforce
Agriculture, forestry and fishing		
1851	2.1	21.7
1891	1.6	10.5
1901	1.5	8.7
1931	1.3	6.0
Manufacturing, mining and building		
1851	4.1	42.9
1891	6.5	43.9
1901	7.7	46.3
1931	9.5	45.3
Trade and transport		
1851	1.5	15.8
1891	3.4	22.6
1901	3.6	21.4
1931	4.7	22.7
Domestic and personal		
1851	1.3	13.0
1891	2.0	15.8
1901	2.3	14.1
1931	1.6	7.7
Other		
1851	0.6	6.6
1891	0.8	7.2
1901	1.3	9.5
1931	2.3	18.3

Source J. Benson, *The Working Class in Britain 1850–1939*, London 1989, p. 10.

the number of women clerks rose by 400 per cent, and domestic and personal service, as opposed to the manufacture of clothing and textiles, continued to provide by far the most common employment opportunities for working-class girls and women (the number 'in service' rising from 1.3 million in 1851 to 2.3 million in 1901).

However, the signficance of this shift should not be allowed to obscure the fundamental and continued importance of manufacturing, mining, building and parts of transport to the working lives of the working class (and, in terms of direct employment, especially to working-class males). For example, between 1851 and 1931 those employed in manufacturing alone increased from 33 per cent (3.2 million) of the recorded labour force to 34.1 per cent (7.2 million). The number of railwaymen rose from less than 100,000 in 1871 to 400,000 in 1911, and, perhaps most spectacularly and importantly, the number of coal miners from 500,000 to 1.2 million in the same period (miners were, of course, increasingly to be at the very heart of the labour movement). The relative decline of textiles and clothing was offset by the rapid growth of metalworking and food processing. And as late as 1911 there were over 600,000 female textile workers in England, Wales and Scotland as compared with 182,782 women clerical workers. In sum, the period under review in Part II marks the growth and increasing ascendancy of the traditional proletarian, as opposed to artisanal, working class rooted in manufacturing, mining, quarrying, building and transport.[3]

The very dominance of proletarians in the economy and society of later Victorian and Edwardian Britain did not, of course, automatically produce widespread feelings of similar or common interests and identity or opposition to other groups, of class consciousness, especially class consciousness of a socialist and/or revolutionary kind. As we have observed throughout this study, the methodological and substantive underpinnings of class identities must be sought not only in occupational profiles and changes but also in wider economic determinations, in politics, culture, ideologies and in institutional arrangements and multifaceted human relations. With respect to concrete historical developments, McKibbin identified, in his important 1984 article 'Why was there no Marxism in Britain?' an important contrast between ascendant proletarian occupational status and the relatively weak presence of socialism, especially Marxian socialism, among British workers and within the organised labour movement. Why, asked McKibbin, did the pre-1914 Labour Party continue to 'exclude a programmatic socialism and any candidate who ventured to stand as "socialist"' while nearly all the major European working-class parties shared at least a nominal commitment to Marxist or 'rejectionist' ideology (that is, rejecting formally the political systems in which they were compelled to work)? And

> why was it that, before the First World War, political Marxism's classical moment, Britain alone of the major European states produced no mass Marxist party, why groups – like the Social Democratic Federation – which could claim at least a vulgar Marxism were either absorbed into the Labour Party or became mere sects without a significant following?[4]

Part of McKibbin's thoughtful and challenging explanation of Britain's unique or peculiar standing in relation to left-wing European experience resided in his insistence upon the highly *fragmented* character of the working class. Thus, nowithstanding common proletarian occupational status, differences and divisions – rooted in unionised and non-unionised labour, in living standards, in the sexual division of labour, in place and type of employment and residence, and in status and life style – combined with the generally small-scale and often scattered nature of industrial organisation and employment, presented formidable obstacles to the development of a rejectionist political party which 'presupposed a unified and ideologically unique working-class interest'. In addition, claimed McKibbin, the continued, indeed expanded, gains made by the organised labour movement and sections of the working class within British capitalism, the seeming class neutrality of the organs of the state (including the monarchy), the generally easy-going relations between employers and workers, the already established associational culture of the working class, and the dominant reformism or 'Lib-Labism' of organised labour's leaders made it extremely difficult for Marxism and other revolutionary doctrines to take root. Large numbers of Britain's workers did possess a strong *cultural* sense of 'us' and 'them', but the sense of being a separate group *within* rather than predominantly *outside* society found political expression far more within the mainstream parties and the newly created

Labour Party (particularly, in the latter case, from the First World War onwards) than in Marxism. The marked tendency of middle-class socialists morally, culturally and politically to set themselves above, and to preach rationality and improvement to, the masses compounded the general divide between socialism and Marxism on the one hand and, on the other, the working class.[5]

McKibbin's identification of patterns of differentiation among workers and organised labour's accommodation to the dominant social order did not, however, preclude the significance of class, conflict and change. British workers may have been largely un-responsive to the revolutionary overtures of Marxism, but many of them did move, albeit unevenly, from Liberalism to the reformism of the Labour Party. Furthermore, the latter was increasingly rooted in the trade union movement and in the associational culture of workers, and constituted the dominant political expression of the distinct, if somewhat modest and lim-ited, sense of class associated with the notion of 'us' and 'them'. Evident in McKibbin's work, the case for class-based political change and close links between the rise of Labour and cultural changes (most notably, the growth of a traditional working class with increasingly standardised and largely separate experiences, life styles and values) has been more pronounced and expressed more forcefully by Hobsbawm.[6]

Emphases upon class-based political, social and cultural changes have, however, been vigorously challenged in one of the most prominent recent works of the 'Cambridge school', Eugenio Biagini's and Alastair Reid's edited collection *Currents of Radical-ism.*[7] Biagini and Reid present four main arguments in favour of continuity and working-class fragmentation. First, a basic con-tinuity is detected in the aims, methods and structures of trade unionism between the third and fourth quarters of the nine-teenth century. Differences between 'old' and 'new' unionism, highlighted by Hobsbawm and many other 'traditionalists', are rejected as resting upon insubstantial empirical founda-tions. Second, the 'substantial continuity in popular radicalism throughout the nineteenth and into the twentieth century' is said to have ensured that there was far more in common between radical Liberals and members of the Labour Party than is often claimed in the historical literature – notwithstanding its rapid growth in confidence, strength and independence from 1914 onwards, the Labour Party assuming, in significant ways, the appearance of the major party of twentieth-century radical liberalism. Third, it is suggested that, in terms of structure and culture, the working class continued to be characterised more by diversity and division than by increased homogeneity and unity, and that older, more home and neighbourhood-based, customary forms of leisure persisted alongside the new commercialised pursuits promoted by the mass entertainment industries.[8] Finally, it is proposed that, much in the manner of the post-Chartist years, the integration into and accommodation of the late Victorian and Edwardian working class and the labour movement to capitalism took place in relatively peaceful, painless and, by implication, largely consensual ways.

As will be evident to the reader, the points of view and areas of debate outlined above revolve around those general issues of continuity and change, class and fragmentation and advance, accommodation and challenge with which we are centrally concerned throughout this study. The following three chapters resume this concern with reference to the workplace, politics and culture. However, before proceeding to an investigation of these areas, we will, in keeping with the procedure adopted in Part I, provide an overview of the main findings which have emerged from our empirical enquiries.

The period from the onset of the great depression, in 1873, to the end of the post-World War I boom, in 1920, saw continuing interaction between the forces of advancement, accommodation and challenge among workers. In terms of advancement, citizenship rights and status were greatly expanded and improved.[9] By the 1920s, as a result of the Reform and Redistribution Acts of 1867–68 and 1884–85 and the Representation of the People Act of 1918, Britain possessed a mass electorate. (The 1918 provision of votes of women over thirty was extended, in 1928, to include all those aged twenty-one or over.) Furthermore, what was, by international standards, an enviably strong and officially recognised labour movement had developed since the mid-Victorian years. This movement had significantly expanded its social base, to include, as exemplified by the 'new' unions, sections of the non-skilled working class. By 1920 organised labour had come to exert a strong presence within society. As James Hinton has observed:

> Between the 1870s and the First World War a mass labour movement was formed in Britain. Trade union membership grew from about half a million in the mid-1870s to over four million by 1914 . . . Membership of the co-operative movement grew, in line with the unions, from about 600,000 in 1880 to over three million by 1914. Trades councils . . . spread rapidly over the whole country . . . The formation of the Labour Party in 1900 gave further expression to this sense of a working-class movement.

The unprecedented demands made by the experience of total warfare upon the resources of the country, especially upon the supply and optimum utilisation of labour power, greatly accelerated labour's progress:

> Trade unions were drawn into the corridors of power at Whitehall, helping to break down their sense of the state as alien and impermeable to working-class interests, a lesson reinforced by the involvement of local trades councils in the administration of labour exchanges, war pensions, food control . . .
>
> Women gained new possibilities of citizenship, not only as war workers, but also as housewives, managing wartime austerity in co-operation with the state.[10]

By 1920 trade union membership had risen spectacularly, to embrace over 8 million workers. Notwithstanding continued and often high levels of industrial conflict, a national system of institutionalised collective bargaining had taken firm root. Furthermore, the Labour Party had replaced the Liberals as the main alternative to the Conservatives. Within four years the Labour Party would achieve the extremely rare feat of becoming a party of goverment within less than twenty-five years of its birth. Finally, the late Victorian and Edwardian years had seen an increasing number of working-class leaders achieve elected office and enhanced status and influence within their local communities.[11]

As we shall observe in due course, organised labour's progress had been far from untroubled and linear during the period under review. But of the overall, accelerated and substantial gains made, and the pride taken in those gains, there can be no doubt. In truth, workers' 'warrening' of British society, centrally involving notions of working-class empowerment and expanded social and political influence, had become far more extensive and intensive than during the mid-Victorian years.

This marked, if uneven and at times discontinuous, transition from outsider to insider or 'citizenship' status can also be seen significantly to have affected, albeit to varying degrees, the lives of the mass of working people, many of whom were either entirely outside or lacked central involvement in the labour movement. (In terms of numbers, if not influence, the labour movement constituted a minority force among workers throughout the period under review.) Attention has already been drawn to the achievement of mass political citizenship. In addition, living standards for the majority of the working class improved dramatically. Between 1850 and 1913–14 'normal' real incomes rose by 90 per cent, and continued to rise substantially during the inter-war period. There was a general shift away from poorly paid labouring and casual work towards more secure and better-paid jobs, increasingly of a semi-skilled nature, which amounted to a general upgrading of labour.[12] Furthermore, the difference in income (particularly during the First World War), experience and life chances between the skilled and non-skilled narrowed significantly. Within the overall context of the 'demographic making of the English working class' (members of the class becoming 'increasingly homogeneous in their origins and destinations'), Savage and Miles thus observe that between 1899 and 1914 'the sons of unskilled men had greatly improved prospects of upward mobility inside the working class'. At the same time, and notwithstanding the fact that more than 60 per cent were still to be found following in their fathers' footsteps, almost one-third of skilled workers' sons 'were now downwardly mobile inside the class, compared with one in seven in the period 1839–54'. The narrowing of the traditional gulf between the skilled elite and the labouring poor was reflected in the development of more standardised working-class patterns of leisure, housing and residence. Increasingly concentrated in cities and towns, the working class developed what Savage and Miles term a distinct urban territorial base. The development of this base, combined with the cultivation of dense and extensive intra- and inter-urban networks, was arguably of key importance both to the economic and spatial remaking of the working class and an intensified sense of class consciousness.[13]

We can agree with McKibbin that the advances outlined above undoubtedly underpinned the great strength of reformism among British workers and their overall rejection of revolutionary alternatives. However, much as we observed in relation to mid-Victorian popular radicalism, working-class reformism of the late Victorian and Edwardian years was generally not synonymous with reconciliation to, or total incorporation into, the 'system' and the conscious and unmediated adoption of the latter's dominant ideas, values and practices. Rather, reformism embraced a range of progessive and, in many ways, challenging ideas and practices.

There were, for example, strong emphases upon working-class pride and independence and the proven benefits and strengths of working-class collectivism and agency – of organisation, determination and mutuality – as against unfettered individualism and competition. Deference was fiercely contested, and workers in general remained largely impervious to direct middle-class attempts to re-remake them in 'rational' and 'improvement-minded' ways. Conflict and struggle were often regarded as the predictable, if unwelcome, result of continued, if unnecessary, employer, landowner and state tyranny and unreason. Points of identity and consciousness did not, however, revolve simply around class and collectivism. A male-dominated labour movement continued to carry within it deeply rooted assumptions about gender and a woman's place. Ethnic, local, regional and national identities interacted, more often than not, in *interdependent*, as opposed to exclusive, ways. As Hinton has argued,

> Class and nation may sometimes place competing claims on individual loyalties, but neither exists alone, and they cannot be fully understood in isolation from one another. Discourses of class involve claims about the place of class in the nation, whether (as with Chartism) the sense of class is partly constituted by exclusion from citizenship, or whether patriotism is being used to advance the claims of excluded groups to full membership of the nation. Imagined communities of class and nation were constructed together.[14]

Such emphases and identities were expressed within the framework of political commitment to the achievement of a more

democratic, equitable, co-operative, civilised and morally informed and regulated society in which workers and other producers would receive their due acknowledgement, protection and
reward. While frequently an expression of class consciousness,
the elastic notion of 'producerism' suggested that the 'productive'
and 'honourable' of all social groups were deserving of due reward and recognition. In such ways did organised labour per-
ceive itself to be possessed of a generous and tolerant plural and
holistic view of society which overshadowed mere self-interest
and sectionalism. Finally, the achievement of organised labour's
social vision involved pragmatic attention to the nuts and bolts of
change, especially in the short and medium terms. But it is also
important to note that reformist socialists and ordinary members
of the Labour Party also frequently possessed long-term goals
of fundamental social transformation which official Labour's
increasing twentieth-century concern with the attainment and
retention of office have often marginalised and obscured.

It was, of course, the case that forward-looking and challenging reformism, rooted in collectivism and class, constituted only
a part of total working-class experience. The rise of Labour was
indeed halting and uneven. Before 1914 the party's parliamentary
presence and progress were far from impressive. Trade unionism
had still not touched the mass of workers. Socialist strength and
influence paled into relative insignificance when set against the
full force of popular Conservatism and Liberalism. Imperialist
and racist sentiments, and all manner of internal differences and
divisions, provided, in some contexts, important counterweights
to the influence of class among workers.[15] Indeed, in their wish
effectively to counter what are perceived to be unduly heroic or
romantic interpretations of working-class life, some notable recent portrayals of late Victorian and Edwardian workers have
presented what may variously be described as starkly realistic or
unduly pessimistic and even embittered accounts.

For example, in a brilliant and provocative essay, Gareth
Stedman-Jones has argued that working-class culture in late nineteenth and early twentieth-century London marked a sharp retreat from the impressive intellectual and political challenge
posed by mid-Victorian artisan radicalism. Increasingly organised around sport and leisure, rather than around the workplace,
working-class culture in London supposedly became largely apo-

litical, passive, defensive, introverted, conservative and resigned to workers' subordinate place in an apparently permanent social hierarchy.[16] Rather than challenging the *status quo*, workers sought consolation for their 'life sentence' of class within the pleasurable and comforting, yet introverted and largely non-threatening, world of 'the pub, the sporting paper, the race course and the music hall'. Furthermore, the formation of the Labour Representation Committee represented, as a form of political association,

> not so much a challenge to the new working-class culture that had grown up since 1870 as an extension of it. If it sang *Jerusalem* it was not as a battle-cry but as a hymn. It accepted *de facto*, not only capitalism, but monarchy, Empire, aristocracy and established religion as well. With the foundation of the Labour Party, the now enclosed and defensive world of working-class culture had in effect achieved its apotheosis.

There is doubtless some truth in Stedman Jones's portrayal. As we indicated at the end of Chapter 5, later nineteenth-century socialists and others committed to fundamental social change often experienced considerable difficulty in establishing and developing the appeal of their ideas among working-class communities seemingly tied to the overriding importance of immediate, and at times smothering, experience – located, as Joanna Bourke informs us, 'in the intimate locale of the body, the home, and the locality'[17] – and the 'common sense' of prevailing ideas and social divisions. Furthermore, the institutions of traditional working-class culture often provided a sound defensive wall against unwelcome middle-class intrusion, and gave workers a sense of security, place and worth within their own chosen social contexts, values and norms and in relation to people of their own kind. However, Stedman Jones's picture is, in the final analysis, too one-dimensional and static to carry total conviction.

As McKibbin has suggested, it is, for example, 'doubtful if the British working class as a whole did cease to be work-centred'. Furthermore, as already emphasised in this study, cultures contain within them a variety of characteristics, meanings and capacities – for example, for change and continuity, for radicalism and conservatism, for passivity and challenge – which are complex, contested and subject to change over time. Within this context

Stedman Jones has attached exaggerated importance to the fatalistic, defensive and largely apolitical features of working-class culture and insufficient significance to its more assertive, confident and challenging characteristics. As Gurney has most recently shown, many reformists involved in the co-operative movement of these years were by no means passive, resigned, apathetic or inert. Rather they prided themselves upon the powers of their own *agency* – upon their proven ability to *create* their own ways of life and institutions, to extract considerable gains from capitalist society, and to press for transformative changes. Furthermore, this sense of purposeful, independent working-class agency was not confined to the organised labour movement and its activists. It penetrated to the heart of working-class culture, whether in factory-based Lancashire or in more casualised London. McKibbin has rightly drawn our attention to an active, if formally non-political, form of working-class culture which

> bred dogs and pigeons, grew flowers, raised canaries, founded angling clubs and cycling societies, put the factory or local football team together (or seized it from the posession of middle-class patrons), preached in church/chapel, attended Pleasant Sunday Afternoons, or forgot what it learned at the fourth standard but amazed the middle classes by its knowledge of football, racing, or even cricket . . .[18]

Furthermore, Stedman Jones has drawn too sharp a dividing line between culture and politics. Traditional working-class culture may not have been political in the formal, organised and narrow party political sense but, as McKibbin observes, 'it was a life in the broadest sense political – the *same kind* of people who founded pigeon-breeding societies also founded the Labour Party'. And 'at the moment when Stedman Jones' "non-political" working class was being formed the Labour Representation Committee was making its first real advances in the metropolis'. As demonstrated by the researches of Susan Pennybacker, Pat Thane, John Marriott and Jim Gillespie, Labour's advance in casualised London was far from insignificant during the pre- and, especially, in the post-war years.[19]

Some of the more recent accounts of Victorian and Edwardian working-class life have not only endorsed Stedman Jones's emphasis upon working-class conservatism and fatalism, but have gone further – to argue that instances of class consciousness were greatly overshadowed by racism, sexism, individualism, growing consumerism and deep-seated and enduring divisions among workers. Often erecting sweeping generalisations upon insubstantial empirical support, mistakenly seeing differences among workers as, *ipso facto*, evidence of division and conflict, and falsely positing necessary antagonisms between class and gender, class and ethnicity, and class and nation, such accounts lack the sophistication of that provided by Stedman Jones. They also present unbalanced and somewhat negative and pejorative pictures of working-class life.[20]

Just as citizenship gains and material advance promoted reformism and negotiated accommodation to capitalism – rather than the incorporation of a largely passive, fatalistic and / or hopelessly divided and reactionary working class – so, in turn, the process of living with capitalism involved considerably more instances of conflict, struggle and challenge and discontinuity than the notion of labour's relatively easy, untroubled and largely consensual integration into the 'peaceable kingdom' of Britain would suggest.

As we shall see in the following three chapters, many of labour's gains were themselves the product of struggle. For example, between the late 1880s and 1920s significant advances in trade union membership and in institutionalised collective bargaining often followed major 'official' battles between labour and capital. Furthermore, as seen in 1888–92, 1910–14, during the war and in the immediate post-war period, Britain was subjected, in the interests of trade union and worker advancement, to intense bouts of widespread labour unrest. The latter was, in numerous instances, 'unofficial' in character and in a minority of cases informed by revolutionary syndicalist and socialist ideas. Equally significant was the fact that hostile or indifferent attitudes and action on the part of some employers, sections of the judiciary and other organs of the state and the mainstream parties towards the claims of workers and organised labour did, as seen in the 1890s and in the immediate pre- and post-war periods, intensify popular grievances, class consciousness and feelings of outsider status, and promote, in part, radical and even revolutionary challenges to the *status quo*. Of particular importance in this context were the turns to independent labour and socialist politics which posed a fundamental challenge to workers' integration into the two-party system. Finally, there were important limits and exceptions to workers' advancement. As revealed in the surveys of Booth and Rowntree, poverty and insecurity continued to deny many working-class families the material benefits of 'true citizenship'. And feelings of relative deprivation and the general unfairness of existing social arrangements intensified between 1910 and 1920. In sum, we are observing in these years not only the growing *presence* of workers and labour movements within society, but also their intensified *challenge* to aspects of that society.

To observe such developments is, finally, to raise questions and revisit debates concerning the relative importance of change and stability in workers' lives between the 1870s and 1920. The argument, simply asserted here and developed in some detail in the rest of Part II, is that elements of discontinuity overshadowed elements of continuity. To summarise: as compared with the third quarter of the nineteenth century, the period from the 1870s to 1920 witnessed the growth of a mass labour movement rooted in a more confident, assertive, outgoing, increasingly independent, united and class-conscious working class. Its class consciousness, while more reformist than revolutionary in character, nevertheless contained within it strong oppositional currents, and constituted a marked departure from the dominant status-consciousness of the mid-Victorian working class. As much recent historiography has been at pains to demonstrate, important areas of continuity existed simultaneously – as reflected in political ideas, in patterns of culture and in trade unionism. But change was of paramount importance. We can begin to demonstrate the validity of this thesis, in Chapter 7, with reference to the area of workplace relations.

Notes

1 R. McKibbin, *The Ideologies of Class: Social Relations in Britain 1880–1950* (Oxford, 1991), p. 2.

2 J. Benson, *The Working Class in Britain 1850–1939* (London, 1989), p. 3.

3 E. Roberts, *Women's Work 1840–1940* (London, 1988), chapter 2; Benson, *Working Class*, pp. 15–16; N. Kirk, *Labour and Society in Britain and*

the USA, II, *Challenge and Accommodation 1850–1939* (Aldershot, 1994), pp. 7–8, 288–9.

4 McKibbin, *Ideologies of Class*, pp. 1–2.

5 *Ibid.*, pp. 2–41, 297–9, chapter 9; C. Waters, *British Socialists and the Politics of Popular Culture 1884–1914* (Manchester, 1990), especially chapter 6.

6 McKibbin, *Ideologies*, pp. 95–6; R. McKibbin, *The Evolution of the Labour Party 1910–1924* (Oxford, 1974); D. Tanner, *Political Change and the Labour Party 1900–1918* (Cambridge, 1990); E.J. Hobsbawm, 'The Formation of British Working-class Culture' and 'The Making of the Working Class 1870–1914', in his *Worlds of Labour* (London, 1984).

7 E.F. Biagini and A.J. Reid, *Currents of Radicalism* (Cambridge, 1991), chapter 1. It should, however, be noted that an emphasis upon political, social and cultural continuity, with respect to the period from the 1870s to 1920, has *not* uniformly characterised the writings of the 'liberal revisionists'. Gareth Stedman Jones, for example, detects the development of a more introverted and depoliticised working class in the late nineteenth century, while, according to Patrick Joyce, popular class consciousness 'developed most markedly in the early twentieth century, especially post-1914'. See G.S. Jones, 'Working-class Culture and Working-class Politics in London, 1870–1900: Notes on the Remaking of a Working Class', in his *Languages of Class* (Cambridge, 1983); P. Joyce, *Visions of the People* (Cambridge, 1991), p. 329.

8 Biagini and Reid (eds.), *Currents of Radicalism*, pp. 18–19; A.J. Reid, 'Dilution, Trade Unionism and the State in Britain during the First World War', in S. Tolliday and J. Zeitlin (eds), *Shop Floor Bargaining and the State: Historical and Comparative Perspectives* (London, 1985); A. Davies and S. Fielding (eds), *Workers' Worlds: Cultures and Communities in Manchester and Salford 1880–1939* (Manchester, 1992), introduction and chapter 5.

9 McKibbin, *Ideologies*, pp. 28–9, 38–9.

10 J. Hinton, 'Voluntarism versus Jacobinism: Labor, Nation and Citizenship in Britain 1850–1950', *International Labor and Working Class History*, 48 (1995) 68–90; J. Hinton, *Labour and Socialism: A History of the British Labour Movement 1867–1974* (Brighton, 1983), p. 24.

11 M. Savage and A. Miles, *The Remaking of the British Working Class 1840–1940* (London, 1994), p. 76; C. Williams, *Democratic Rhondda: Politics and Society 1885–1951* (Cardiff, 1996), pp. 72–83, chapter 3; B. Lancaster, *Radicalism, Cooperation and Socialism: Leicester Working Class Politics 1860–1906* (Leicester, 1987); K. Laybourn and J. Reynolds, *Liberalism and the Rise of Labour 1890–1918* (London, 1984).

12 Benson, *Working Class*, pp. 55–6.

13 Savage and Miles, *Remaking*, pp. 34–7, 72; Hobsbawm, *Worlds of Labour*, pp. 202, 204–5.

14   Hinton, 'Voluntarism Versus Jacobinism', 68.

15   J. Bourke, *Working Class Cultures in Britain 1890–1960* (London, 1994), chapter 6.

16   Stedman Jones, 'Working-class Culture', pp. 179–238.

17   Bourke, *Working Class Cultures*, p. 213.

18   P. Gurney, *Co-operative Culture and the Politics of Consumption in England 1870–1930* (Manchester, 1996), pp. 22–5, Part I; McKibbin, *Ideologies*, p. 14.

19   J. Marriott, *The Culture of Labourism: The East End between the Wars* (Edinburgh, 1991); McKibbin, *Ideologies*, p. 15; J. Gillespie, 'Popularism and Proletarianism: Unemployment and Labour Politics in London 1918–34', in D. Feldman and G.S. Jones (eds), *Metropolis: London Histories and Representations since 1800* (London, 1989), pp. 163–88; S. Pennybacker, ' "The Millenium by Return of Post": Reconsidering London Progressivism', in *ibid*; P. Thane, 'Labour and Local Politics: Radicalism, Democracy and Social Reform 1880–1914', in Biagini and Reid, *Currents of Radicalism*.

20   Renson, *Working Class*, chapters 6 and 7.

7

The workplace:
conflict and compromise

Specific developments in workplace relations – in patterns of conflict and compromise and of change and continuity between workers and employers – can most fruitfully be approached and understood if first situated within the wider context of the changing political economy of British capitalism from the early 1870s to 1920. The substantive core of this chapter accordingly begins with a brief description of the relevant economic developments of this period. It then proceeds to an examination of the responses and initiatives undertaken by employers and their organisations and the state in relation to these developments, paying particular attention to questions concerning the position and the transformation of labour within the workplace. In the course of this examination ideological and political considerations are brought into play with purely economic factors. Finally, questions concerning workers' consciousness, responses, powers of agency and developments within trade unionism are incorporated into the politico-economic framework of analysis.

The central arguments of the chapter may be summarised in the following way. First, mounting economic problems promoted, on the one hand, numerous instances and sustained periods of industrial conflict, accelerated employer and state attempts to reduce labour costs and subordinate labour to the will of capital, and growing opposition to trade union 'excesses', immunities and, in some instances, recognition. On the other hand, hostile official intentions and actions towards workers and trade unionism were limited and uneven; especially from the 1890s onwards,

they were accompanied by growing attempts to contain and reduce conflict by means of the more widespread development of
systems of institutionalised collective bargaining and the cultivation of amicable relations with 'responsible' trade unionism and
its leaders. In sum, workplace relations were characterised by the
complex interplay of forces of conflict and compromise.

Second, and taking due account of the undoubted importance
of threats to workers' standing and security in the workplace, the
period did not witness the wholesale transformation of labour.
Contrary to the well known thesis of Harry Braverman, workers
were not reduced to a uniformly de-skilled, non-unionised and
machine-dependent mass, rendered largely defenceless in the
face of capital by the ravages of new managerial practices
(Taylorism), technological change and uniformly ruthless and
American-style open-shop (i.e. non-union) policies on the part of
employers.[1] Many workers demonstrated great tenacity and resilience in their defence of customary skills, workplace controls
and practices and continued assertiveness in their attempts to
influence the effect of new technologies and practices upon the
division of labour.[2] Far from being destroyed or weakened, trade
unionism greatly increased its constituency and influence during
this period. And, while committed to profit maximisation and
management's full 'right to manage', many employers were less
and less intent upon the wholesale extirpation of trade unionism
or the total transformation of the existing division of labour.
Finally, on balance, the state was concerned to play a mediatory
and conciliatory role between organised labour and capital than a
policy of outright union repression.

Third, within the world of trade unionism changes outweighed
continuities. Notwithstanding some undoubted similarities between the 'new' and 'old' unions, differences revolving around
constituency, size and structure, outlook, leadership and threat
to the *status quo* were correctly perceived by contemporaries to
be of more significance. The increasingly widespread and arguably more challenging, class-conscious nature of trade unionism
as a whole provides a further telling point of contrast with
the relatively small, predominantly sectional and the more
moderate, narrow and limited perspective of the mid-Victorian
movement.

The changing economic context

Traditionally many economic historians drew a sharp contrast between the heady optimism accompanying the 'great Victorian boom' of the middle decades of the nineteenth century and the widespread pessimism and gloom prevalent in business circles during the long years of the great depression, between 1873 and 1896. Indeed, it was often claimed that the roots of Britain's twentieth-century relative economic decline, and especially of 'entrepreneurial failure', were to be traced to the depressed final quarter of the nineteenth century. More recent research has, however, successfully challenged or heavily qualified the conventional wisdom with respect to a number of key issues.

We know, for example, that the economy as a whole continued to perform respectably. There was some slowing down of the rate of growth of total output – from 2.5 per cent between 1831 and 1860 to 1.9 per cent between 1873 and 1907 – and of output per head – the respective figures being 1.3 per cent and 1.0 per cent – but 'this was partly to be expected in a mature economy' and, in any case, antedated the great depression. Despite generally downward, if variable, pressures upon profits, rents and interest there were, furthermore, sufficient variations in prices, levels of production and employment between 1873 and 1896 to 'invalidate the notion of unrelieved depression'. We can observe a general fall in the price of foodstuffs during the same period, but it had the positive effect of reducing the cost of many of the necessities of life for the majority of the population. For those in work prices generally fell faster than wages: the result was the most marked and sustained increase in living standards for the mass of the working class during the entire century. Similarly, there exists evidence to support the view that the period of the great depression saw an increase in labour's share of the national income. Finally, just as most of the evidence fails to support the notions of sudden economic retardation and general doom and gloom, so it also invalidates the theses of entrepreneurial failure and the ascendancy of an aristocratic anti-industrial spirit among the business classes. Thus:

> British employers continued to act 'rationally' (i.e. profit-maximise and cost-minimise, subject to prevailing constraints). And the tenac-

ity of 'aristocratic' style within the British ruling elite should not obscure the close interpenetrations between different kinds of wealth, the powerful self-confidence of the bourgeoisie, and the overriding commitment of the economy to full-blown commodity production.

We may conclude, therefore, that

the term 'Great Depression' is an ideological construct, rooted in the growing problems of those late nineteenth-century contemporaries dependent upon profits, rent and interest . . . It is significant that once prices, profits and (in all probability) capital's share of the national income rose between 1896 and 1914, at a time when real wages remained pretty stable, talk of depression largely disappeared from middle-class dinner tables.[3]

As Roderick Floud and Peter Clarke have recently reminded us, it is, furthermore, all too tempting from a position of hindsight to exaggerate the nature and extent of Britain's economic weaknesses and relative decline on the eve of the First World War and beyond.[4] We must remember that, notwithstanding the growth of competition from the United States and Germany and the advent of the former country to a position of world leadership in the sphere of manufacturing production, Britain remained, by the end of the war, in possession of a world-wide empire, internationally renowned industries and skills and pre-eminent in the fields of shipping and finance. Not many early twentieth-century Britons would have accepted the pessimistic judgement passed on them and their era by their late twentieth-century counterparts.

Yet we would be equally guilty of misrepresentation, and, additionally, complaceny, to suggest that the economy between the 1870s and the 1920s did not face growing and increasingly serious problems which did expose significant structural, attitudinal and behavioural deficiencies. For example, having discarded the notion of the great depression, we can still usefully adhere to the view that the late nineteenth century saw a crisis of 'competitive capitalism'. The latter resided in sqeezed profit margins resulting from falling prices, increased competition, more hostile product markets, a decline in the rates of increase of productivity and total output, and the growing power of workers and trade unions to prevent wages from falling as quickly as prices. In addition, government legislation of the 1870s afforded legal protection to trade unionism and, as such, placed important restrictions upon the scope for effective anti-union action of the North American type on the part of employers and the judiciary. What these combined factors amounted to was not only an economic crisis of accumulation but also, as observed independently by Arthur McIvor and myself, 'a *class-based* or social crisis in which a successful resolution to their problems demanded that labour be more fully subordinated to the will of capital'. 'Nothing less than a marked shift in the blance of class forces was required.'[5]

From the point of view of capital, matters improved somewhat from the mid to late 1890s almost to the end of the 1900s. Prices rose, industrial unrest declined, and, in general, the balance of power within the evolving system of institutionalised industrial relations rested far more with the employers than with the workers. This state of affairs did not, however, persist. From 1908 onwards strike activity increased and, as observed by John Lovell, 'the whole period down to 1926 – with the exception of some of the war years, when an industrial truce was in operation – was one of unprecedented industrial conflict'.[6] As Bernard Waites has suggested, it was during the war and the immediate post-war years that the language of class, of experiential and structured conflict between labour and capital, grew substantially in importance and appeal. Part of the reason lay in the fact that the total national effort and sacrifice increasingly demanded by the war raised serious doubts about the national, as opposed to the purely sectional, selfish and greedy, interests and concerns of private capital.[7] More generally, Hinton has shown that the wartime experience offered a fundamental challenge to the doctrines of economic individualism and *laissez-faire* which had dominated the nineteenth century, and gave a boost to organised labour's growing, if by no means uncontested, belief in the superiority of collectivism and regulation over voluntarism. The immediate post-war years saw Labour's adoption of Clause IV and massively increased popularity at the polls, a further upsurge in popular radicalism and industrial conflict and the significant growth of revolutionary ideas.[8] Post-war British capitalism was faced with painful choices concerning economic, social and political reconstruction and 'readjustment'. The staple export industries went into serious decline in the face of growing competition from the developed and less developed countries of the world, and the United States continued its seemingly inexorable march towards world economic dominance. In sum, as argued by Hobsbawm, the world had changed fundamentally from the previous century. Britain was no longer the workshop of the world, and the economic liberalism upon which British hegemony had been premised would be further ravaged by inter-war depression, the rise of economic and political nationalism and fascism and the Second World War.[9]

Responses: British traditionalism

How did Britain's employers responded to what McIvor has termed 'the conjuncture of rising worker militancy – an ability and will to sustain resistance – with intensifying competition, more hostile product markets and changes in state and public attitudes towards industrial relations'?[10] By way of introduction to the formulation of a response, it is important to take serious note of Zeitlin's and Tolliday's argument that employers and their organisations did not constitute a uniform, undifferentiated group with respect to interests, actions or attitudes, and that the concept of social class is of extremely limited value in explaining the complex and varied nature of employer behaviour. Rather, suggest these scholars, primary importance should be attached to historical contingency and elements of diversity, fragmentation and division among employers. In contrast to such an approach, however, this chapter takes the view that, notwithstanding the importance of complexity, variety and contingency, and without assuming complete uniformity of interests, actions or beliefs, nevertheless we can detect among employers in this period patterned, indeed often class-based, responses to the conjuncture highlighted by McIvor.[11]

In overall terms, and with a minority of notable exceptions, the dominant response was to maximise profits, minimise costs and ensure employer control in the workplace by resort to what has become known as 'traditionalism'. Unlike many of their North American counterparts, British employers reacted to the crisis of competitive capitalism less by the rapid adoption of the practices and structures of corporate or 'monopoly' capitalism – mass production carried out in very large, non-unionised, integrated, bureaucratic and Taylorised corporate firms, complete with close links between finance and industrial capital – than by adherence to the 'tried and trusted' customs and structures of small-scale, competitive and largely fragmented nineteenth-century capitalism. It is the case that the factory had become the dominant site of production in late nineteenth-century Britain, that the First World War in many cases accelerated trends towards 'bigness' and integration, and that in some sectors of the economy, such as the newer industries of engineering, motor car manufacturing and boot and shoe production, thoroughly transforming American methods were introduced. In the final analysis, however, concentration, giant corporations, Taylorism and close ties between investment banks and industry remained, up to the end of our period, much less marked in Britain. As observed by Hobsbawm, by the end of the nineteenth century Britain was becoming 'a parasitic rather than a competitive economy', largely wedded to the increasingly archaic structures and practices of the first industrial revolution, and 'living off the remains of world monopoly, the underdeveloped world, her past accumulations of wealth and the advance of her rivals'.[12] Herein lay the roots of Britain's relative decline.

Traditionalism was also the dominant feature of British capital's response to the specific problems of increasing labour costs and the growing confidence and assertiveness of workers and trade unions. (Ironically, given our marked differences of approach and emphasis, my general thesis is, in this respect, consistent with Zeitlin's specific findings for engineering.[13]) As we shall see below, and as demonstrated in the cases of cotton, engineering and most other industries, employers in Britain tended to push existing methods of labour management 'to the maximum limits of productivity' rather than, as in the United States, to 'fundamentally transform existing plant layout and the division of labour by means of Taylorism and technological exchange'. In Britain there was, for example, more concern with 'cheapening and intensifying skilled labour within the existing division of labour' than with experimentation with new forms of capital-intensive investment. Capital-intensive and, in some instances, anti-union methods did prevail in sectors (such as motor cars, footwear and cycles) in which a mixture of mass standardised demand, technological imperatives and acute international competition did induce employer radicalism. However, within the confines of our chosen period of study, such methods constituted exceptions to the traditionalist rule.[14]

Within this hegemonic framework of traditionalism, employers sought to increase profits, output and productivity, reduce costs and protect the 'right to manage' by resort to two distinct, if closely interrelated, strands of labour management. The first strand was explicitly aggressive and coercive in character. The second, while still fundamentally designed to protect the 'rights of capital', was more accommodating. It is to an examination of these contrasting, if often complementary, aspects of labour policy that we can now usefully turn.

Coercion and conflict

As we observed in Chapters 2 and 3, hostile and coercive employer attitudes and actions towards workers and their organisations constituted a staple feature of mid-Victorian workplace relations. The aggressive actions of capital, combined with the worker resistance and industrial conflict which frequently ensued, have, however, been either ignored or underplayed in many recent political and intellectual accounts of the development of mid-Victorian 'consensus, continuity and stability'. In similar ways we can observe continued, and in some instances intensified and expanded, employer aggression and serious workplace conflicts in the late Victorian and Edwardian periods, and their underestimation, even marginalisation, in much of the literature which puts the case for post-1880s Britain as a stable and largely consensual, integrated and ordered society.[15]

Employer opposition to trade unionism and strikes, the use of the lockout, the blacklisting of strikers, the 'document' (a written renunciation of trade unionism), strike breakers ('scabs', 'knobsticks' or 'blacklegs') and attempts to enlist state aid in anti-union endeavours thus constituted important, if recently unduly neglected, features of workplace relations in a number of places and instances throughout the period under review. For example, in his very thorough and original research into the expanding field of the social history of employers, McIvor has clearly shown that employers' associations 'usually originated as coercive strikebreaking organisations, concerned above all else to root out and destroy trade unions'. Confrontational origins and purposes stretching from the eighteenth century to the mid-Victorian years were modified significantly by the widespread development of collective bargaining between the 1890s and 1920. But even in this latter period the associations generally retained their coercive character. As McIvor declares,

> One of the major functions of employers' organisations before 1914 was forcibly to break strikes, either as an initial reaction, or as a second line of defence when established procedures to settle disputes without a stoppage of work were either exhausted or ignored.[16]

During the first and second waves of new unionism, in the early 1870s and from the late 1880s to the mid-1890s, employer anti-unionism manifested itself strongly in agriculture, in coal mining, in the docks and ports, on the railways and in more established centres of trade unionism such as cotton and engineering. At times receiving significant support from the forces of law and order and other official sources, employers and their organisations notched up some important anti-union successes. For example, the Revolt of the Field of the early 1870s, in which Joseph Arch's National Agricultural Labourers' Union attracted between 100,000 and 150,000 members, was effectively destroyed by a combination of economic downturn, the formation of Defence Associations among farmers, the anti-union fulminations of Anglican ministers and the Eastern Counties Lock out of 1874.[17]

By the mid-1890s adverse economic conditions and a fierce employer counter-attack had halved the new unionist membership upsurge of 1888–92. Coal mining, cotton, slate quarrying, engineering and the boot and shoe industries experienced major strikes or, more often, lock-outs during the 1890s in which issues of employer and official resort to violence, the very existence and standing of trade unionism, and the attempted importation of 'scab' labour by employers were, albeit to varying degrees, of cricial importance. Two coal miners were shot dead by troops at Featherstone during the extremely bitter four-month dispute of 1893. In cotton, observes McIvor, the master cotton spinners' and weavers' federations continued, after the adoption of formal collective bargaining and dispute procedures, to 'fall back on more coercive methods, including labour replacement, when the formal conciliation machinery broke down'. Significantly, the major advances in the uneven development of collective bargaining machinery in cotton followed closely upon the heels of the major conflicts of the early 1850s, 1878 (involving 100,000 workers) and the late 1880s and early 1890s 'when labour had illustrated its power to resist'. Indeed, as late as the 1900s employers in cotton 'continued to withhold full recognition to the relatively poorly organised cardroom operatives, female ring spinners, cloth-lookers and warehousemen'.[18] The lock-out in the engineering industry in 1897–98 revolved in part – much like its counterpart of 1852 – around the right of employers to employ non-union black-leg labour at individual rates of pay. In both lock-outs the engineering employers formally achieved their goal. Around the docks and ports anti-union activity was rife, whether in the form of the messianic National Free Labour Association (formed in 1893), one of the other 'specialist labour replacement agencies', or the notorious Shipping Federation, founded in 1890. The latter was 'one of the most militant of pre-1914 employers' organisations, established explicitly as a "permanent battle-axe" to protect shipowners against the strike weapon'. A number of seamen's strikes were broken, and the forcible defeat of the Hull dockers' strike in 1893 ('where 95 per cent of the men were in the union') constituted 'a clear indication of the power of the Shipping Federation's strikebreaking machinery'.[19] A series of adverse legal verdicts, climaxing in the Taff Vale decision of 1901 – which negated the widespread belief that the Acts of 1871 and 1875 had rendered trade unions, as collective organisations and agents, exempt from claims for damages – and the seeming inability and/or reluctance of the established political parties adequately to defend the interests of the trade union movement added significantly to organised labour's growing list of grievances and renewed worker feelings of outsider status.

Finally, notwithstanding their widespread geographical presence, anti-trade union sentiments and action were particularly marked in Scotland and South Wales. The heavy industries of the west of Scotland, less productive, more undercapitalised and more prone to acute cyclical fluctuations than their English counterparts, were owned by employers who generally 'fought long and hard against trade unionism'. As shown by Joseph Melling and John Foster, trade unionism in and around Glasgow developed later than in England, was relatively weak, and was frequently 'accompanied by much bitterness and deeply held suspicion towards the employers'.[20] In South Wales the rapid growth in membership and workplace influence of the South Wales Miners' Federation was accompanied, from its formation in 1898, by a 'remarkably high level of strike activity' and mine owners who were predominantly anti-union by tradition and inclination. According to Roger Fagge, in the face of mounting world competition, these owners placed increasing pressure on wage costs and miners' customary rights and allowances, and turned to 'the vigorous use of the courts in an attempt to stifle the growth of the SWMF'. As seen most acutely in the violent Cambrian dispute of 1910–11 – which resulted in several injuries and a fatality following police baton charges – conflict between miners and owners was a chronic feature of workplace relations in the South Wales coalfield up to the General Strike and beyond.[21]

During the third, and most successful, wave of new unionism – from 1910 to 1914 – demands for union recognition and improved pay and conditions constituted 'the overriding goal of the vast majority of (non-skilled) participants'.[22] Furthermore, as demonstrated most sharply in the national railway strike and the mass transport strikes of 1911, many employers and (at least in the first instance) government representatives reacted with hostility and violence to workers' demands. In response to the human resource demands of total warfare and growing worker strength and increasing radicalism, the war and immediate post-war years saw major gains in the strength of trade unionism. But these gains involved the human sacrifices and official 'no strike' costs of wartime, and the renewed, indeed heightened, industrial and political conflicts of 1918–21 – the latter revolving around radical post-war reconstruction in the full interests of the 'people'.[23]

Implicit in the foregoing discussion is the fact that many employers retained their dislike of trade unionism on the grounds that it constituted potential and, in numerous instances, actual bases of competing power and control within the workplace. These issues of power and control, and especially of management's 'right to manage' – to have control over and to change working patterns and conditions in order to protect and advance capital's interests without 'undue' or 'illegitimate' worker and trade union interference – assumed added, indeed urgent and widespread, importance in a period of worsening market conditions, adverse pressures upon capital accumulation, and growing worker confidence, strength and militancy. Thus the vast majority of employers in this period, whether pro- or anti-union in character, markedly quickened and intensified their attempts aggressively and unilaterally to exert control over workplace matters and to increase the 'squeeze' on labour. The aim was to reduce labour costs, increase output, productivity and profits and to subordinate labour more effectively to the will of capital. These controlling endeavours constituted another crucial site of coercion and conflict.

Examples of such endeavours abound.[24] In cotton the employers variously increased work loads, speeded up mules and looms, utilised cheap and inferior raw cotton and yarn (which in turn made the work more onerous, hazardous to health and time-consuming, and reduced earnings), reduced wages, opposed the closed shop in weaving, condemned in trade journals such as the *Textile Mercury* (See document 11) trade union 'tyranny' and 'excessive' demands, put greater pressure upon overlookers to 'drive' the operatives, and attempted, with marked success in the wake of Taff Vale, to subject striking local unions to financial penalties. Attempted wage reductions, opposition to the minimum wage, the eight-hour day and adjusted payments for working difficult seams ('abnormal places'), attacks on customary rights, extensive fining and the prosecution of strikers for breach of contract characterised the actions of coal-mining employers in various parts of the country.

In rapidly and successfully transforming production methods – from those based on outwork and craft control to the mechanisation and semi-skilled labour of the factory – footwear employers in Leicester sparked off fierce industrial and political conflict in the town, as witnessed most acutely in the acrimonious 1895 lock-out and the growing socialist challenge to Lib-Labism. In engineering, where craft-based control issues were particularly prominent, employers fought very hard to undermine craft and union regulation and control of the labour process. As a result of the successful 1897–98 lock-out, employers won the the right 'to introduce piecework at rates agreed with individual workers . . . to have full control over the employment of apprentices, to enforce overtime, and to place any worker on any machine at a mutually agreed rate'. The issues of dilution, manning and the appropriate rate for the job aroused fierce and persistent passions and conflicts in engineering during the war and inter-war years. Notwithstanding tenacious worker resistance, Zeitlin records that engineering employers were

> able to undermine the long-term future of craft regulation through the increasing employment of semi-skilled and female labour; the multiplication of apprentices and the subversion of the technical content of their training; and the rapid extension of payment by results.

As in the case of the footwear industry, 'transformed' labour became a particularly marked feature of the newer, more standardised and Taylorised sectors of engineering. In keeping with their pronounced anti-unionism, many employers in Scotland demonstrated an impetus towards increased innovation and management. As Melling concludes, in all the major sectors of the Scottish economy there occurred, albeit unevenly, 'tighter workplace controls, heavier workloads, fresh incentive systems, mechanisation and rationalisation'.[25]

As we shall observe in more detail below, employer aggression towards workers and unions was by no means an unqualified success. In coal mining, for example, notwithstanding considerable employer opposition, the Miners' Federation of Great Britain, formed as late as 1889, had become by 1914 the largest bargaining unit in the country, and the miners had achieved the statutory eight-hour day and government acceptance of the principle of a minimum wage for the industry. However, especially between the 1890s and 1910, employer resort to conflict and coercion had, on balance, brought more success than failure.

> in a number of crucial battles – in cotton between . . . 1891 . . . and the Brooklands Agreement of 1893; in north Wales slate quarrying during 1896–97 and 1900–03; in the 1895 lockout in the boot and shoe industry; in most spectacular fashion in the engineering lockout of 1897–98; and (to a lesser extent) in the miners' lockout of 1893 – the employers won most of their demands. Above all, they won

the 'right' to impose unilateral changes in working conditions and practices, to defeat craft control, to stabilise and limit wage costs, and to reduce unwanted risks to production runs and profits.[26]

Accommodation and detente

Notwithstanding the numerous examples of coercion and conflict cited above, the capitalist transformation of labour in Britain during this period was a limited and uneven process. Aggressive and coercive employer strategies generally operated within the guiding framework of traditionalism. As we shall see below, in the vast majority of cases in which employers had won – often as a result of industrial conflict – the right unilaterally to control the workplace, they did not totally transform the existing division of labour along 'American' lines. Rather they increasingly adopted, from the mid-1890s onwards, more conciliatory and accommodating policies towards labour and the trade unions. (See documents 12–13.) In consequence, Braverman's notions of uniformly transformative employers and a de-skilled and defeated working class stand in need of serious correction. However, in pursuing the objective of detente, employers sought simultaneously to maximise profits and to hold formal and informal sway over labour.

Brief references to workplace experiences in specific industries may serve to illustrate the general points made above. In cotton employers generally reacted to their growing problems far more by attempting to protect and extend their markets and push customary methods of labour management to the full than by following the American path of vertical integration, rapid and widespread technological innovation (in the form of ring spinning) and the introduction of more direct managerial control over hiring. Unlike the predominant pattern in the United States, subcontracting English cotton minders retained their labour management functions over the piecers. In addition, and again in marked contrast to much of the experience in cotton in the United States, English cotton employers moved, often in the wake of periods of bitter industrial conflict, willingly to embrace, indeed increasingly to initiate, union recognition and sophisticated mechanisms of collective bargaining. Such was famously the case in 1893 when, following the general spinning lock-out of the previous year, the Brooklands Agreement was drawn up. The agreement set a ceiling of 5 per cent on wage movements per annum, involved a wage reduction, and introduced a centralised disputes procedure in spinning which 'stated that unresolved local disputes had to be referred to a central joint committee before strike action could be considered'. In effect, Brooklands represented an attempt to institutionalise shop-floor grievances, to delay their resolution and to avoid costly and wasteful interruptions of production. It is with such considerations in mind that Keith Burgess can reach his conclusion that Brooklands represented a turn to detente and collective bargaining on the employers' terms. Significantly, a national, industry-wide procedural agreement had arisen in cotton weaving in 1881 in response to the costly and damaging effects of the 1878 dispute.[27]

As Hugh Clegg and John Lovell have shown,[28] the national resolution of grievances and disputes by means of conciliation machinery and industry-wide procedural agreements became a marked feature of the overall British industrial scene between the 1890s and 1920. Boots and shoes in 1895, engineering in 1898 and building and shipbuilding in the first decade of the new century thus followed the example of cotton. Frequently, if not invariably, procedural agreements were adopted in the aftermath of periods of workplace conflict. (Before 1914 industry-wide substantive agreements, dealing with conditions of employment, usually took place at the local or district level within each industry.) In engineering, where employers had won their famous victory in the 1897–98 lock-out, they nevertheless continued to recognise and negotiate with trade unions. And the attempts of the engineering employers to cheapen and intensify skilled labour took place 'invariably within the parameters of the existing technology and traditional division of labour'. McIvor notes that in engineering 'No evidence has been unearthed of the Lancashire employers' organisations promoting Taylorism', and that 'the main protagonists of pseudo-scientific managerial ideology' in the period under review were 'maverick employers like Mather, Renold, Ford and British Westinghouse' which were either non-members or dissociated themselves from their industry associations.[29] In a similar vein, Zeitlin has convincingy shown that a marked difference existed between the newer, Taylorised areas of engineering and its more established sectors. In the latter, based on small and unspecialised firms catering to diverse customer requirements, new technologies and methods of working were thus introduced 'within a workshop organisation that remained structurally unchanged'. Furthermore, and notwithstanding important setbacks and outright defeats, skilled workers in the more traditional areas of engineering displayed remarkable tenacity in defence of workgroup loyalties and in relation to control issues (whether manning, dilution, levels of pay, leaving certificates or employer 'tyranny') throughout the years from the 1890s to 1920.[30]

Much the same conclusions may be reached – with respect to the issue of employer practices and worker responses – in shipbuilding, iron and steel, the building industry and other traditional craft sectors of the pre-1914 economy. In all these cases employers, while insistent upon managerial prerogative and at times resorting to coercive strategies, 'sought to eliminate "excesses" of craft and union power, rather than, geneally speaking, trade unionism *per se*'.[31]

Explanations

Why did employers turn to traditional, and increasingly accommodating, rather than transforming methods and strategies? In the first place, employer experience and assessments of the relative costs and benefits involved in the choice and exercise of a particular strategy were undoubtedly of major importance. For example, by the mid-1890s many employers had come to the conclusion that more was to be gained from detente and institutionalised collective bargaining, if conducted *largely upon their own terms*, than from extended periods of conflict. As McIvor has suggested, 'Coercive control – via pitched battle trials of strength – proved increasingly costly in terms of production time lost as trade unions consolidated themselves.' Furthermore, having gained the upper hand as a result of their victories in industrial struggles, employers felt confident that they could use the resilient, if weakened, trade unions as controlling and regulating mechanisms in a number of ways. Regulation of wages would bring order and stability into imperfect and unpredictable market conditions. 'Responsible' trade union leaders, grateful for recognition and a recognised bargaining role, would 'play cricket' with the employers, avoid, if at all possible, strikes and police the more 'unruly' and 'extreme' among their members. Unions would be kept 'firmly out of the workplace' by means of 'prescribed collective bargaining on a limited range of issues on the employers' terms', and labour militancy and interruptions of production contained by protracted dispute procedures.[32]

Between the late 1890s and the late 1900s the employers' strategy worked extremely well, as reflected in the facts that institutionalised collective bargaining made rapid advances and that the years 1899–1907 'were in fact the quietest in the whole period from 1891 (when adequate strike statistics start) to 1933'.[33] However, as seen, for example, in the cases of cotton and shipbuilding, centralised grievance procedures proved too slow and unwieldy adequately to address workers' mounting grievances concerning poor materials, overwork, speed-up and various aspects of craft regulation. Such pent-up frustrations, allied to economic buoyancy and increased demand for labour, the failure of money wages to catch up with price inflation, and renewed confidence and strength on the part of the non-skilled, underlay the labour unrest between 1910 and 1914. And the successes achieved by workers during these years, especially in terms of union recognition, posed a serious challenge to the dominance achieved by capital between the 1890s and the 1900s. Furthermore, and notwithstanding government opposition to 'extreme' and 'irresponsible' forms of workers' action on Clydeside and elsewhere during the war and the immediate post-war years, tight labour market conditions, workers' sacrifices on behalf of a nation at war and the threat of growing popular radicalism ensured that state support for official trade unionism, mediation and conciliation and collective bargaining would increase markedly during the period from the Munitions of War Act of 1915 to 1920. In sum, by the end of our period workers and their unions were in a much stronger position than during the 1890s. Ironically, the system of institutionalised collective bargaining and accommodation initiated by the employers primarily to preserve and/or increase their power at the workplace had, in the changing politico-economic climate from 1910 to 1920, worked increasingly to labour's advantage. By the onset of depression in 1921, and notwithstanding a general hardening of employer attitudes and practices during the depressed periods of the inter-war years, trade unions had achieved sufficient strength and legitimacy in the eyes of the nation at large to render their total destruction unthinkable to the majority of employers and politicians. During the period of the 1926 General Strike employers and state agencies would thus adopt the role of lion-tamer rather than big-game hunter.[34]

Second, market conditions and patterns of trade also played a crucial role in the determination of employer strategies. For example, standardised wage determination by means of institutionalised collective bargaining appealed to a growing number of employers faced with uncertain markets and wage and price competion from other employers. As illustrated most clearly in the case of cotton, the promotion of standard wage and price lists helped employers to regulate and stabilise market conditions. The cotton trade unions could be employed effectively to police wage agreements and help to bring rogue employers and workers into line. In some industries matters were less straightforward. In engineering and the building trade, for instance, employer competition and individualism could, as emphasised by Zeitlin, seriously obstruct attempts to hammer out common employer strategies. However, we have seen that common problems elicited similar responses from employers across a range of industries. Furthermore, faced with growing foreign competition, most employers in the traditional export industries effectively retreated into empire markets rather than meet the new-found competition head-on. The fact that such markets were vast and safe, and that large profits continued to be derived from them, meant that there was relatively little pressure upon employers radically to transform the organisation and management of their concerns. By way of contrast, in the newer sections of engineering and footwear, where foreign competition could not be sidestepped, employers introduced far more radical and transforming business and labour strategies.[35]

Third, employer attitudes, actions and influences did not exist in isolation. They interacted with, and were balanced against, the perceived interests and values of the various organs of the state, the trade unions, the workers and the wider public. As will be evident from this chapter, the state adopted, on balance, a positive and accommodating rather than a negative and hostile stance towards the issues of trade union recognition and voluntary collective bargaining. The period did see judicial challenges to the favourable trade union legislation of the 1870s. But we must remember that the punitive anti-union judgement of Taff Vale was soon reversed by the Trade Disputes Act of 1906, which once again legitimised trade union immunities and rights. And, as against the restraints imposed by the Osborne judgement of 1909 upon the spending of union funds for political purposes, the Trade Union Act of 1913 stated that a union had to ensure, by means of a ballot, that a majority of members were in favour of such purposes. Instances of state coercion of trade unionists and those suspected of being revolutionary socialists and syndicalists must not be underestimated. Simultaneously, however, they should not be allowed to overshadow the outstanding fact of the state's overall acceptance of the mainstream labour movement as an 'estate of the realm'. Within this context there is perhaps no more telling contrast than that between the British and US situations. Samuel Gompers, the president of the American Federation of Labour, looked with envy and longing at the official recognition, freedom of action, immunities and membership strength enjoyed by British trade unions. The pronounced and persistent anti-unionism of the courts and chronic employer and state repression placed major obstacles in the way of the realisation of the 'British way' in the pre-1930s United States.[36]

The very strength and resilience of British trade unionism also markedly influenced the increased employer preference for accommodation. Notwithstanding a number of setbacks and major defeats, the union movement as a whole increased its membership from approximately 500,000 in 1870 to a staggering 8,348,000 by 1920, or 45 per cent of the labour force. As such, the unions not only enjoyed an enviable international reputation for strength and depth but also constituted a solid fact of life for the employing class.

As is well known, union membership advanced by three pronounced leaps: from 750,000 in 1888 to 1.5 million in 1892; from 2.5 million in 1910 to 4 million in 1914; and thence to 8.3 million in 1920. There is general agreement among labour historians that the second and third of these great leaps forward saw the consolidation of the new unionism and its numerical dominance of the trade union movement as a whole. Conversely, lively debates still rage over three issues of the period 1910–20: the precise influence of syndicalism and other revolutionary ideas upon workers and trade unionism; the effects of the First World War (as accelerator or transformer) upon labour; and the role of the state (as coercive or conciliatory force) during the war and the immediate post-war years. However, these issues have been somewhat overshadowed by long-standing and continuing debates concerning elements of continuity and change in the development of the old and the new unionism during the first period of advance, from 1888 to 1892. It is to a brief evaluation of this latter area of debate that the final part of this chapter now turns.[37]

The case in favour of continuity between the new and the old unionism may be summarised in the following way. First, the numerically most significant and lasting gains between the late 1880s and the mid-1890s were made not by the new, non-skilled unions but by the old unions – the latter embracing both the closed, 'new model' organisations of the craft and skilled and the more open or mass unions in coal and cotton. Second, about half the 'new' unions formed in this first period of advance failed to survive the economic depression of the mid-1890s and the employer and judicial counter-attack. Third, those new unions which did survive the difficult 1890s did so by resort to the cautious and sectional tactics of the old unions rather than by the 'new' tactics of militant mass action, open membership and low dues. Finally, the diverse patterns of leadership (socialist and non-socialist), structure and policy characteristic of the new unions mean that the latter did not constitute a uniform whole.

We can endorse many of these points. We may also add that, as we observed in Part I, the 'new model' unions were neither so pacifist nor so capitalist-minded as is traditionally claimed. What all this amounts to is, indeed, the rejection of a simple black-and-white distinction between 'old' and 'new' unionism, and support for the persistence of significant areas of continuity in trade union affairs. Simultaneously, however, we must insist that a conventionally exaggerated view of discontinuity does not, *ipso facto*, clinch the case in favour of continuity.

Rather, it is a case of striking a proper balance between elements of continuity and change. For the new unionism, as contemporaries recognised, marked some very important departures in the development of organised labour and the working class.

These departures were at least sixfold in character. To summarise: there was the massive (if ephemeral) growth of trade unionism among previously unorganised or weakly organised workers; an increase in the average size of unions; a casting off of deference and fatalism among the non-skilled and the growth of the mass confidence, independence and assertive radicalism characteristic of the Chartist years; a marked advance in socialist leadership and influence, as compared with the mid-Victorian period; growing union support for increased state intervention and independent labour representation, as opposed to the predominant volun- tarism and Lib-Labism of the old unions; and the fusion of elements of the new organisations which 'could provoke conster- nation in respectable circles'. Thus during the late 1880s and early 1890s mass assertiveness, strikes and militancy and the influence of socialism led many establishment figures 'to complain of union "dictation" and "tyranny" on a scale and with an intensity far more reminiscent of the 1830s and 1840s than the 1860s and 1870s'.

Taken together, these six changes do, in fact, strongly support the view that change outweighed continuity and that 'a funda- mental change was occurring in British trade unionism'. In any event, the initial growth of the new unionism, combined with its consolidation between 1910 and the 1920s, persuaded many em- ployers and politicians to step with increasing care and considera- tion in relation to the 'labour problem'.

Finally, in its parallels with Chartism – in terms of mass organi- sation, optimism, radicalism and the attempted exertion of influ- ence beyond the work-based world of skilled male workers – the new unionism raised the spectre of class consciousness in the 'peaceable kingdom' of Britain. As we shall see in the following two chapters, this issue of class consciousness, allied to the themes of change and continuity, stood at the heart of develop- ments in politics, ideology and culture.

Notes

1   N. Kirk, *Labour and Society in Britain and the USA*, II, *Challenge and Accommodation 1850–1939* (Aldershot, 1994), chapter 1.

2   J. Zeitlin, 'Engineers and Compositors: A Comparison', in R. Harrison and J. Zeitlin (eds), *Divisions of Labour: Skilled Workers and Tech- nological Change in Nineteenth-century Britain* (Brighton, 1985).

3   Kirk, *Challenge and Accommodation*, pp. 11–13.

4   R.C. Floud, 'Britain 1860–1914: A Survey', in R.C. Floud and D. McCloskey (eds), *The Economic History of Britain since 1700*, II (London,

1981), p. 1; P.F. Clarke, *Hope and Glory: Britain 1900–1990* (Harmondsworth, 1996).

5   Kirk, *Challenge and Accommodation*, pp. 13–14; A.J. McIvor, *Organised Capital: Employers' Associations and Industrial Relations in Northern England 1880–1939* (Cambridge, 1996), chapter 1.

6   J. Lovell, *British Trade Unions 1875–1933* (London, 1977), p. 43.

7   B. Waites, *A Class Society at War: England 1914–18* (Leamington Spa, 1987).

8   J. Hinton, 'Voluntarism versus Jacobinism', *International Labor and Working Class History*, 48 (1995) 74–8.

9   E.J. Hobsbawm, *Age of Extremes: The Short Twentieth Century 1914–1991* (London, 1995), chapters 3 and 4.

10   McIvor, *Organised Capital*, p. 6.

11   For these conflicting approaches see S. Tolliday and J. Zeitlin (eds), *The Power to Manage?* (London, 1991); McIvor, *Organised Capital*, pp. 25–6; Kirk, *Challenge and Accommodation*, chapter 1.

12   E.J. Hobsbawm, *Industry and Empire* (Harmondsworth, 1971), pp. 186–92.

13   J. Zeitlin, 'The Labour Strategies of British Engineering Employers 1890–1922', in H.F. Gospel and C.R. Littler (eds), *Managerial Strategies and Industrial Relations: An Historical and Comparative Study* (Aldershot, 1983); Zeitlin, 'Engineers and Compositors'.

14   See, in addition to the listings for Zeitlin in note 13, Kirk, *Challenge and Accommodation*, p. 21; B. Lancaster, *Radicalism, Cooperation and Socialism* (Leicester, 1987); B. Elbaum and W. Lazonick (eds), *The Decline of the British Economy* (Oxford, 1986).

15   Clarke, *Hope and Glory*; McKibbin, 'Why was there no Marxism in Great Britain?', in his *The Ideologies of Class: Social Relations in Britain 1880–1950* (Oxford, 1991).

16   McIvor, *Organised Capital*, pp. 6, 54.

17   Kirk, *Challenge and Accommodation*, p. 76.

18   A.J. McIvor, 'Cotton Employers' Organisations and Labour Relations 1890–1939', in J.A. Jowitt and A.J. McIvor (eds), *Employers and Labour in the English Textile Industries 1850–1939* (London, 1988), pp. 9–10; Kirk, *Challenge and Accommodation*, p. 6.

19   McIvor, *Organised Capital*, pp. 94–5.

20   Kirk, *Challenge and Accommodation*, p. 36; J. Melling, 'Scottish Industrialists and the Changing Character of Class Relations in the Clyde Region', in T. Dickson (ed.), *Capital and Class in Scotland* (Edinburgh, 1982); J. Foster's comments in *Labour History Review*, 55:1 (1990) 64–8.

21   R. Fagge, *Power, Culture and Conflict in the Coalfields: West Virginia and South Wales 1900–22* (Manchester, 1996), chapter 4; D. Gilbert, *Class, Community and Collective Action: Social Change in Two British Coalfields*

1850–1926 (Oxford, 1992); C. Williams, *Democratic Rhondda: Politics and Society 1885–1951* (Cardiff, 1996).

22 Kirk, *Challenge and Accommodation*, p. 108.

23 *Ibid.*, pp. 150–4.

24 See, for example, *ibid.*, pp. 14–21; Fagge, *Power*, pp. 170–84; Lancaster, *Radicalism*, chapters 8 and 11; Zeitlin, 'Engineers and Compositors'.

25 Melling, 'Scottish Industrialists', pp. 80, 96–101.

26 Kirk, *Challenge and Accommodation*, p. 102.

27 *Ibid.*, pp. 15–16, 104–5.

28 Lovell, *British Trade Unions*, chapter 4; H.A. Clegg, A. Fox and A.F. Thompson, *A History of British Trade Unions since 1889*, I (Oxford, 1964).

29 McIvor, *Organised Capital*, pp. 129–30.

30 Zeitlin, 'Engineers and Compositors'.

31 Kirk, *Challenge and Accommodation*, p. 37.

32 McIvor, *Organised Capital*, pp. 18, 122.

33 Lovell, *British Trade Unions*, p. 41.

34 J.E. Cronin, *Labour and Society in Britain 1918–1979* (London, 1984), chapter 3.

35 Hobsbawm, *Industry and Empire*, pp. 191–2; Kirk, *Challenge and Accommodation*, p. 39.

36 Kirk, *Challenge and Accommodation*, 42–5, 134–41.

37 *Ibid.*, pp. 98–115.

8

Politics: competing loyalties

Chapter 4 was concerned with the demise of independent working-class politics, in the form of Chartism, and the growth of popular Liberalism and Conservatism in the mid-Victorian years. In this chapter we resume and develop the story of organised labour's and workers' diverse political and ideological allegiances and fortunes with reference to the period from the late 1860s to 1920.

The years from the Second Reform Act of 1867 up to the Representation of the People Act of 1918 saw – notwithstanding the continued disfranchisement of women and some 40–5 per cent of Edwardian adult males – the growth of mass politics which were often expected to lead to the more or less automatic renaissance of independent labour politics. The Reform Acts of 1867 and 1884 enfranchised borough householders and householders in the counties, respectively, and the 'fourth' Reform Act of 1918 introduced manhood suffrage and the vote for women over thirty years of age. As McKibbin, Matthew and Kay have noted, the manhood suffrage provision of the latter Act marked an important rupture in British political history in that it divorced possession of the franchise from the qualification of property – whether owned, occupied or economically related – and vested it in the adult male person.[1] Furthermore, the secret ballot imposed in 1872, limits on personal expenditure by candidates in 1883 and the effects of redistribution in 1885 meant, as suggested by Ewen Green, that the electorate was 'less open to "influence" than in former times', that 'informal networks of patronage and personal authority were increasingly ineffective as the sole basis of political organization', and that, as a result, 'new structures and a professionalized party bureaucracy at both central and local level were requirements for coping with "the democracy" '.[2]

Significantly, in the wake of the 1867 Act the two established parties sought to come to terms with, and gain further advantage from, the advent of mass politics by strengthening their popular bases of support. These aims were to be realised by means of the creation of Liberal and Conservative clubs and associations, increasingly social and recreational in character, and politically partisan friendly, burial and even co-operative societies among workers. Such creations were initially designed to appeal to working-class adult males (up to 1918 women were excluded from the two main party organisations). However, from the 1880s onwards the Conservative Primrose League (founded in 1883) and the Women's Liberal Federation (1887) and the Women's Liberal Unionist Association (1888) massively extended the partisan embrace to women.

Notwithstanding their quickened attempts to reach the people, many politicians and commentators saw the advent of mass politics as synonymous with the revival of an independent, threatening, untrustworthy and inherently radical popular political and social presence. Assumed to derive their primary motivation from the narrow material interests and desires of class, rather than from wider concern with community, religion and nation, the newly enfranchised masses were believed to pose a serious threat to property and the balance of power and status. Thus

> Like Sidney Webb, Conservatives felt that the political enfranchisement of the lower orders was bound to be followed by a demand for their social and economic enfranchisement . . . they felt that 'If you transfer the power in the State to those who have nothing in the country, they will afterwards transfer the property'.[3]

In accord with these sentiments, the leader of late nineteenth-century Conservatism, Lord Salisbury, was of the strong opinion, during the period of the Reform Act of 1884, that 'there was no possibility of converting "the democracy" to Conservatism: all that could be done was to discipline the masses on their inexorable march to political ascendancy'. As Green observes,

Salisbury's view of the future of British politics was almost vulgar Marxist, insofar as he saw the triumph of democracy and radicalism, even Socialism, as almost inevitable. From this perspective, Salisbury saw the Conservative party as a sort of guard's van of the revolution – there to apply the brake where possible but otherwise simply being pulled along by a runaway radical train.[4]

From a directly conflicting, if similarly deterministic, ideological perspective Engels wrote, during the 1880s and 1890s, that in England 'democracy means the dominion of the working class, neither more nor less'; and that the erosion of Britain's 'monopoly of the world market' would surely, 'though slowly and in zigzags', divest English workers of their 'sense of imaginary national superiority', their 'essentially bourgeois ideas and viewpoints' and their ' "practical" narrowmindedness', and pave the way for the mass development of socialism.[5]

However, neither the fatalistic dread of Salisbury nor the ultimate confidence of Engels was fully to come to pass. The Marxist Social Democratic Federation (1884) and the socialist Fabian Society (1884) and Independent Labour Party (1893) all failed to exert mass appeal in the period under review.[6]

Independent labour politics, in the form of a predominantly non-socialist Labour Party, were, indeed, once again placed on the agenda of British politics. And there were continuing – indeed, in some cases, strengthened – instances of independence, opposition, challenge and transforming class consciousness within working-class life. But the progress of the Labour Party was, at least up to 1914, relatively slow and uneven. Strong organisational and ideological ties with Liberalism remained in place. And the Conservative Party continued to attract, well into the inter-war years and beyond, a large minority of working-class voters. In sum, enfranchisement and projected class interest plainly did not, in and of themselves, push a majority of workers into independent politics of a socialist kind.

Confounded by the complexity and diversity of concrete historical developments, Salisbury's and Engels's predictions also suffer greatly from their rootedness in deeply flawed deterministic and reductionist methods of reasoning. As already indicated, the key assumption guiding their views was that an externally defined notion of workers' material interests and goals would inevitably produce, under conditions of mass enfranchisement, predetermined political outcomes. But history rarely, if ever, moves in such mechanistic ways. Furthermore, little or no recognition was afforded by either Engels or Salisbury to the complex and varied nature of the material and extra-material needs and interests of working people, the similarly complex and diverse, if patterned, ways in which experience is handled in consciousness and the shaping influences of consciousness, institutions and agency, including political agency, upon the apparent given-ness of interests, needs and structures. Finally, proper attention to the full influence of non-material forces upon political developments was similarly lacking.

The following sections of this chapter will attempt to remedy such defects, primarily by drawing the reader's attention to the rich and varied nature of, and the broad underpinnings of, late Victorian and Edwardian popular politics. We will, firstly, address the issue of 'radicalism', and especially its diverse manifestations and the continuities and ruptures between Liberal and Labour politics. Secondly, our attention will turn to a topic which, until recently, has been seriously neglected by many historians: the post-1868 growth and development of working-class Conservatism. Our enduring concern with change and continuity, class and fragmentation, and the relative importance of the political and the social as areas of historical influence and explanation, permeate this chapter.

Radicalism: consensus and contestation, continuity and change

Late Victorian and Edwardian radicalism may be seen as an umbrella movement which covered a variety of viewpoints and organisations. Between the late 1860s and the 1890s Gladstonian Liberalism constituted the hegemonic, rather than the sole and completely uncontested, form of radicalism. Thereafter radicalism found its main expression in 'new Liberalism', the pre-1914 Westminster-based Progressive Alliance between the Liberals and the Labour Party, and Progressivism, a broad reforming political and social movement which brought together in parts of Lancashire, London and elsewhere 'advanced' Liberals, socialists, trade unionists and members of the Labour Party. Whether the emergence of the Labour Representation Committee in 1900 and its development into the Labour Party, the Progressive Alliance and Progressivism, and, indeed, Labour's impressive post-World War I electoral advances can accurately be seen to belong to a continuous, if evolving, tradition of radicalism – as suggested by Biagini and Reid – is a crucial matter which will accordingly occupy a good deal of our time in the pages that follow. (Whether the 'socialist' agitations of the 1880s signalled 'a major shift away from older, established political forms' or can also be assimilated to 'an earlier stage of radical development' constitutes another important aspect of debates concerning political continuity and discontinuity.[7]) For the moment it is sufficient simply to note that our overall findings rest more upon the complex and *increasingly* – that is, from the late nineteenth century onwards – diverse, discontinuous and contested nature of radicalism than upon uniformity, continuity and consensus. The validity or otherwise of these findings – which are consistent with the conclusions reached in Chapter 4 in relation to the mid-Victorian politics – will become manifest both during and in the light of the substantive discussion conducted in this chapter.

Gladstonian Liberalism and 'Victorian consensus'
Many of the increasingly distinctive characteristics of mid-Victorian popular Liberalism identified in Chapter 4 revealed themselves most completely in the full glow of Gladstonian Liberalism during the two decades following the second Reform Act. In this latter period there was continuing Liberal identification with pragmatism, with open government and the rule of law, with the further extension of political, civil and religious liberties and with religious Dissent, with community-centred democracy, free trade, social and political reform and opposition to the bloated 'tax-eater' state, with independence, voluntarism, self-help, temperance and respectability, with the state as the facilitator rather than the primary guarantee of happiness and with the virtues of the 'producers' and the vices of the 'parasites'. Gladstone's own massive contribution to the Liberal tradition may be seen to have resided in his crusading, moral appeal and charisma, in his elevation of the interests of the community or humankind above those of selfish class, section or clique, in his support for Irish disestablishment and Home Rule and in his advocacy of a peaceful foreign policy. As Belchem has recently

observed, 'Gladstone represented a new form of gentlemanly leadership in which ethical substance and ethical character were fused in a poweful platform of moral populism'.

> Embodying the moral claims of the people's cause, Gladstone's campaigns facilitated popular incorporation in liberty, retrenchment and reform, in joint and zealous struggle for self-government, economy and Christianization. Eschewing any crude appeal to class at elections, Gladstone invoked a wider frame of reference, a single overarching issue in the struggle between good and evil . . . The foe of sinfulness, selfishness and fiscal extravagance, Gladstone campaigned against the abuse of power and privilege, attracting the votes of those who had neither.[8]

Yet pragmatism was also a key feature of Gladstone's populist message. There was, for example, no blind and unbending allegiance to the principles of *laissez-faire* and the minimalist state. Self-help, independence and voluntarism constituted the preferred methods of individual and social action and advancement. However, in cases of demonstrable necessity and/or the public good, the democratically accountable state was to be called upon to promote self-help. As Biagini has noted, 'At every level *laissez-faire* was applied in a pragmatic way and with due attention to what economists called the "exceptions" to its principles.' Furthermore, the latter 'were quite wide and included the establishment of public hospitals, the organisation of a national system of education, and the nationalisation of "natural monopolies" like the telegraphs'. Factory legislation (which was cheap), Irish and Scottish land reform, and the extension of the powers of local government constituted further important examples of Gladstoninan interventionism and 'collectivism'.[9] Intervention, collectivism and the promotion of independence figured prominently in Joseph Chamberlain's 'Unauthorised Programme' of 1885 which, by means of the compulsory purchase of land by local authorities, held out the promise of 'three acres and a cow' to newly enfranchised householders in the counties. And Chamberlain's 'gas and water socialism' in Birmingham, whereby 'public enterprise was responsible for gas, water, sewerage, lighting and slum clearance', foreshadowed increasingly widespread concern among radical Progressives with municipal reform in the quarter-century before 1914.[10]

Gladstonian Liberalism appealed directly to the organised labour movement and its supporters on a number of counts. At the most general level Liberalism promised the eradication of the unfair privileges and returns derived by parasitical landowners, speculators and other 'monopolists' from unearned wealth and income in the form of excessive rents, interest and other payments. Liberalism, it was believed, sought to achieve fair play and just rewards for all industrious members of the community by a number of means. For example, cuts in central government expenditure promised to reduce the amount of money spent on the repayment of the national debt – and 'the exploitation allegedly exercised by *rentier* bond-holders through their receipt of interest' on that debt – on the army, the navy, the police, the diplomatic service and other establishments which were also 'favourite targets for radical criticism'. As Biagini has written,

> central government expenditure appeared mainly aimed at providing 'fuel' for a 'class' machinery whose purposes were war abroad, repression and economic exploitation at home, and the general preservation of a system based on privilege and injustice . . . 'Light taxation – other things being equal – implies unfettered industry, enterprising and profitable trade, a well-fed, well-clothed, and well-educated people.'

As part of this perspective, radical working men strongly supported direct taxation and taxes on property as essential to fiscal and social justice – entertaining, in the process, some doubts concerning Gladstone's proposed abolition of income tax – reductions in the rates and, above all, the abolition of all 'surviving taxes on foodstuffs and the necessities of life'.[11] Biagini makes a convincing case in favour of his claim that 'Historians of the labour movement have generally undervalued the importance of the Gladstonian finance and fiscal system in the making of the "liberal consensus" in Victorian Britain'. Yet, as Biagini himself has also made clear in his impressive book-length study *Liberty, Retrenchment and Reform: Popular Liberalism in the Age of Gladstone 1860–1880* (1992), and as other contributors to Biagini's and Reid's stimulating edited collection, *Currents of Radicalism* (1991), have demonstrated, there was more to Gladstonian Liberalism's appeal to organised workers than government retrenchment and low taxation. For example,[12] the Liberals' 'sympathetic regard for the aims and objectives of the "new model" craft unions', their 'far more positive' support for the legal rights of trade unions between 1873 and 1875 'than historians have hitherto recognised' (Jonathan Spain), and their advocacy of conciliation and arbitration in the sphere of industrial relations, carried considerable weight. The representation of the 'labour interest' in the House of Commons, from 1874 onwards, by a small, 'but distinct', group of Lib-Lab MPs who sat 'as labour members but were ardent Gladstonian Liberals in politics' (John Shepherd) was of major importance in the further strengthening of formal political ties. Similarly, with their strong belief in independence, voluntarism, 'collective self-organisation to regulate the market' (Alastair Reid) and, in many cases, active Nonconformity (Kenneth Brown), labour leaders such as Robert Knight, general secretary of the Boilermakers' Society, found a natural home within Liberalism. The Home Rule issue and Liberal endeavours to encourage more small-scale property ownership and limit the powers of 'landlordism' in Scotland and Ireland – by means of the 'three Fs': fixity of tenure; fair rents; freedom to inherit a holding – likewise generated considerable popular support.[13] Finally, the full extent of organised labour's endearment to 'the people's William' was seen in the great demonstrations preceding the Reform Act of 1884–85, of which Gladstone was the author. As T.C. Smout has observed, these demonstrations and the mass processions in the run-up to the Second Reform Act were 'pure street theatre, encapsulating more than anything else in the nineteenth century the character of proletarian Liberalism, and emphasizing its civic and craft pride, its class feelings against landlords' and 'its sense of belonging to a coherent tradition of reforming zeal'. The massive Glasgow demonstration of 1884, involving an estimated 64,000 marchers and an additional 200,000 gathered to meet them on Glasgow Green, to protest against the Tory House of Lords' obstruction of political reform, was a vivid illustration of the crusading march of the masses against the classes. Thus Smout:

> They carried countless pictures of Gladstone and many of Bright, a flag from as far back as 1774, banners from 1832 and from Chartist days, and models and mottoes old and new. The french-polishers, for example, carried a miniature wardrobe first borne in 1832 and a flag inscribed, 'The french-polishers will polish off the Lords and make the cabinet shine' . . . the sawyers a banner with the device of

two circular saws and the words, 'The crooked Lords – we'll cut them straight' . . . The executive of the Scottish Land Restoration League passed with the motto, 'God gave the land to the people, the Lords took the land from the people' . . . The basic message was clear – the 'class' obstructed reform, the 'masses' were here to demand it.[14]

Yet we must be careful not to present an exaggerated impression of Gladstonian Liberalism as all-consuming and all-embracing of the people's radical passions and actions. While there is undoubtedly a good deal of truth in John Belchem's recent statement that 'In its heyday, Gladstonian liberalism left little space for independent radicalism', we should also heed the findings of a growing body of research which suggests that the tradition of mainly *independent* popular radicalism was far from extinguished between the late 1860s and the 1880s.[15]

Independent radicalism

As we observed in Chapter 4, especially in London and parts of Yorkshire and Lancashire forms of largely Chartist-inspired independent radicalism survived the decline of mass Chartism in the late 1840s and constituted, at significant points, an alternative form of political allegiance to mainstream Liberalism during the mid-Victorian years. We also observed that by the time of the second Reform Act the labour movement in general and erstwhile advocates of working-class political independence, such as Ernest Jones, were making their peace with, and indeed becoming a part of, the Liberal Party. And, as already shown in this chapter, the labour movement remained wedded to Liberalism up to the end of the century – indeed, we might add, beyond. However, the researches of Edward Royle and, more recently, Anthony Taylor, Mark Bevir and Jon Lawrence (the latter notwithstanding his general 'liberal revisionism') suggest – in opposition to Biagini's and Reid's emphasis upon the enveloping effect of Gladstonian Liberalism upon radicalism, and in qualification of Belchem's view of radical confinement – that, while probably constricted by the mass appeal of mainstream Liberalism, nevertheless independent popular radicalism did continue to exert itself in vibrant and significant ways.

Drawing mainly upon a study of the radical press, Jon Lawrence can thus point to 'the continued vitality of the Radical subculture in British politics' and the 'uneasy relations with organized Liberalism'.[16] In particular, notes Lawrence, 'old-style Radicalism retained a powerful hold over large sections of the popular press throughout the 1870s and 1880s'. According to Thomas Wright, 'over three hundred thousand workers bought *Reynolds's Newspaper* during the mid-1870s, while many more became acquainted with its extreme Radical doctrines through informal readings in pub, home, and workplace'. Sections of the radical press outside London likewise 'tapped "a radical provincial sub-culture" that "stubbornly maintained a sense of class"'. And, as clearly shown by Anthony Taylor,[17] *Reynolds's* became, during the 1880s, the chief vehicle for those continuing popular anti-monarchist and radical-patriotic sentiments which, contrary to received historical wisdom, continued to have a significant popular presence during the last quarter of the century. The radical case was based not only upon specific concern with the future Edward VII's 'incompetence', 'immorality' and 'corruption', but also upon a general critique of monarchical and aristocratic rule as being anti-democratic and parasitical upon 'honest industry'.

It is also important to note that by the mid-1880s *Reynolds's* had converted to 'collectivist social reform' and 'bellicose support for the Social Democratic Federation militancy of this period'. As Lawrence and Bevir indicate, drawing upon the impeccably democratic sentiments to be found in the radical press, upon the proposed currency and land reforms of the O'Brienites, upon the 'single tax' proposal of the American radical Henry George (to be levied upon the incremental value of land), and upon the secularist and freethinking ideas popular in artisan clubs in mid-Victorian London, both the SDF and the Fabians grafted their demands for collective ownership of the means of production on to the predominantly political and anti-aristocratic ways and means of traditional, independent radicalism.[18] In such ways did the varied strands of radicalism inform the late-century 'socialist revival'.

Finally, independent radicalism continued to strike a special chord among the 'excluded people' and their leaders. The Tichborne case, 1867–86 – concerned with 'restoring the property of a long-lost aristocrat' – elevated the issue of fair play to a position of national importance and, as demonstrated by Rohan

McWilliam, underpinned 'one of the largest (if not *the* largest) popular movements between the end of Chartism and the development of socialism and independent Labour politics in the 1880s and 1890s'.[19] The Paris Commune of 1871 gave a stimulus to the 'latent republicanism' within working-class radicalism.[20] Considerable opposition was expressed by old-style 'direct democracy' radicals, such as Joseph Cowen and his supporters in Newcastle, to the 'wealthy cliques of landowners and businessmen who increasingly controlled Liberal politics in the localities' and their 'wire-pulling' and 'dictatorial activities'.[21] And the impressive campaign, conducted mainly by 'the excluded' in the early 1880s, in opposition to the exclusion from Parliament of the atheist Charles Bradlaugh, the elected member for Northampton, constituted another important example of the radical masses directing their fire against the governing classes.[22]

There were undoubtedly considerable swings in the fortunes of later nineteenth-century independent radicalism. For example, a republican *movement* – as opposed to a somewhat inchoate anti-monarchical 'ultra-radical state of mind' – fell away badly after the early 1870s. Furthermore, Gladstonian Liberalism's generally favourable ideological and legislative record regarding the 'interests of the people' did much to diminish feelings of popular outsider status and, correspondingly, strongly to enhance citizenship or insider standing among both organised and unorganised workers. Nevertheless, the continuing, if fluctuating and minority, appeal of independent radicalism merits further investigation on the part of historians. As we shall observe in the next section, some of the growing conflicts between Liberalism and organised labour were to be traced not only to conditions specific to the late nineteenth and early twentieth centuries but also to long-rooted contradictions and tensions within the traditions and currents of radicalism itself. Such contradictions and tensions constitute, ironically, a basic point of continuity within this particular study which is, of course, concerned to demonstrate the overarching importance of political and social change.

Liberalism and independent labour

Our emphasis so far in this chapter has rested upon the predominant, rather than total, containment of late ninteenth-century radicalism within the broad framework of Liberalism. Between the 1890s and the immediate post-World War I years there was, however, evidence of growing tension and open conflict within radicalism. Questions concerning workers' and organised labour's continued commitment to the Liberal Party and radical liberalism arose in a variety of contexts and out of a number of concrete experiences. There were, for example, the 'threatening developments in labour law which culminated in the Taff Vale case' and 'local Liberal resistance to the selection of working-class candidates and national Liberal reluctance to institute the payment of MPs'.[23] The very mixed responses of both the Liberal and the Conservative parties to the rise of a mass, and increasingly self-confident and assertive, labour movement within the context of the 'crisis of competitive capitalism' and rapidly increasing foreign competition (see Chapter 7), allied to the 'socialist revival' and the increased appeal of *independent* labour politics – as manifested most prominently in the formation and development of the Labour Party – also indicated that Victorian cross-class political consensus and accommodation were being, to say the least, severely tested. (See document 14.) Tests, tensions and open ruptures were also manifest in the growing number of local political and industrial conflicts revolving around issues such as the recognition of the new unionism, conditions of work, employer 'tyranny', living standards, unemployment and 'relief without pauperisation', 'the right to work, minimum wages and the eight-hour day' and the closed shop.[24] Finally, the wartime and immediate post-war experience with respect to the issues of 'individualism versus collectivism', the positive and negative features of the massive increase in state intervention and control, the 'increased significance of shared features in working-class economic experience', and 'the establishment of a class-based discourse at the heart of local politics' – undoubtedly introduced, as suggested by Tony Adams, 'a profound shock to the character of local politics' and, in some areas, 'the foundations of a new form of two-party politics'.[25]

Yet such instances of questioning, tension, conflict and shock did not, according to Biagini and Reid, signify either marked breaks in the radical tradition or the triumph of 'class-based' (defined by these authors as socio-economic) forces over political factors in the shaping of political allegiances and identities.[26] For example, the early twentieth-century Labour Party is held by

Biagini and Reid to have owed far more to the continuity of radicalism, albeit in its increasingly collectivist and socially reforming, or 'new' and Progressive, form, than either the 'religion of socialism' or the 'ideology of labourism'.[27]

This debt of gratitude, we are informed, manifested itself both organisationally and ideologically. Thus there did not exist 'any major difference in political aims or values' between Liberals and early Labourites. Indeed,

> labour activists still retained a strong sense of loyalty not only to radical traditions but also to the Liberal party itself, even as they were establishing their own independent organisations.

And

> This can only be fully understood if we appreciate how much organised labour had been able to gain from its alliance with Gladstonian Liberalism, even after the end of the triumphant reforms of the 1860s. For not only had the 'final settlement' of the central questions of financial policy and labour law been achieved by the Liberals, this was also long remembered by activists within the labour movement.[28]

Furthermore, and notwithstanding the damaging blows suffered by Peter Clarke's pioneering thesis of 1971 that the 'new Liberalism' of progressive welfare and other reforms effectively contained, in Lancashire and elsewhere, the rise of class-based politics, a modified case for radical continuity up to and beyond the war continues to be articulated with great force. For example, Duncan Tanner's massively documented study *Political Change and the Labour Party 1900–1918* (1990) and his most recent piece of work, 'Class Voting and Radical Politics', argue, respectively, that, while less successful than claimed by Clarke, 'new Liberalism' and the Progressive Alliance were relatively strong up to 1914; and that 'Labour's progress up to 1914 was far more limited, and far more contingent upon particular configurations of circumstances, than those who identify a simple class-based advance would suggest'.[29]

Tanner and Reid recognise that the Labour Party's fortunes did improve during and especially after the First World War. But once again important objections are lodged to a picture of class-based discontinuity. Reid, for example, largely discounts the ef-

fects of wartime class conflict upon Labour's improved performance in 1918 in favour of the supposed benefits accruing to an
increasingly 'statist' post-war Labour Party from the positive effects and appeal of increased state intervention during the war.
And Labour's post-war advances in London and elsewhere are
attributed far more to its inheritance of the reforming values and
policies of pre-war Progressivism – revolving around qualitative
and quantitative improvements in the municipal provision of
services and employment opportunities at union-sanctioned rates
of pay and conditions of work – than to any new ideological
initiatives amid policies.[30] Tanner maintains that Labour 'developed a positive but limited appeal during the war, which enhanced but did not revolutionize its position'; that it became the
second largest party in 1918 more as a result of its 'established
core of support, most notably in the coalfields' than, *pace*
McKibbin, Matthew and Kay, owing to its appeal to the newly
enfranchised; and that the party 'did not perform particularly
well between 1918 and 1923, although it formed a minority government in 1924'. Significantly, concludes Tanner, Labour 'did
exceptionally well between 1923 and 1929', a performance
attributed to 'the role of national politics' rather than the rise of
class.[31]

It would be foolish to deny the partial validity of the case in
favour of continuity made by Biagini and Reid and Tanner, especially with reference to the years before the First World War. The
creation of the Labour Party had far less to do with the influence
of socialism than with the pragmatic political response of the
trade unions to adverse legal decisions and Liberal reluctance
more actively and extensively to support working-class parliamentary candidates. Ideological affinities and organisational
links with Liberalism were initially strong. As Belchem has
observed,

> the formation of independent Labour was not a dramatic or decisive
> break. In its public political language, independent Labour kept
> within the mainstream current of radicalism, drawing upon conven-
> tional . . . idioms and motifs.[32]

And with respect to voting patterns, the Labour Party's pre-1914
'rise' was in fact slow and uneven. The Progressive Alliance between Labour and the Liberals was generally maintained up to

1914, with Labour very much the junior partner at Westminster. And, notwithstanding some successful results at the municipal level, instances of growing support in parts of the country where the Liberals had always been weak, and the consolidation of its strength in areas dominated by occupational groups such as coalminers and railwaymen, 'it was not until the early post-war years that Labour became more than a sideshow to Conservative and Liberal dominance in the major urban centres'.[33] For example, Trevor Griffiths has concluded that the strength of traditional allegiances across coal and cotton Lancashire in the pre-1914 period suggested that 'the rise of the Labour Party . . . had wrought no fundamental change in the terms of political debate', and that 'Far from being complete, the transition to class politics had barely begun by 1914'.[34]

At the same time we must, however, be careful not to elevate a partial truth into the whole truth. Indeed, an overall assessment of the evidence concerning the balance of power between the forces of continuity and change between the 1890s and 1920 suggests that the latter forces increasingly overshadowed the former. Furthermore, short-term tactical and strategic considerations were accompanied by class-based issues and sentiments, with the latter manifesting themselves in a variety of economic, political and cultural ways and increasingly assuming a position of major importance in independent Labour's development.

The validity of our assessment may be demonstrated in the following ways. First, the very acts of placing the idea of *independent* labour politics on the political agenda, and successfully translating that idea into concrete practice, constituted, in themselves, major political discontinuities: they offered fundamental challenges to organised labour's and workers' mid- and late Victorian accommodation to the domination of politics by the Liberal and Conservative parties. The presence of important political continuities should, therefore, 'not obscure the important fact that the issue of *independent* labour politics had by 1900 assumed a degree of importance lacking since the days of Chartism'.[35] Second, and taking full account of Tanner's and David Howell's demonstration of the awesome complexity and diversity of local political arrangements and developments, and the partial successes of Liberalism in retaining workers' allegiance, it was, in the final analysis, 'the overall failure of Liberalism to prevent the rise of Labour which mattered most'. Conflicts between new and old Liberalism, the far more limited influence of new Liberalism upon the party as a whole than suggested by Clarke, the reluctance of *laissez-faire* old Liberalism to countenance change and concessions to labour, and the inability of new Liberals in London and elsewhere fully to translate fine, reforming words into concrete policy commmitments – these were all factors which contributed to Liberalism's overall failure. And integral to that failure in a number of localities were issues of economic and social policy, of power, authority and control, and of political style and culture informed by the question of class. Thus

> From Scotland to South Wales there arose, albeit unevenly, areas of disagreement which, while not generally manifest in the political deals of Westminster and in national voting patterns, nevertheless were of major importance in modifying and transforming local political cultures, allegiances and, increasingly, voting patterns. The 'right to work', to relief 'without pauperisation' for the unemployed, to the eight-hour day, to (especially for women) a minimum wage, to trade union wages and conditions, to decent housing at fair rents, to efficient, expanded and accountable public services, and opposition to local 'Taff Vales', to the antagonistic policies of employers, and to collusion between the latter and local political establishments – these were the key issues which, time and time again, variously moved workers to champion independent labour representation in preference to Liberalism.[36]

In such closely interrelated ways did the social and the political deeply affect politics, often under the inspiration and guiding hand of those local socialists and even revolutionaries who have largely been written out of radical liberalism's forward march.

If Labour and Liberalism had less and less in common in the pre-1914 years than suggested by Biagini and Reid, then differences and conflicts escalated sharply between 1914 and 1920. The war time split between Asquith and Lloyd George did much to weak the Liberal cause. And, as Adams has astutely observed, 'The war ... brought wider endorsement of the need for independent political action to protect working-class interests.'[37] Grievances accumulated and shared during the war – high food prices, profiteering, poor housing, shortages and, *pace* Reid, the widespread belief that 'government was acting deliberately against working-class interests' – induced a feeling of common identification on the part of many working-class people. In the immediate post-war years this feeling was heightened by mounting industrial conflict, considerable labour movement advances in terms of numbers, organisation and confidence, and expanded popular expectations concerning the rewards to be received for the considerable sacrifices made during the war. The language of structured conflict between labour and capital and of organised labour's transforming 'moral–economic' perspective grew apace. At the local political level Labour made significant strides in important urban centres. Nationally, the wartime period 'established a trend of improvement for Labour . . . which cut across local peculiarity'. Labour's advance was, of course, by no means complete. Local diversity persisted. In Lancashire, for example, while mining constituencies 'provided a solid core of support for Labour from 1918', progress in neighbouring cotton towns was 'faltering by comparison': community politics by no means expired in the face of the undoubted advances of class politics.[38] But we must not underestimate the very real extent of Labour's overall progress. From rather inauspicious foundations at the beginning of the century the Labour Party had, within twenty years, replaced the Liberals as the main national rival to the Conservatives. Within the next ten years Labour would form two minority governments. And these very considerable achievements were closely linked with expressions of class. As John Belchem has concluded,

> Gradual and uneven as it was, the rise of Labour undermined the cross-class constituency of progressive Liberalism. Labour acquired a distinct image and identity, linked in cultural and organizational style to the much-expanded ranks of organized labour, to the 'traditional' . . . 'representation' of the working class which, having emerged in the late nineteenth century, remained little altered until post-Second World War 'affluence'.[39]

Popular conservatism

In a review article, published in 1991, Ewen Green observed the relative neglect among historians of 'the most successful political party of the modern era', the British Conservative Party.

The Conservatives have been in Government, either alone or in coalitions dominated by their party, for sixty-seven of the past 100 years, and their share of the vote at general elections has rarely fallen below 40 per cent. No other party of the right operating within a mass electoral system has equalled this achievement . . . The enduring appeal of the Conservatives is undoubtedly one of the most important political phenomena of the twentieth century; and yet both the party as an institution and the nature of British Conservatism remain relatively understudied.[40]

Green's observation certainly holds true in relation to the subject of working-class Conservatism. As we saw in Chapter 4, the appeal of Conservatism to workers grew strongly in some parts of the country from at least the mid to late 1860s; yet, in comparison with late Chartism and mid-Victorian Liberalism, the subject of popular Toryism has attracted relatively little attention from labour historians. In the course of the present chapter reference has been made to the voluminous literature concerning Liberalism and Labour and even the 'socialist revival'. Yet it is a curious fact that, while there were as many members of the Conservative Party's Primrose League Habitation in Bolton in 1900 (approximately 6,000) as there were in the Independent Labour Party nationally, it is the ILP which has been far more widely studied than the League.[41] In a similar vein, while the Conservatives' domination of inter-war politics was rooted in considerable working-class as well as massive middle and lower middle-class support – 'the Tories (probably) had a majority of the working-class preferred vote' throughout the 1920s and 'in the 1930s (almost certainly) a majority of the actual vote' – nevertheless labour histories of this period have concerned themselves far more with the fluctuating fortunes of trade unionism and the Labour Party than with hegemonic Toryism.[42] The researches of Martin Pugh into the Primrose League, of H.J. Hanham, Peter Clarke, Philip Waller, David Walsh, Neville Kirk, Patrick Joyce and Geoffrey Trodd into features of Victorian and Edwardian Conservatism and, more recently, of Ross McKibbin, Ewen Green, Jon Lawrence and David Jarvis into various aspects of popular Conservatism between 1867 and 1939, have gone some way towards filling the large gaps in the literature.[43] Much, however, remains to be done. What follows is a brief synthesis and evaluation of the patchy state of current knowledge.

We can usefully begin with an outline of the fortunes of popular Conservatism in the period following the second Reform Act. As we observed in Chapter 4, the general election of 1868 revealed to shocked Liberals significant areas of electoral support, on the part of newly enfranchised workers, for Conservative candidates. We also noted that popular support for Conservatism was particularly strong in Lancashire, and that between 1874 and 1906 the Conservatives overturned the Liberals' mid-Victorian electoral domination of the county. Even more significant, however, was the fact that the political trend in Lancashire mirrored developments in a number of urban areas throughout the country. It is true, as recorded by McKibbin, that, in terms of power at Westminster, matters were fairly evenly balanced – with the Conservatives in office sixteen and a half years and the Liberals twelve and a half between the Home Rule crisis of 1886 and the formation of the Asquith–Bonar Law coalition in 1915.[44] But as an effective counterweight we must set the facts that the Conservatives had held national office for only eight years between 1846 and 1884, and that between 1886 and 1900 the Conservatives recorded three outstanding victories out of the four elections held. Furthermore, a seismic political shift was taking place in many of the key cities and towns. As Lawrence has noted, 'For most of the Victorian era the major cities of England were bastions of political Liberalism, but between the mid-1870s and 1900 many increasingly fell under the sway of a revitalized Conservative party'.[45] For example, Wolverhampton, Lawrence's specific focus of attention, 'witnessed a major transformation of political allegiance during the late Victorian period'. 'After decades of almost unchallenged Liberal dominance,' observes Lawrence,

> the town's political culture changed rapidly during the 1880s and 1890s as the Liberal party found itself squeezed between the genteel Conservatism of the new suburbs and the increasingly strong populist Toryism of central working-class districts.

And, as such,

> Wolverhampton stands alongside Birmingham, Manchester, Sheffield and Nottingham as one of those important, urban, manufacturing communities whose lurch towards Conservatism in the late nineteenth century effectively killed the 'Liberal Dream' of an inexorable march towards an enlightened, progressive polity.[46]

The Liberals did, nevertheless, stage a spectacular come-back with their landslide victory in the 1906 general election (which had been preceded by a run of good by-election results). And two further Conservative defeats in the January and December general elections of 1910, and 'few signs that the party was in a position to break out of this enclave' by 1914, have led Green to identify a 'Crisis of Conservatism' during this period.[47] However, and notwithstanding considerable internal unease and lack of confidence, the Conservative Party came to dominate inter-war politics. Electoral landslides were registered in 1924, 1931 and 1935, and the party remained in office, either independently or with other parties, 'for all but three years of the inter-war period'.[48] In sum, between the 1870s and the 1930s, and taking into account fluctuations in electoral performance, the Conservatives constituted the dominant force in British politics.

As numerous historians have shown, the ability of the late nineteenth-century Tory Party to attract the support of increasingly large numbers of middle and lower middle-class urban property owners ('villa Toryism'), many of whom abandoned their traditional allegiance to Liberalism, constituted a vital factor in the party's improved fortunes. When set alongside its traditional bedrock support among the aristocracy, county squirearchy and important sections of the *haute bourgeoisie*, this new-found urban-based support fully justified the Conservatives' claim to represent the interests of property. And Conservative claims that the radicalised Gladstonian Liberal Party was careless of the rights of property owners (as manifested especially in its land reform policies in Ireland and Scotland), combined with portrayals of the Liberal Party as 'unpatriotic and anti-imperial' (especially in relation to the Home Rule issue), undoubtedly struck a warm response among large sections of the conservatively patriotic and imperialistic propertied groups.[49] Simultaneously, however, and as will already be evident to the reader, Conservative success was rooted in popular, as well as propertied, support. It is to an examination of the factors underlying this popular support that we will now turn.

Of fundamental importance to late Victorian Conservative working-class supporters and voters was the ability of party locals and notables effectively to pose as the *defenders* of traditional values and a traditional way of life, especially at a time when

Liberalism was 'still generally equated with the relentless pursuit of "progress" and economic efficiency'.[50] This was by no means a new phenomenon. We observed in Chapter 4 that mid-Victorian Conservatives frequently set themselves up as the defenders of the local people's 'robust pleasures, habits and customs' (as manifested in drink, sport, sociability, informality, practical as opposed to book knowledge, 'natural' patriotism and respect for property) in opposition to the 'killjoy', 'improving' and 'transforming', and 'hypocritically elitist' schemes of morally earnest, temperance-minded and often militantly Nonconformist Liberals. But this *laissez-faire* defence of a particular way of life – of the purportedly autonomous local community against the interfering Liberal other – probably grew in importance in the later Victorian period. For example, Lawrence has demonstrated the ways in which Wolverhampton's Conservatives set themselves, in their informal club life and the extension of that life to embrace (in the Primrose League) large numbers of women and their concerns, vigorously to champion the politics of self-validation in opposition to the regulatory politics (as manifested particularly in the areas of gaming and licensing) of the Liberals.

> During the 1880s Wolverhampton witnessed the emergence of a new type of populist Tory politician. Conservative councillors . . . used their unusual proximity to working-class life . . . to identify themselves unequivocally with 'the pleasures of the people' in opposition to the interference of state or municipality . . .
> Pledged to defend the right of working people to carry on their lives untroubled by outside authority, these populist Conservatives might almost be thought of as the true *laissez-faire* liberals of late nineteenth-century politics.

Furthermore, although posessed of organisation, Wolverhampton's communitarian Conservatives were keen to present themselves as above mere party, as totally opposed to the Liberals' alleged calculative manipulation of politics and the voters by means of political caucuses and 'wire-pullers'. Whereas Liberalism 'was associated with the dry procedural debate of the branch meeting, Conservatism was associated with entertainment and spectacle', with 'the importance of "the social element" over formal party politics'. In Wolverhampton and numerous other urban centres throughout the country Conservative working men's clubs and Primrose League Habitations thus catered more to the leisure-based, albeit respectable, needs of members than to their self-improving concerns.[51] The constituencies addressed also went beyond the confines of party membership to include members of the wider local community. In Blackburn, for example, members of the politically dominant Conservative family, the Hornbys, had local and county-wide cricketing, racing and footballing connections (see Chapter 4). And in Wolverhampton the Conservatives' 'proximity to, and pronounced sympathy for, working-class life and culture' were clearly illustrated in 'the strong association between the local Conservative Party and Wolverhampton Wanderers Football Club'. When the Wolves reached the FA Cup Final in 1889 it was Sir Alfred Hickman, Wolverhampton's former Tory MP and the club president, who organised a reception for the returning players. 'The favour was repaid at the 1892 general election,' observes Lawrence, 'when Tory politicians toured working-class districts of the town accompanied by prominent Wolves players.' And by 1895

> relations between the terraces and Toryism were so close that the entire Wolves team was seen attending a Primrose League demonstration, and the local Tory newspaper claimed that working-class voters showed their support for Hickman by chanting, 'Play up, the Wolves.'[52]

Conservative defences of 'local ways' often involved strong links between local notables and the people. As we observed in Chapter 4, the more widespread and accelerated development of employer paternalism during the mid-Victorian period and the more active involvement of employers in the life of the factory locale helped to forge strong bonds of inter-class community. Significantly, and notwithstanding the decline of the family firm and the growth of the limited liability company, the growing impersonalisation of workplace relations and the increasingly segregated character of much working-class life between the 1880s and the 1920s, such inter-class bonds of community and popular identification with the personality, style and tone set by leading local family firms often remained strong. As was the case with the Hill-Wood cotton family in Glossop, leading Tory (and Liberal) paternalistic employers continued to evoke, into the post-World War I years and beyond, a warm response from their employees. Such employers were the recipients of much working-class gratitude, not only on the grounds that they provided employment and other material comforts and protection, but also as a result of the fact that they were key figures in setting the tone of much of the social, cultural, religious and political life of the locality and in stimulating civic pride.[53]

So far our emphasis has rested upon the largely *defensive* appeal of Conservatism to working people – in particular as against unwarranted intrusion, organisation and change from outside; and in defence of traditional patterns of culture, social and personal relations, employment and more general material protection and rewards. And, as suggested by Green, community solidarity – 'the "us" of popular Conservatism' – was increased by emphasising ' "hostile" communities – the "them" of popular Conservatism'.[54] Militant Nonconformists, 'faddish' Liberals, temperance and teetotal advocates, opponents of empire and voluntary religious education, Irish Catholics, republicans, secularists, socialists and atheists, 'alien' Jews and many other immigrants, all manner of 'foreigners' (including those classed as non-local) and people of colour, especially those in a dependent relationship with Britain, feminists and 'extreme' members of the labour movement – these constituted some of the main demoniacal 'others' of nineteenth and early twentieth-century Conservatism. It is true that antagonism towards 'them' varied in time, place and intensity – opposition to Irish Catholic immigrants, for example, moderating somewhat in many instances in the post-Murphyite years[55] – but of the general power of negative stereotyping in forging the bonds and identities of popular Conservatism in this period there can be no doubt. Furthermore, this *laissez-faire* and in many ways negative and hostile brand of popular Conservatism complemented Lord Salisbury's high Tory belief in 'the limited, negative role of Conservative politics' and that 'organizational efficiency could control the democracy'.[56]

The march of time and local and regional peculiarities did, however, force some adjustments and even constructive changes upon the more negative and seemingly immobile features of working-class Conservatism. We have earlier drawn attention to the far more positive, if often limited and uneven, tradition of early to mid-Victorian Conservative social radicalism which manifested itself in support for factory legislation, trade unionism and the paternalistic protection of labour (see Chapter 4). Conservative involvement in the labour laws of the mid-1870s, support for workmen's compensation, and, in Liverpool and elsewhere, for trade unionism and fair wages for council employees constituted important later nineteenth-century continuities within this tradition. Simultaneously, however, the increasingly 'hard-headed' and sectional character of late nineteenth-century Toryism imposed severe limits upon the extent and depth of its social radicalism. The warm welcome given by the Conservative press and many within the party to the Taff Vale decision, combined with the party's general prescription of 'large doses of economic liberalism and tough anti-trade unionism as the only effective remedies for Britain's growing economic ills', did much to dent Conservatism's reputation seriously as the party of the community and much to increase its reputation as the bosses' party.[57] Similarly, the growth of mass politics from the second Reform Act onwards did see the Tories make serious and in many instances successful organisational and ideological efforts to play down their reputation for aristocratic exclusiveness in favour of a more inclusive appeal to the people. However, as Joyce astutely noted, 'Tory Democracy ... had more to do with the Toryism of the democracy than any democracy in Toryism'. 'In the clubs ... and on the town councils representatives of industry and wealth continued to operate the levers of power while simultaneously streamlining "the machinery of a make-believe democracy"'.[58]

The election defeats of 1906 and 1910, the more collectivist character of Liberalism, the birth and development of the Labour Party, and the statist and levelling threats posed by socialism forced the Conservative Party to reconsider its strategical and tactical options seriously during the early part of the twentieth century. In addition, the 'waning influence of Nonconformity in politics' and the increasing depoliticisation of the drink issue (as a result of the rapid development and mass appeal of the non-political working men's club movement) 'undermined the credibility of late Victorian beer-barrel populism' and 'made old-style urban Toryism appear distinctly anachronistic'.[59] Finally, mounting economic problems on the international front and the close identification of the Conservatives, as the party of empire, with the debacle of the Boer War, compounded the party's problems.

Once again, Conservative responses were a mixture of the constructive and the negative. First, the adoption of tariff reform – as the means to steady employment and the funding of social reform without any of the social levelling costs inherent in the Liberals' tax-based welfare measures – was a central, if deeply flawed and divisive, feature of the new Conservative programme.[60] Second, 'an alternative, more domestic-centred politics became the dominant face of popular Toryism'. Concern with, and reconstructions of, gender, nation and home – as opposed to local community and work – lay at the heart of this new political identity. As argued by Lawrence, 'The typical "Tory working man" of Conservative discourse was transformed from the honest labourer who had earned the right to a quiet pint, to the honest family man who had earned the right to a quiet home life.' Central to this positive construction of the Tory working man as the champion of the Englishman's castle was, however, the presence of the negative other, or 'them'. In place of the fanatical Nonconformist Liberal, there now appeared the equally fanatical and demoniacal statist, atheistic, libertarian socialist, intent upon 'nationalising' the family and undermining the respectability and virtue of women, family life and Christian religion.[61] Third, an increasingly politicised labour movement was presented as selfish and sectional, as being little concerned with the interests of the nation as a whole, as being increasingly informed by alien ideas and at odds with the hard-working decency, moderation, patriotism and sense of fair play of the typical working man and his family.[62] Alongside concern for tight controls over government expenditure, low inflation, low taxation and the protection of property and investments, these three economic, gender-based and political motifs would go a long way towards promoting Conservative hegemony throughout the inter-war years.[63]

In conclusion, this chapter has highlighted, on the one hand, continued diversity in relation to the political allegiances and ideas of working people between the 1870s and the 1920s. As such, a simplistic picture of the linear development of 'class politics' is wide of the mark. Workers supported Liberal and Conservative politicians for perfectly rational reasons. Socialism was of very limited influence, and the development of the Labour Party was far from smooth and even. Furthermore, workers' politics could not be explained by reference to economic and social factors alone. On the other hand, we have seen that the revived notion and increasingly wide appeal of *independent* labour politics did mark something of a rupture in political life. Notwithstanding its fluctuating fortunes and its early links with Liberalism, the Labour Party did become a national political force in its own right within a relatively short period of time. And, as seen in both the previous and the present chapters, class-based feelings, rooted in politics and economics, constituted an important factor in Labour's development. Whether the same can be said in relation to questions of culture and leisure is a matter to which we will turn in the final chapter.

Notes

1 R. McKibbin, *The Ideologies of Class: Social Relations in Britain 1880–1950* (Oxford, 1991), p. 70.

2 E.H.H. Green, *The Crisis of Conservatism: The Politics, Economics and Ideology of the British Conservative Party 1880–1914* (London, 1995), pp. 15–16.

3 *Ibid.*, p. 124.

4 *Ibid.*, p. 125

5 K. Marx and F. Engels, *On Britain* (Moscow, 1953), pp. 480, 516, 517, 519, 525, 531, 533, 536–7.

6 N. Kirk, *Labour and Society in Britain and the USA*, II, *Challenge and Accommodation* (Aldershot, 1994), pp. 240–3; K. Hunt, *Equivocal Feminists: The Social Democratic Federation and the Woman Question 1884–1911* (Cambridge, 1996); J. Hill, 'Requiem for a Party: Writing the History of Social Democracy', *Labour History Review*, 61:1 (1996) 102–9.

7 Much depends, of course, upon *which* 'earlier stage of radical development' for example, mainstream Chartist, O'Brienite, or radical-liberal – is taken as the basis of comparison with 1880s socialism. See A.D. Taylor, ' *Reynolds's Newspaper*, Opposition to Monarchy and the Radical Anti-jubilee: Britain's Anti-monarchist Tradition Reconsidered', *Historical Research*, 68:167 (1995) 318–19; M. Bevir, 'The British Social Democratic Federation 1880–1885: From O'Brien to Marxism', *International Review of Social History*, 37 (1992) 207–29; J. Lawrence, 'Popular Radicalism and the Socialist Revival in Britain', *Journal of British Studies*, 31 (1992) 163–86, especially 165–85.

8 J. Belchem, *Popular Radicalism in Nineteenth-century Britain* (London, 1996), pp. 128–9.

9 E.F. Biagini, 'Popular Liberals, Gladstonian Finance, and the Debate on Taxation 1860–1874', in E.F. Biagini and A.J. Reid (eds), *Currents of Radicalism* (Cambridge, 1991), p. 140.

10 Belchem, *Popular Radicalism*, p. 137; P. Thane, 'Labour and Local Politics: Radicalism, Democracy and Social Reform 1880–1914', in Biagini and Reid, *Currents of Radicalism*, pp. 244–70.

11 Biagini, 'Popular Liberals', pp. 138–9, 158–9.

12 The following section is heavily indebted to the essays in Biagini and Reid, *Currents of Radicalism*, by Jonathan Spain ('Trade Unionists, Gladstonian Liberals and the Labour Law Reforms of 1875'), pp. 109–10; John Shepherd ('Labour and Parliament: The Lib-Labs as the First Working-class MPs 1885–1906'); Alastair J. Reid ('Old Unionism Reconsidered: The Radicalism of Robert Knight 1870–1900'), pp. 217, 221; Kenneth D. Brown ('Nonconformity and Trade Unionism: The Sheffield Outrages of 1866'). See also J. Parry, *The Rise and Fall of Liberal Government in Victorian Britain* (New Haven, 1993).

13 T.C. Smout, *A Century of the Scottish People 1830–1950* (London, 1988), pp. 71–3.

14 *Ibid.*, pp. 245–6.

15 Belchem, *Popular Radicalism*, p. 128.

16 Lawrence, 'Popular Radicalism', 170–5.

17 Taylor, *'Reynolds's Newspaper'*, 318–37. See also D. Thompson, *Queen Victoria: Gender and Power* (London, 1990), chapter 6; D. Nicholls, *The Lost Prime Minister: A Life of Sir Charles Dilke* (London, 1995), chapter 4.

18 Bevir, 'British Social Democratic Federation'; Lawrence, 'Popular Radicalism', 179–85.

19 R. McWilliam, 'Radicalism and Popular Culture: The Tichborne Case and the Politics of "Fair Play" 1867–1886', in Biagini and Reid, *Currents of Radicalism*, p. 44.

20 Thompson, *Queen Victoria*, p. 105.

21 Lawrence, 'Popular Radicalism', 172–3; N. Todd, *The Militant Democracy: Joseph Cowen and Victorian Radicalism* (Whitley Bay, 1991).

22 E. Royle, *Radicals, Secularists and Republicans: Popular Freethought in Britain 1866–1915* (Manchester, 1980), chapter 3. See also Royle's comments in *Labour History Review*, 61:3 (1996) 346–8.

23 Biagini and Reid, *Currents of Radicalism*, p. 16.

24 Belchem, *Popular Radicalism*, p. 140. See also Chapter 7 above.

25 T. Adams, 'Labour and the First World War: Economy, Politics and the Erosion of Local Peculiarity?', *Journal of Regional and Local Studies*, 10:1 (1990) 40. This is an important article which merits close attention.

26 It is suggested that Biagini and Reid's unduly narrow confinement of class to the area of 'the economic' (i.e. social production) severely limits the force of their arguments. It is perhaps worth reminding ourselves that throughout this study class identity is located not only within the material aspects of life (to include numerous sites and modes of production, and the spheres of distribution, consumption and reproduction as well as social production) but also within politics, culture and social structure and relations. For such matters see N. Kirk, *Labour and Society in Britain and the USA*, I, *Capitalism Custom and Protest 1780–1850* (Aldershot, 1994), pp. 8–12; N. Kirk (ed.), *Social Class and Marxism: Defences and Challenges* (Aldershot, 1996), p. 5.

27 Biagini and Reid, *Currents of Radicalism*, p. 17.

28 *Ibid.*, pp. 16–18.

29 D. Tanner, *Political Change and the Labour Party 1900–1918* (Cambridge, 1990), pp. 419 ff., 431–2, 441–2; D. Tanner, 'Class Voting and Radical Politics: The Liberal and Labour Parties 1910–31', in J. Lawrence and M. Taylor (eds), *Party, State and Society: Electoral Behaviour in Britain since 1820* (Aldershot, 1997), p. 112. Much in the manner of Biagini and Reid, Tanner's use of the term 'social class' appears to be predetermined, or structurally given, within a narrowly defined notion of 'the economic'. Any sense of class as a broad and interactive process – between conditioning *and agency* – is largely absent from Tanner's usage.

30 A.J. Reid, 'Dilution, Trade Unionism and the State in Britain during the First World war', in S. Tolliday and J. Zeitlin (eds), *Shop Floor Bargaining and the State* (London, 1985); A.J Reid, 'The Division of Labour and Politics in Britain 1880–1920', in W.J. Mommsen and H-G. Husung (eds), *The Development of Trade Unionism in Great Britain and Germany 1880–1914* (London, 1985); Kirk, *Challenge and Accommodation*, p. 257; Thane, 'Labour and Local Politics', pp. 253–4.

31 Tanner, 'Class Voting', pp. 116, 122–3. See also J. Turner, *British Politics and the Great War: Coalition and Conflict 1915–18* (London, 1992), pp. 400–25; J. Lawrence, 'The Dynamics of Urban Politics 1867–1914', in Lawrence and Taylor, *Party, State and Society*, p. 87.

32 Belchem, *Popular Radicalism*, p. 147.

33 Adams, 'Labour and the First World War', 24; Tanner, 'Class Voting', p. 112.

34 T. Griffiths, 'Work, Class and Community: The Structure and Values of Working-class Life in Coal and Cotton Lancashire, with Particular Reference to Bolton and Wigan c. 1880–1930' (Ph.D. thesis, Oxford University, 1994), p. 387.

35 D. Howell, *British Workers and the Independent Labour Party 1888–1906* (Manchester, 1984), pp. 123–8, 277–82; Kirk, *Challenge and Accommodation*, p. 176.

36   Kirk, *Challenge and Accommodation*, pp. 258–9.
37   Adams, 'Labour and the First World War', p. 32. The following section is heavily indebted to Adams's article.
38   Griffiths, 'Work, Class and Community', chapters 8 and 9.
39   Belchem, *Popular Radicalism*, p. 187.
40   E.H.H. Green, 'The Strange Death of Tory England', *Twentieth Century British History*, 2:1 (1991) 67.
41   Kirk, *Challenge and Accommodation*, p. 203.
42   R. McKibbin, 'Class and Conventional Wisdom: The Conservative Party and the "Public" in Inter-war Britain', in McKibbin, *Ideologies of Class*.
43   See the references to Walsh (n. 39), Joyce (nn. 57, 59, 60), Waller (n. 47), Trodd (n. 60) and Lawrence (n. 53) in Chapter 4 above. See also M. Pugh, *The Tories and the People 1880–1935* (Oxford, 1985); H.J. Hanham, *Elections and Party Management* (Brighton, 1959); P.F. Clarke, *Lancashire and the New Liberalism* (Cambridge, 1971); N. Kirk, *The Growth of Working Class Reformism in Mid-Victorian England* (Beckenham, 1985), chapter 7; J. Lawrence, 'Class and Gender in the Making of Urban Toryism, 1880–1914', *English Historical Review* (July 1993) 629–52; McKibbin, 'Class and Conventional Wisdom'; E.H.H. Green, *Crisis of Conservatism*; D. Jarvis, 'The Shaping of the Conservative Electoral Hegemony 1918–39', in Lawrence and Taylor, *Party, State and Society*.
44   McKibbin, 'Class and Conventional Wisdom', p. 259.
45   Lawrence, 'Class and Gender', 629.
46   Lawrence, 'Popular Politics and the Limitations of Party', in Biagini and Reid, *Currents of Radicalism*, p. 66.
47   Green, *Crisis of Conservatism*, p. 1.
48   Jarvis, 'Shaping', p. 131.
49   Green, *Crisis of Conservatism*, chapters 2 and 3.
50   Lawrence, 'Popular Politics', p. 75.
51   *Ibid.*, pp. 75–6; Green, *Crisis of Conservatism*, p. 127.
52   Lawrence, 'Class and Gender', 640.
53   A.H. Birch, *Small Town Politics: A Study of Political Life in Glossop* (Oxford, 1959).
54   Green, *Crisis of Conservatism*, p. 127.
55   Griffiths, 'Work, Class and Community', pp. 380–3.
56   Green, *Crisis of Conservatism*, pp. 128, 156.
57   *Ibid.*, p. 139; Kirk, *Challenge and Accommodation*, p. 254.
58   P. Joyce, *Work, Society and Politics* (Brighton, 1980), pp.268–9, 324; Kirk, *Challenge and Accommodation*, pp. 206–7.
59   Lawrence, 'Class and Gender', 634, 648; Green, *Crisis of Conservatism*, 76–7.

60 Green, *Crisis of Conservatism*, introduction and conclusion.
61 Lawrence, 'Class and Gender', 634.
62 McKibbin, 'Class and Conventional Wisdom', pp. 270–93.
63 *Ibid.*, p. 269; Green, 'Strange Death', 87.

9

Culture: custom, commercialisation and class

In seeking, in this final chapter, to provide the reader with an overview of the main features of working-class culture between the 1870s and the 1920s and a critical guide to the historical literature, we are immediately faced with a number of issues and questions which have been raised, albeit in relation to different contexts and chronologies, at various points in this study. Were, for example, late Victorian and Edwardian workers' lives characterised more by cultural differences and divisions than by common, similar and unifying processes? Did the 'respectable' versus 'rough' divide of the mid-Victorian period retain its dominance? Or did developments referred to briefly in previous chapters in Part II, such as the overall improvement in working-class living standards, combined with the narrowed gap between the skilled and the non-skilled, the growing self-confidence and organisation of the latter group and the growth of a more separate working-class way of life, induce strengthened feelings of working-class unity? In a similar vein, what were the relative strengths of elements of conflict and co-operation and individualism and mutuality among workers with respect to time and place and change over time? What were the places and roles of women in working-class communities, and what forms did constructions of femininity and masculinity take? More generally, to what extent did the development of commercial forms of leisure, such as the music hall and football as a mass spectator sport, overshadow the customary or traditional leisure pursuits of workers rooted in largely non-cash-paying activities in and around the household and local

212

community? Are we indeed witnessing – alongside the 'growing national integration and concentration of the national economy and its sectors' and the 'growing role of the state in both'; the rise of a mass labour movement (Chapter 6); the development of a national system of institutionalised collective bargaining (Chapter 7); and mass politics and the rise of the Labour Party to national prominence (Chapter 8) – the growth, to quote Hobsbawm, of a 'single, fairly standardized, national pattern of working-class life'?[1] If so, is it possible to establish links and causes with respect to these developments? Do, for example, the emergence of the traditional 'Andy Capp working class' and the rise of 'Labour with a capital L' (Hobsbawm) go hand in hand? Or was the relationship between culture and political developments more varied and complex in character?[2] Finally, what were the implications of the more extensive national development of economics, politics, industrial relations and culture for the local sense of place and identity so central to nineteenth-century working-class life?

Issues relating to cultural process, habits and links with other aspects of thought and behaviour are accompanied by difficult and complex questions concerning the meanings and perceptions which workers brought to and developed out of their engagement with their structured cultural (and extra-cultural) conditions of existence. We are obliged, in attempting to reconstruct cultures, to pay careful attention to ways of seeing as well as ways of being. And sociological surveys, based upon questionnaires and the compilation of statistics, are of limited help in the reconstruction of structures of seeing and feeling. As Richard Hoggart argued some forty years ago in his marvellously evocative and insightful book, *The Uses of Literacy*, in relation to such structures:

> A sociological survey may or may not assist us here, but clearly we have to try to see beyond the habits to what the habits stand for, to see through the statements to what the statements really mean (which may be the opposite of the statements themselves), to detect the differing pressures of emotion behind idiomatic phrases and ritualistic observances.[3]

In attempting properly or fully to 'see through' in an historical sense, we encounter, as already demonstrated in Chapters 5–6, considerable difficulties, not only in terms of the limited and patchy nature of the evidence, but also in terms of the bewildering complexity of meanings which inhabit cultures and historians' reading of those cultures. For example, with reference to both the 1830–70 period and the years between 1870 and 1920, we are continually forced to identify, unravel and assess the relative importance in the overall scheme of things of the jumble of conservative, defensive, introverted, negative, consolatory, fatalistic, purposeful, positive, challenging and indeed transforming values, ideas and attitudes which informed, and have been observed by historians to have informed, 'working-class consciousness'.

This chapter will seek to address the questions and difficulties raised above by means of a critical engagement with the relevant historical literature. We will begin by considering those works which have placed greatest emphasis upon the diverse, divided and, by and large, depoliticised and conservative features of working-class life and ideas in the late Victorian and Edwardian periods. We will then move to an evaluation of Hobsbawm's theses concerning the growth of traditional working-class culture, its increasingly class-conscious character and its links with the 'rise of Labour'. While by no means totally in agreement with Hobsbawm, our conclusions will be seen to reside far more with his emphases upon change and class than with those of his various critics.

As in our earlier discussion of mid-Victorian working-class culture (see Chapter 5), a number of key assumptions and propositions inform the present chapter. These, we may briefly recall, consist of the following: the presence, in the midst of seeming chaos, of dominant, subordinate, new and residual elements in cultures; the necessity firmly to situate ideas, attitudes and values in their full and changing historical contexts; the multi-faceted and often contested nature of ways of being and seeing; and the emergence of meanings in the course of active engagement between cultural and other social structures and practices. It will be evident from the latter that an integrated, as opposed to isolated or compartmentalist, approach to the study of culture is adopted.

Approaches: diversity, division and continuity

Any attempt to present working-class culture of this period as a *totally unified* or *finished* whole is doomed to instant failure.

Neither the working nor any any other class is ever a completely unified and undifferentiated entity, fixed or frozen in time. Indeed, from a structural point of view, diversity is 'given', irrespective of human volition, by the very existence of the (increasingly sophisticated) division of labour, including the sexual division of labour, and variations in terms of income, skill and so forth, among workers. However, it is useful to remind ourselves that such structural underpinnigs of difference do not, in themselves, necessarily give rise to divisions and conflicts. The latter may, of course, develop. But they are contingent upon the play of historical forces rather than determined by structure alone. Similarly, the notion that diversity more or less automatically rules out class-based mutuality and solidarity is wide of the mark. Elements of diversity and similarity, and of division and unity coexist among workers. And historical skills reside in teasing out and investigating the continuing, as opposed to fixed or static, interplay and overall balance of power between these elements. These basic methodological propositions are offered at this initial stage of our investigation immediately to counteract the marked tendency in much of the (especially recent) literature improperly to conflate the diverse and divisive/conflicting aspects of working-class culture, and to attribute to materialist historians, such as Hobsbawm, a picture of an undifferentiated and 'finished' working class.[4]

It is, of course, true that diversity, and in some instances divisions and conflicts, were not only present but also marked features of working-class experience between 1870 and the inter-war years. For example, in identifying the importance of speech, dress and the 'thousands of other items from daily experience' which helped to distinguish a 'recognisably working-class life', Hoggart was at the same time fully attentive to 'the great number of differences, the subtle shades, the class distinctions, within the working classes themselves'. For Hoggart's Hunslet inhabitants a variety of status hierarchies pervaded daily life. For instance,

> there is a fine range of distinctions in prestige from street to street. Inside the single streets there are elaborate differences of status, of 'standing', between the houses themselves; this is a slightly better house because it has a separate kitchen, or is at the terrace end . . . There are differences of grade between the occupants; this family is doing well because the husband is a skilled man and there

is a big order in at the works; the wife here is a good manager and very houseproud, whereas the one opposite is a slattern; these have been a 'Hunslet family' for generations, and belong to the hereditary aristocracy of the neighbourhood.[5]

The son of corner shopkeepers, Robert Roberts also highlighted the central importance of the street and household, occupation, gender roles and 'respectable' values to one's local standing in the 'classic slum' of Salford during the first quarter of the twentieth century. 'In our community, as in every other of its kind', recalled Roberts in 1971,

> each street had the usual social rating; one side or one end of that street might be classed higher than another. Weekly rents varied from 2s 6d for the back-to-back to 4s 6d for a 'two up and two down'. End houses often had special status. Every family, too, had a tacit ranking, and even individual members within it; neighbours would consider a daughter in one household as 'dead common' while registering her sister as 'refined'.[6]

Occupational standing was judged by Roberts to be of primary importance in the determination of social status. Divisions in Roberts's own society were held to range from 'an elite . . . composed of the leading families' of shopkeepers, publicans and skilled tradesmen, 'through recognised strata' of regularly employed semi-skilled workers to 'a social base whose members one damned as the "lowest of the low", or simply "no class"'. Among the semi-skilled Roberts drew special attention to female cotton operatives and the ways in which they were ranked by 'we' – presumably Roberts's own ('leading'?) family. Female weavers were accepted as '"top" in their class', followed by winders and drawers-in and, finally, spinners. This ascribed status hierarchy duly reflected the differential earning capacities of women employed in the various occupational grades of cotton. But more was at issue than simply occupation and earnings. Religion and ethnicity, dress, appearance and bearing, the nature and requirements of the job, all constituted important complications. Thus female spinners 'lacked standing on several counts':

> first, the trade contained a strong Irish Catholic element, and wages generally were lower than in other sections. Again, because of the heat and slippery floors, women worked barefoot, dressed in little more than calico shifts. These garments, the respectable believed,

induced in female spinners a certain moral carelessness. They came home, too, covered in dust and fluff; all things which combined to depress their social prestige.

It was, however, 'women employees of dye works' who 'filled the lowest bracket'. According to Roberts, 'their work was dirty, wet and heavy and they paid due penalty for it'.[7]

Below the ranks of the semi-skilled, the unskilled workers 'split into plainly defined groups according to occupation, possessions and family connection'. Scavengers and night-soil men were followed by casual workers, such as dockers, then local street sellers – 'of coal, lamp oil, tripe, crumpets, muffins and pikelets, fruit, vegetables and small-ware' – and, finally, 'among the genuine workers', firewood choppers, bundlers and sellers and rag-and-bone merchants. Workhouse paupers, along with bookies' runners, prostitutes, idlers, part-time beggars and petty thieves, 'odd homosexuals, kept men and brothel keepers', formed the base of Roberts's local social pyramid.

In many, if by no means all, cases respectable habits and values – as manifested in temperance, unremitting commitment and endeavour, good workmanship, honesty, a positive commitment to one's family and kin, a clean and tidy household, a 'clean' rent book, well scrubbed and well brought-up children, and overall 'decency' – were, in Roberts's opinion, closely attendant upon occupational standing. But the onset of drunkenness, rowing or fighting in the streets, and known connections with low Irish Catholics, the workhouse or prison could bring instant disrepute upon the heads of formerly respectable families, however well-off and skilled they might be.[8]

Within the classic slum, concluded Roberts, people were generally far more concerned with their place in the local status hierarchies outlined above, and with competition with other members of the community for such places, than with working-class solidarity or radical social and political change, or even politics *per se*. Hyndman Hall, home of the local branch of the socialist Social Democratic Federation, 'remained for us mysteriously aloof and through the years had, in fact, about as much political impact on the neighbourhood as the near-by gasworks'.[9] Similarly, the Conservative Club, duly reflecting the political apathy and the traditional and dominant cultural and social 'common sense' of the neighbourhood, did not, 'except for a few days at election time . . . appear to meddle with politics at all'. Rather, 'it was notable usually for a union jack in the window and a brewer's dray at the door'. Notwithstanding the many examples of neighbourliness, especially on the part of women, competition and self-interest ruled the roost. And resigned conservatism and fatalism were everywhere apparent. 'Class divisions were of the greatest consequence,' wrote Roberts, although 'their implications remained unrealised' and, at least in the pre-First World War period, 'the many looked upon social and economic inequality as the law of nature'. Localism and place, complete with notions of family-, neighbourhood-, workplace- and gang-based territoriality, boundaries and competition with, and, often, physical opposition to, the 'other' – as seen in 'drunken Saturday night brawls' to settle scores – prevailed in Roberts's almost Hobbesian depiction of his community.[10]

Roberts's findings for Salford prefigured in various ways the conclusions reached by many studies of late Victorian and Edwardian working-class culture published in the last two decades. For example, in his impressive and detailed 1985 study of national working-class patterns of saving and spending between 1870 and 1939, Paul Johnson highlighted the competitive and personal motivations which underpinned such behaviour, even when undertaken by collective agencies such as the co-op or friendly society. In Johnson's account, concern to 'keep up with the Joneses' and with self and ostentation took precedence over the perceived interests of class and commonalty.[11] From another perspective, the self-enclosed and largely fatalistic and conservative features of Roberts's Salford bear a striking resemblance to the introverted, defensive and consolatory picture of London's late Victorian and Edwardian working-class communities drawn by Stedman Jones (see Chapter 6). Seemingly less deferential and less susceptible to middle-class influences than their counterparts in Salford, workers, and especially casual workers, in London nevertheless apparently inhabited the same limited mental universe.

Finally, Roberts's emphases upon diversity and divisions, and upon the predominantly depoliticised, introverted and conservative features of working-class life, figure strongly in Carl Chinn's fascinating study of women of the urban poor in Engand, published in 1988, and Andy Davies's excellent work on aspects of working-class life in Manchester and Salford which appeared in print in 1992. Interestingly, both Chinn and Davies convey, on the whole, more positive impressions of workers' consciousness and actions than Roberts and Stedman Jones. A sense of purposeful *agency* – as manifested in the ability actively to shape and enjoy life and to derive satisfaction and pride from one's determination and achievements, rather than a mainly passive, dispirited, profoundly depressing and consolatory process of 'making do' – is seen centrally, and convincingly, to have informed the lives of workers in Manchester and Salford, Birmingham and elsewhere. But the enduring battles fought in pursuit of survival and 'some sort of life' were conducted, by Chinn's and Davies's subjects, within a determining framework in which making ends meet and the smothering embrace of immediate experience left precious little time for interest in politics or working-class movements. Intra-class divisions, rooted in gender, and differences in culture and living standards further placed severe restrictions upon the potential for working-class solidarity and the adoption of radical goals. Thus Chinn:

> The poorest women did not have the time to consider the merits of organised co-operation, to debate a different social and political system, to demand a more comprehensive medical system or to seek an improved education for their children. Neither did they have the time to unite, to march, to protest, to write or to make their opinions heard. Poverty alone united the women of the urban poor.

Davies's interviews revealed that political meetings did form part of street activities, but that other activities occupied 'a more central place in accounts of life in the two cities' and that 'activists were to a degree atypical within working-class districts'.[12] In sum, and notwithstanding their powers of agency in matters of everyday life, the vast majority of workers covered by Chinn and Davies closely resembled those studied by Roberts and Stedman Jones in that they largely accommodated themselves to, and indeed saw as an inevitable fact of life, the wider structures of power, authority and social relations.

Both Chinn and Davies also make extensive use of oral evidence significantly to advance the insights provided by Roberts into the influences of poverty and gender upon working-class culture. As we observed in Chapter 6, there is no doubt that the period in question saw a substantial improvement in working-class living standards. Simultaneously, however, as recognised by contemporaries such as Charles Booth and Seebohm Rowntree, and by many historians subsequently, poverty and insecurity remained at the heart of working-class life. (See document 15.) Booth estimated that 30 per cent of London's late nineteenth-century population was living in 'actual poverty', and in his study of York, published in 1901, Rowntree arrived at the comparable figure of 27 per cent (with 15 per cent of working-class households having a total family income insufficient to meet the basic requirements of food, clothing and shelter and therefore deemed to be in 'primary' poverty). Furthermore, the loss of the income of the main breadwinner through childbirth, old age, illness, death or unemployment could easily reduce those families used to regular earnings and relative comfort (40 per cent of Booth's total) to 'irregularity' and poverty.[13]

Davies and Chinn confirm the enduring and marked character of poverty. In Manchester and Salford between 1900 and 1939 oral and social survey evidence reveals that poverty was widespread. And, according to Chinn, poverty was the most pervasive of those aspects of the lives of the urban poor which remained pretty much the same between 1880 and 1939. 'The effects of poverty were everwhere apparent,' notes Chinn.

> So too were its symbols: the pawnshop; the moneylender; the 'strap' at the corner shop; a poor education, and ill-paid jobs and unemployment. This meant that the new generation of women, in spite of crucial differences, still led their lives much as their mothers and grandmothers had before the First World War, and indeed were to do so right up to the early 1960s.[14]

Confirmation is also accompanied by the advance of our knowledge in three important ways. First, in the process of his admirable attempt, along with Ellen Ross, Melanie Tebbutt, Elizabeth Roberts and Joanna Bourke, to fill some of the massive gaps in our knowledge of the lives of 'the women of the urban poor', Chinn advances the thesis that, while not belonging to 'a closed caste', the urban poor, especially poor women, 'were distinguished as a separate section of the working class as much by their cultural distinctiveness as they were by their impoverishment'.[15] It remained the case that respectable and non-respectable habits could be found at all socio-economic levels within the working class. But, argues Chinn, poor urban working-class women became, in many ways because of their poverty and the necessity of seeking employment and their key role as mothers, 'arbiters of their own and their families' lives, as well as emerging as dominant influences within their communities'. These 'hidden matriarchs' thus largely managed and ensured the survival of the family and the household, took care of most of the children's and many of the men's needs, exerted real power over community affairs (for example, as 'gaffers' in matters concerning communal self-regulation and self-control), acted as unofficial midwives and doctors, learned how to take care of themselves in family feuds and street fights, and by virtue of their paid employment, enjoyed a relatively high degree of self-respect and independence, especially *vis-à-vis* the menfolk of the local community. In contrast to women in the upper strata of the working class and the middle class, where notions of female domesticity, the family wage and separate spheres were extremely strong, women of the urban poor are seen by Chinn as 'more self-reliant and less dependent on men' and as being, 'in many respects, already in control of their own destinies'.[16]

Second, Davies presents the convincing arguments that poverty and the gendered nature of poverty – with women sacrificing most in the interests of the family – greatly limited the extent to which workers could partake of the pleasures of commercialised leisure. As a result, maintains Davies, working-class leisure continued to be 'largely rooted in neighbourhood life'. A variety of domestic and neighbourhood activities which cost little or nothing – 'sitting out' or playing in the street, talking, visiting markets in order to obtain cheap food and free entertainment, street gambling, football, visiting the park, the Whit walks and Sunday school outings, corner gangs and monkey parades – are thus shown, at least for Manchester and Salford, to have maintained their dominant appeal between 1850 and 1939. Notwithstanding the growth of the cinema, the pub, the music hall, the dance hall and mass spectator sports, Davies can claim, therefore, that 'the commercialization of leisure was clearly a partial process, and in the communal life of working-class areas, continuities were much stronger'. Working-class life and leisure continued to be characterised by diversity more than uniformity. (See document 16.) 'In this light, the late Victorian period appears to represent much less of a turning point in the history of popular leisure than has hitherto been assumed.'[17]

Third, in highlighting the importance of working-class women to family – and neighbourhood – life, both Chinn and Davies open up, along with a host of other historians, important questions concerning the ways in which we should interpret women's behaviour and consciousness. To put the matter somewhat schematically, the issue is whether women should be regarded as possessing substantial power, authority and choice – Chinn's notion of 'hidden matriarchy' – albeit within a patriarchal society in which 'male supremacy was enshrined in the law, in religion and in social mores' – and whether the home held positive attractions for them, or, conversely, whether women were, in most cases, effectively 'put upon' by their male oppressors. In contrast to Chinn, Roberts and Bourke, Davies tends to weigh the evidence in favour of the latter, 'patriarchy first', position, advocated by Rose, Sylvia Walby, Pat Ayers and Jan Lambertz.[18] This debate also raises wider issues concerning the extent to which patriarchal assumptions of masculinity pervaded the labour movement to the detriment and effective marginalisation of women.

The position adopted by the present author is critical of both Chinn and Davies. It is suggested that Chinn offers a somewhat idealised picture of poor working-class women and underestimates the severe material and patriarchal limits and pressures within which they were literally compelled either to sink or swim. Equally, Davies tends to be insufficiently appreciative of the fact that, as revealed in their written and spoken 'voices', home and housework held a positive attraction for a number of women (especially as compared with ill-paid work), that women could perform their domestic tasks without feeling inferior to, our totally dependent upon men, and that, as demonstrated by Tebbutt, gossip and neighbourhood life did offer women the opportunity to cultivate genuine networks of frienship and neighbourliness.[19] In sum, as suggested in Chapter 5, women did inhabit patriarchal structures, but they were not passive victims in life. Rather they frequently exerted their 'agency' to modify and even subvert such structures. And these processes of conscious modification and transformation were, as demonstrated by Deborah Thom, at work in women's relations with the labour movement (in which there was growing female participation in this period) as well as in their domestic and neighbourhood lives. Equally, Bourke clearly shows us that by no means all men conformed to a dictatorial and even violent stereotype, largely interested in the company of 'mates', the pub and sport, rather than the pleasures of life in and around the home. In sum, as suggested by Thom, 'notions of patriarchy are inadequate and ignore the activties and ideas of women themselves'.[20]

Notwithstanding their contrasting evaluations of the position of women, both Chinn and Davies are in agreement that the issues of poverty and gender among workers strongly illustrate the key features of intra-class cultural diversity and division, whether in the form of the labouring poor versus the upper working class or women pursuing activities and interests different from, and often in conflict with, those of men. According to Davies and Fielding, such divisions reinforce 'a growing recognition of the limitations of a class-centred approach'.[21] It would be pointless to deny that the working-class family was the site of violence, and especially male violence and hostility towards women, as well as consensus and mutuality. But, once again, there is considerable oral evidence to suggest that, notwithstanding its failings and gender-based inequalities, the working-class family was the site far more of affection, love and mutuality between the sexes and the means of collective survival and advancement than of division and conflict.[22] We are thus left with the overall conclusion that the gender-based differences could, and in the majority of cases probably did, exist relatively painlessly alongside co-operation between men and women.

In addition to living standards and gender, politics and religion often constituted further sources of difference in working-class communities. The reader's attention has already been drawn – in Chapter 8 – to the ways in which split political allegiances continued to characterise the late Victorian and Edwardian working class. There is also no doubt that many politically active workers often bemoaned the seeming apathy and 'commercialised mindlessness' of the masses. Gurney observes that within the discourse of the co-operative movement 'participation and membership were counterposed . . . to the passive and homogenised "masses" so beloved by capitalist entrepreneurs'.

> Not infrequently a feeling of distance and coldness, a rather hu-
> mourless lack of sympathy can be discerned amongst co-operators
> impatient with the 'failings' of the poor. The obvious attraction of
> 'low' domains like the music hall and the seaside resort continued to
> cause concern in the inter-war years and was joined by a new threat
> – the cinema – the appeal of which . . . depended on 'rudeness, or
> "cheek", or vulgarity'.[23]

Similarly, the unremittingly earnest, improving and rational, and in many cases somewhat joyless and elitist, tone and stance of a number of socialists towards 'the people' undoubtedly did the socialist cause harm and probably pushed some ordinary workers into the receptive arms of the more relaxed and amiable Tories. Within this context Chris Waters has clearly shown that, while critical of the capitalist purveyors of commercialised leisure, many socialists also blamed the passive, politically quiescent and 'vacant' workers who consumed commercial leisure and who were 'mentally incapable of understanding their own needs and rights'.[24]

Hugh McLeod notes that 'between about 1880 and 1930 there was a gradual weakening of the position of social influence enjoyed by the churches'.[25] The growth of alternative, secular sources of leisure provision and social life, the general diminution in the importance of sectarian identity to politics, and the decline of the family firm with its close links with church and chapel were among the factors which accounted for the diminished social importance of organised religion. At the same time, however, in counties such as Lancashire the influence of organised religion was by no means erased. As Griffiths has observed of the Red Rose county:

> Despite declining levels of attendance and the rise of alternative,
> secular agencies, the church retained its importance as a leading
> source of economic and cultural provision . . . the promotion of
> thrift through Sunday School Sick Societies ensured that the princi-
> pal denominations continued to be identified with working-class
> aspirations to independence. Organised leisure remained centred,
> in large measure, on places of worship. Competitive sports, from
> cricket to association and Northern Union football, were run

from church and chapel, rather than from the mill or the mine. Most significantly, the church provided the majority of school places across south central Lancashire. The question of control over education continued to excite political controversy in the years to 1914.[26]

A shared commitment to cultural and social provision was, however, accompanied in many cases by the continued cultivation of distinct denominational identities and rivalries. There is no doubt that, in comparison with the mid-Victorian period, sectarian violence and conflict were generally far less marked in the period under review. But this did not mean that religious and ethnic divisions disappeared from sight. Indeed, in some places – Roberts's Salford, Liverpool and other parts of west Lancashire and in parts of Scotland – there persisted, albeit to varying degrees, divisions and conflicts between Protestants and Catholics.[27] Furthermore, such divisions were accompanied in parts of Leeds, Manchester and London and some of the ports by instances of 'host' hostility towards Jews and other new immigrant groups and West Indian workers.[28]

Mutualism, class and change

Notwithstanding their undoubted presence, we must be careful not to exaggerate the influence of elements of difference and division within working-class life. We must also exercise equal care not to fall into the common trap of treating culture and leisure as fixed and isolated subjects, as improperly divorced from other aspects of workers' lives, and, as a consequence, to present the reader with a partial, if by now familiar, picture of a largely unchanging, defensive and depoliticised working class. Indeed, as against the predominantly narrow or 'compartmentalist' readings of working-class culture so far considered in this chapter, Hobsbawm has offered us a more integrated and satisfactory holistic picture which situates trends in culture and leisure within their wider societal context, and which engages diversity and division with other aspects of working-class life. Furthermore, Hobsbawm cogently argues that during this period workers' lives were characterised more by mutuality, collectivism and class consciousness than by divisions.[29] It is to a brief consideration of Hobsbawm's case that we finally turn.

Many of the collectivist and class-engendering influences highlighted by Hobsbawm have been noted in this and previous chapters in Part II. Our purpose here is not to rehearse Hobsbawm's
case in full, but briefly to identify and bring together those influences which were sometimes at work 'behind people's backs' and
at other times were fully present in consciousness. Of fundamental importance was the continued centrality of the family and the
household to working-class life. The family stimulated, despite
the presence of internal tensions and inequalities, a powerful
sense of collective unity and purpose – of men and women, parents, children and kinfolk pulling together in order to survive,
cope and, with a bit of luck, 'put aside a few pennies'. Furthermore, the demographic (Savage and Miles) and wider socio-
economic (Hobsbawm) 'making' of the working class – manifested in its 'greatly increased . . . absolute size and concentration', its predominantly urban and factory-based character, its
increasingly standardised and segregated housing, in the enhanced 'life chances' of the non-skilled, mounting pressures upon
the skilled and the narrowing of the traditional gap between the
skilled elite and the rest – were conducive to a heightened or
'remade' sense of class consciousness. Third, the latter was clearly
present and increasingly infuential within the mass labour movement which developed between the 1870s and 1920. Fourth, class
awareness and a mass labour movement acted as very powerful
counterweights to the extensive development of debilitating ethnic and other divisions among workers. Fifth, the 'total' experience of the First World War and its immediate aftermath fed and
enriched the sense of 'us' and 'them'. (See document 17.) Finally,
by 1920 Britain was characterised by mass politics, a mature
national and international economy, and the development of a
national system of collective bargaining.

It was within this context of the growing ascendancy of the
national within the political economy of Britain that Hobsbawm
duly and importantly located the rise of a more standardised and
national pattern of traditional working-class culture. Hobsbawm
did not argue that the commercialised world of 'Andy Capp'
totally eliminated tradition and custom. Strong attachments to
seemingly unchanged notions of local place and custom provided, and have continued to provide, security in the midst of
what were in fact rapid, if uneven, changes at both the local and

the national levels. Furthermore, Davies and Cunningham are right to identify the material and gender-based difficulties of access to the world of commercialised leisure. However, one-dimensionally to concentrate upon custom and divisions at the expense of the structural and experiential dimensions of change and unity is falsely to inflate the importance of continuity. Of the novel and increasingly pace-setting role of mass spectator sports, palais de danse, fish and chips,[30] the annual holiday treat and many other features of commercialised leisure among workers there can be little doubt.

Furthermore, the traditional culture which emerged and developed in these years was predominantly class-based and committed to radical change. We have thus seen throughout Part II that the late Victorian and Edwardian working class was far more united, in terms of both structure and consciousness, than its mid-Victorian counterpart. Traditional working-class culture could indeed act as a defensive shield against what was perceived to be a largely unknowing and hostile outside world; and the association between such culture and the growth of Labour with a capital L has been overdrawn by Hobsbawm (Conservatism being supported by large numbers of 'traditional' workers). But Labour did increasingly set down firm and enduring roots among those traditional working-class communities in which the co-op, the trade union and the friendly society were strong.[31] Furthermore, many of those workers partaking of the delights of commercialised leisure who also supported the Labour Party, the trade unions and the co-operative society were actively seeking the goal of a fairer society in which they would receive their 'due reward and recognition'. Defensiveness, introversion and resigned acceptance of the *status quo* were hardly the defining characteristics of those 'traditional' workers who were involved in pre- and post-war labour unrest or who struggled to build up the Labour Party or revolutionary political organisations committed to radical changes in, or the complete transformation of, capitalist society.[32] Even in Roberts's erstwhile conservative and fatalistic classic slum, important changes were at work in the post-World War I years: 'Men were changing their minds ... Poor families, dyed-in-the-wool Tories, who had voted Conservative since getting the franchise, were talking now not "Liberal" but "Labour".'[33] In sum, working-class culture provided, along with the workplace and the political arena, an important site for a reawakened class consciousness. The inter-war years would witness both the further development of, and important modifications and changes to, 'traditional' working-class culture.

Notes

1 E.J. Hobsbawm, 'The Making of the Working Class 1870–1914', in his *Worlds of Labour* (London, 1984), pp. 198, 204.

2 N. Kirk, ' "Traditional" Working-class Culture and "the Rise of Labour": Some Preliminary Questions and Observations', *Social History*, 16:2 (1991) 203–16.

3 R. Hoggart, *The Uses of Literacy* (Harmondsworth, 1958), p. 6.

4 For such an attribution see the introduction to A. Davies and S. Fielding (eds), *Workers' Worlds: Cultures and Communities in Manchester and Salford 1880–1939* (Manchester, 1992). It is instructive in this context to quote a passage (p. 194) from Hobsbawm, 'The Making': 'If I call this chapter "The Making of the Working Class" it is not because I wish to imply that the formation of this or any other class is a once-for-all process like the building of a house. *Classes are never made in the sense of being finished or having acquired their definitive shape. They keep on changing'* (emphasis added). Similarly, for an emphasis upon the narrowing, as opposed to total, elimination of divisions within the working class see *ibid.*, pp. 204–8.

5 Hoggart, *Uses of Literacy*, p. 10.

6 R. Roberts, *The Classic Slum: Salford Life in the First Quarter of the Century* (Harmondsworth, 1973), p. 17.

7 *Ibid.*, p. 20.

8 *Ibid.*, pp. 21–3.

9 *Ibid.*, p. 16.

10 *Ibid.*, p 17; J. White, *The Worst Street in North London: Campbell Bunk, Islington, Between the Wars* (London, 1986), pp. 86–8.

11 P. Johnson, *Saving and Spending: The Working-class Economy in Britain 1870–1939* (Oxford, 1985), conclusion.

12 C. Chinn, *They Worked all their Lives: Women of the Urban Poor in England 1880–1939* (Manchester, 1988), p. 22; A. Davies, *Leisure, Gender and Poverty: Working Class Culture in Salford and Manchester 1900–1939* (Buckingham, 1992), pp. 7, 136–8.

13 D. Englander and R. O'Day (eds), *Retrieved Riches: Social Investigation in Britain 1840–1914* (Aldershot, 1995); Chinn, *They Worked all their Lives*, pp. 2–3.

14 Chinn, *They Worked all their Lives*, p. 166; Davies, *Leisure*, p. 171.

15 E. Ross, *Love and Toil: Motherhood in Outcast London 1870–1918* (Oxford, 1993); M. Tebbutt, 'Women's Talk? Gossip and "Women's Words" in Working-class Communities 1880–1939', in Davies and Fielding (eds), *Workers' Worlds*; E. Roberts, *A Woman's Place: An Oral History of Working-class Women 1890–1914* (Oxford, 1984); J. Bourke, *Working Class Cultures in Britain 1890–1960* (London, 1994); Chinn, *They Worked all their Lives*, p. 4.

16 Chinn, *They Worked all their Lives*, chapters 1 and 3, p. 162.

17 Davies, *Leisure*, chapter 5 and pp. 169–70; A. Davies, 'Leisure in the "Classic Slum"', in Davies and Fielding, *Workers' Worlds*, pp. 126–7. For a similar view see Hugh Cunningham's 'Leisure', in J. Benson (ed.), *The Working Class in England 1875–1914* (London, 1985).

18 Chinn, *They Worked all their Lives*, chapters 1 and 2; Roberts, *Woman's Place*; Bourke, *Working Class Cultures*, pp. 64–7; Davies and Fielding, *Workers' Worlds*, pp. 10–12; Davies, *Leisure*, pp. 171–2; S.O. Rose, *Limited Livelihoods* (Berkeley, Cal., 1992); S.O. Rose, 'Gender and Labour History: The Nineteenth-century Legacy', *International Review of Social History*, 38, supplement 1 (1993) 145–62; S. Walby, *Patriarchy at Work* (Cambridge, 1986); P. Ayers and J. Lambertz, 'Marriage Relations, Money and Domestic Violence in Working-class Liverpool 1919–39', in J. Lewis (ed.), *Labour and Love* (Oxford, 1986). See also Ross, *Love and Toil*.

19 Bourke, *Working Class Cultures*, chapter 3; Tebbutt, 'Women's Talk?', pp. 68–9.

20 D. Thom, 'The Bundle of Sticks: Women Trade Unionists and Collective Organisation before 1918', in A.V. John (ed.), *Unequal Opportunities: Women's Employment in England 1800–1918* (Oxford, 1986); E. Gordon, *Women and the Labour Movement in Scotland 1850–1914* (Oxford, 1991); Bourke, *Working Class Cultures*, pp. 81–9.

21 Davies and Fielding, *Workers' Worlds*, p. 10.

22 Bourke, *Working Class Cultures*, chapter 2; Chinn, *They Worked all their Lives*, pp. 14–18.

23 P. Gurney, *Co-operative Culture and the Politics of Consumption in England 1870–1930* (Manchester, 1996), pp. 22, 78.

24 C. Waters, *British Socialists and the Politics of Popular Culture 1884–1914* (Manchester, 1990), p. 35.

25 H. McLeod, *Religion and the Working Class in Nineteenth-Century Britain* (London, 1984), pp. 65–6.

26 T. Griffiths, 'Work, Class and Community' (Ph.D. thesis, University of Oxford, 1994), pp. 408–9.

27 See, for example, S. Fielding, 'A Separate Culture? Irish Catholics in Working-class Manchester and Salford, c. 1890–1939', in Davies and Fielding, *Workers' Worlds*; R. Swift and S. Gilley (eds), *The Irish in Britain*

1815–1939 (London, 1989); P.J. Waller, *Democracy and Sectarianism* (Liverpool, 1981).

28 K. Lunn (ed.), *Hosts, Immigrants and Minorities: Historical Responses to Newcomers in British Society 1870–1914* (Folkestone, 1980); K. Lunn (ed.), *Race and Labour in Twentieth-century Britain* (London, 1985); C. Holmes, *John Bull's Island: Immigration and British Society 1871–1971* (London, 1988); P. Panayi, *Immigration, Ethnicity and Racism in Britain 1815–1945* (Manchester, 1994).

29 Hobsbawm, *Worlds of Labour*, chapters 10 and 11.

30 J.K. Walton, *Fish and Chips and the British Working Class 1870–1940* (Leicester, 1992).

31 Kirk, ' "Traditional" Working-class Culture', 216.

32 R. McKibbin, *The Ideologies of Class: Social Relations in Britain 1880–1950* (Oxford, 1991), conclusion; J.M. Winter, 'Trade Unions and the Labour Party in Britain', in W.J. Mommsen and H-G. Husung (eds), *The Development of Trade Unionism in Great Britain and Germany 1880–1914* (London, 1985).

33 Roberts, *Classic Slum*, p. 219.

Selected documents

Document 1

Oldham co-operators' address to Mr Gladstone and Gladstone's views on co-operation. *Source: The Co-operator* 128, 11 January 1868, pp. 17–19

WEDNESDAY, Dec. 18, 1867, will be a memorable day in the history of Oldham, on account of the visit of the Right Hon. WM. EWART GLADSTONE, M.P., late Chancellor of the Exchequer, who on that day went through, with apparent ease, and certainly with cheerfulness, the surprising amount of physical and mental labour involved in visiting the principal industrial establishments of the town, the Hartford Machine Iron Works of Messrs. Platt Brothers, and Co., the Sun Mill (called Co-operative), the Co-operative Store, King-street, &c., and in addressing three public meetings.

Our pleasant duty will be discharged by confining this report to the inspection by Mr. Gladstone of the Co-operative store, noticing one or two incidents of that visit, and transcribing from our notebook some of Mr. Gladstone's remarks on Co-operation, which were made at the evening meeting, when he distributed the prizes to the students of the Oldham School of Science and Art.

Mr. Gladstone was accompanied to the store by his host, Mr. John Platt, M.P., and Mr. J.T. Hibbert, M.P. (the members for Oldham.) These gentlemen were received by the officers of the 'Industrial' and 'Equitable' stores (King-street and Greenacres-hill), and shown through the grocery store, the extent, stock, arrangement, and neatness of which were noticed. Passing into the secretary's office, an address was presented to Mr. Gladstone. It was engrossed on vellum, and illuminated. The following is a copy: –

231

Selected documents

HONOURED SIR, – We, the committees of the Oldham Co-operative Societies, beg to convey to you, on behalf of our members, the expression of gratification and welcome on your visit to our town, and inspection of one of our principal stores. We have much pleasure in having an opportunity to state that your deep interest in, and great exertions for, the welfare of the operative class – particularly your efforts to free our industry and food from oppressive taxation – are reciprocated by them in grateful feelings of attachment to you, and desires for your continued prosperity and success. We feel assured that you will be pleased to hear a statement of our views and endeavours to advance ourselves, socially and intellectually, by the aid of Co-operation. We view labour as the parent of wealth, and believe that the happiness of nations depends, not upon its amount, but upon its distribution. We look upon Co-operative societies as the first step to attain this end. Mutual Co-operation is as far in advance of unrestricted individual competition, as that was in advance of forced or slave labour. In the earlier part of Mr. Owen's days, Co-operation was looked upon as a dream of enthusiastic theoretical writers; now, such of our friends as Mr. Mill, who have long echoed the noblest aspirations of the people, and who view Co-operation as the most promising of all agencies in operation to elevate the working class, have the pleasure of finding it the fêted theme of Social Science Congresses, and looked upon as the mediator between capital and labour. As a proof of this view being well founded, we may briefly cite the rise, progress, and present position of our own societies in Oldham: – The two societies of this town commenced business in Dec. 1850. During their first five years little progress was made. The number of members at the end of 1855 was 300, their capital £1,000, and their sales during the year £6,000. Their progress during the next five or six years was much more rapid; the members had increased to 2,500, the capital to £22,000, or twenty times the previous sum, and the sales to £100,000 during the year – or seventeen times the amount of 1855. At the present time, the members number 4,500, representing a population of upwards of 20,000, the capital is £65,000, and the sales during the present year have been £200,000. While at the end of 1856 we had only 2 grocery branches, now we have 11 grocery, 4 butchering, 2 tailoring, and 2 shoe and clog branches. There are 8 news-rooms, free to members and their families, and 1 library of 1,500 volumes. An allowance of $2\frac{1}{2}$ per cent is made for these educational purposes each quarter from the profits. To carry on the business of the societies, £14,000 is invested in buildings, upon which an average deduction of 10 per cent per annum is made. £28,000 of our capital is invested in other Co-operative and Joint-Stock companies, in addition to £15,000 in the banks. The reserve funds amount to £2,300. We have a penny savings bank connected with one society, in which 1,200 children have over £1,000 invested. The net profits divided among the members during the year have been £17,500, averaging 2s. on each £1 of purchases; and to non-members £1,300, or an average of 1s. 8d. on each £1 of purchases. Since their commencement, the business done has been £1,099,743; the amount paid in interest on members' shares being £11,000, and in dividends £94,434. – We are, yours most respectfully,

THE COMMITTEES.

Mr. GLADSTONE accepted the address with thanks, and made several inquiries respecting the history and management of the Oldham Co-operative societies, his questions being of a nature that showed he had watched with interest the progress and leading incidents of the Co-operative movement. Mr. Gladstone's attention was called to the grievance inadvertently entailed upon Co-operative societies by the amended Act of last session, in their having to make income tax returns, while exempted from payment of the tax. We have reason to believe that the short Act to rectify this mistake – for such Mr. Hughes, M.P., acknowledged it to be – to be introduced at the earliest opportunity, will receive the support of Mr. Gladstone, who said he thought such a requirement 'very unreasonable.' The great financier expressed his gratification at hearing that there was now less opposition, and that the business of the stores worked more smoothly. Of Co-operation in general he said: – 'It is a thing that is most excellent, and to which everyone must wish well.' The success of Co-operation (he remarked) would entirely depend upon the degree of intelligence which the working classes brought to bear upon it. Co-operation required a self-educated people to carry it on, and it was a great misfortune when it was tried prematurely, before the people were fit for it. It was unfortunate (he thought) that the same name of Co-operative was applied to the mills of production, which were totally different. – [Mr. Gladstone had just left the Sun Mill, Limited, cotton spinning and doubling, with a share capital of £50,000, nearly all paid up, and owned chiefly by working men, and a loan capital of above £40,000.] – Mr. Gladstone said that this misuse of the word created a great deal of confusion. He again highly commended Co-operation, particularly for its tendency to make men prudent and temperate. Mr. Gladstone next asked the managers if they had ever considered the question –

which had been entertained in some Co-operative societies, where it had been decided in the negative – of selling strong liquors? The directors replied that they had never entertained the idea; and further, that they would not allow intoxicating drinks to be sold in their meeting room by persons who engaged it. Mr. Gladstone said the determination of Co-operative societies not to sell strong liquors, was at least a curious fact, seeing that considerable profits were to be made thereby. The reply given to Mr. Gladstone was to the effect that Co-operative societies did not desire profits from anything that would degrade the people, but only from legitimate trade and sources of self-elevation. Mr. Gladstone then asked if the Oldham societies were composed in large proportion of temperance men? explaining that he meant by that term teetotalers. The answer given was that the principal part of the managers were temperance men, if not strict teetotalers; on the other hand, almost all teetotalers were Co-operators. Mr. Gladstone evinced evident pleasure on hearing this testimony to the fellowship of Temperance and Co-operation.

Hearing that $2\frac{1}{2}$ per cent of the profits was devoted to educational purposes, Mr. Gladstone signified his wish to see one of their newsrooms. The news-room and library on the opposite side of the street were then visited. On re-entering Mr. Platt's carriage Mr. Gladstone was heartily cheered.

At a meeting held in the Working Men's Hall, the same evening, Mr. Gladstone said: –

But, gentlemen, there is a great deal more beside direct teaching that is to be had either in schools or in colleges, or in a lyceum, or a mechanics' institute, such as you have in this town – excellent as those institutions are; there are likewise other and very powerful agencies that are at work with a view to raising the mass of the community – influences to which I think we must all heartily wish well. One of those, one of the most remarkable and most characteristic of the age and of this part of the country, is that which is called the Co-operative system. I do not know that the name is a very happy name, simply for this reason, – that it appears not to convey the clearest idea of the nature of the operations carried on, and to be applied to institutions all of which may be excellent, but which really are essentially different. To-day I have had the satisfaction of seeing two institutions in Oldham, one of them a Co-operative mill, the other, I believe, the largest Co-operative store in the town. Both of these fall under the name of Co-operation, yet they are essentially different. The one is a machinery for taking into the hands of the consumers the operations of retail dealing; the other is a joint-stock company with limited liability, and the shares reduced to an amount such as to place them within the reach of the operative community. I am not in the least drawing any distinction between these institutions to the prejudice of the one or the other; both of them appear to me to be excellent institutions in cases where the intelligence of the labouring community enables them to carry them on with safety to themselves; and I am persuaded that in Oldham, if in any place in England, they can be so carried on. There is, however, a distinction between them in this respect. The Co-operative store competes with the retail tradesman, and rather aims at correcting something imperfect in the manner in which retail trade is carried on, than at any wider object. I do not doubt that it has very important reflex effects, if I may so call them, and especially that it is most highly advantageous by giving the habit of dealing with ready money. That habit, however, of dealing with ready money might be combined with the old system of retail trade. It has not been so combined; it would be an immense advantage if it could be so combined; and I sometimes hope that one of the good effects of Co-operative stores may be to bring private retail trade to the very same rule of action, and cause it to be carried on for ready money only. But, however, there is no doubt at all that very great good has been done by these Co-operative stores in the towns of Lancashire, where they have been well organised and well managed. But there are certain functions belonging to a Co-operative mill that are rather of a different character. By a Co-operative mill the operative becomes a capitalist – a small capitalist, it is true, but still a capitalist; and having acquired in the Co-operative mill something beyond the wages of his labour, he has got the nucleus of that which may grow into comparative wealth – he has got a resource over and above that on which the ordinary labouring population depend for daily bread. Now, I do not enter into the question whether it is possible for the labouring class in this community exclusively to undertake the management of these Co-operative mills; all that I say is, that I devoutly hope it may prove to be so, because I think the advantages are enormous of the state of things in which the operative is thus enabled to assume the character of a capitalist. He becomes a link between the two great classes; he at once tends to soften and mitigate whatever there is of collision in the relations of labour and capital. I can conceive nothing more likely to exercise a healing influence upon any tendencies to difference between those two great classes, than the existence of a considerable body of men who belong to both. They will learn, they will know, in this practical experience, what are the feelings of each: and depend upon it, most of our difficulties arise from this – that we are not so capable as we ought to be of placing ourselves in the position of the men with whom we have to do. We look at things from our own point of view; we are not so apt and not so able as we ought to be, to look at them likewise from the point of view of the men with whom we are dealing; and therefore the union of these interests, if it can be effected co-extensively with economical advantage to those who carry on the mills, I think will be a social influence of the greatest possible value and importance.

Document 2

Moderate trade unionism. *Source*: National Association for the Promotion of Social Science, *Report of the Committee on Trades' Societies and Strikes* (1860, reprinted New York, 1968), pp. 77, 78, 88–9, 119–20

VARIOUS Typographical Societies throughout the kingdom were united in January, 1845, and formed the National Typographical Association. The affairs of the Association were managed by a Central Board or Committee, consisting of five District Boards collectively – in which resided the executive power, a majority of whose votes decided every question – and the Committees of each Local Society or Branch belonging to the Union.

A case of dispute between employer and employed being brought before a Local Society's or Branch Committee, their decision was submitted to the District Board of Direction, for approval and confirmation; if the question was thought too important for the decision of the District Board, it was laid before the Central Board, which finally gave or refused the support of the Association according to its own judgment. The appeal to the Executive was final so far as the Association was concerned, but each District Board could act independently, if it thought fit to do so, in any matter, but without the support of the Association and use of its funds. It was the aim of the Association to produce, as far as possible, a uniformity of trade usages throughout the country, to bring the profession to a common understanding on all questions arising between employers and employed, especially in relation to the number of apprentices or boys in proportion to journeymen printers, and the prices of labour, and to support the unemployed to a limited extent while in search of work.

It was thus hoped that strikes would become less frequent, or at least shortened in duration, and that the tramp system would be abolished, by the substitution of a weekly payment made in the town to which the hand belonged while unemployed.

The leading unionists in the printing trade seem to be convinced that the interests of masters and men are mutual; and that what tends to the injury of the interests of either, must ultimately prove detrimental to both; and in combining to protect themselves from the unprincipled masters who would take advantage of the isolated position of an individual or a few, aim to regard the permanent interests of the trade as a whole. Large associations, although more powerful for evil when ruled over by injudicious counsel, exercise, when wisely led, a greater controling power in the circuit under their influence than small ones. A trade united in any extensive union is less likely to fall under the leadership of men fluent in speech but deficient in judgment, and more likely to have within it men of education and ability above the common level, worthy of the trust committed to them by their fellow men. It seems to be gener-ally admitted, that society men in the printing trade are, as a rule, superior both in ability and steadiness to non-society men; and taking non-society men at a lower rate of wages is not by any means equivalent to getting the work done cheaper, especially if quality is a consideration. An employer of about twenty hands in a large provincial town, says, 'Some years ago my men became so careless and unruly, that the overseers received a month's notice, and when a fortnight had elapsed, every man and boy (not under indenture) received a fortnight's notice, the whole leaving the premises at one time. Others, non-society men, took their places. They were easily obtained, and paid variously, some 5s., 3s., and 2s. each less than the unionists. Their services were retained some three years. I am of opinion that the inferiority of these men, as workmen, more than counterbalanced the difference in wages, although they certainly were a more satisfied and manageable class of persons. About twelve months ago, on the entreaty of the unionists, they were again admitted. By this trial I feel satisfied that the unionists are the better workmen, so far as my particular trade is concerned, and confining my observations to this locality.'

The Smiths' Society appears to us especially to be worthy of notice. The preface to its rules states, that among the objects to which its funds are to be applied is, 'To advance the interests of the operatives of the trade generally, both in a pecuniary and in a moral sense of view, by every legal means within its reach, and to resist aggression in whatever shape it may present itself as an antagonist to its members or to the trade at large,' – but further on it states, 'that the Society had an early origin (1827), and, like most of its kind, became imbrued with and indulged more or less in the category of strikes, which expensive item, in all probability, tended more than anything else to repress and to reduce its funds and its members to a very low ebb. In the year 1845 a delegate meeting assembled, at which it was unanimously considered and determined, that strikes of all kinds, however seemingly just in their nature, were in the aggregate an unpremeditated evil on the part of the operatives, and an unmitigated one to all concerned – in fact, an infliction upon society at large – the immediate enactors being the proximate sufferers in all cases, the ultimatum of which was beyond calculation. At this meeting it was most wisely determined, for the future, to avoid all such contests, and in furtherance of the same, a law was enacted, and thus this Society became incorporated, in point of fact, as the original anti-strike society, a fact (although put forth, perhaps, a little before its time, and which may in some respects have militated against the society), yet a fact of which we have no cause to be ashamed; a fact which in the short space of eight years has nearly trebled the number of our members, and has enabled us to meet every demand honourably, which certainly was at one time rather doubtful, and above all, has put us, in a pecuniary sense of the word, in such position that perhaps no other society of the kind can boast of. So much for anti-strike principles. Want of intelligence on the part of both man and master induces and precipitates strikes. They are battles between the employers and the employed which are too often unwisely got up by one or both parties, and continued more for the purpose of trying which shall gain the mastery over the other than otherwise, at no trifling sacrifice both to themselves and to the public at large; when a small spice of intelligence would convince both that it is impossible for the wages of labour or its concomitants to be permanently regulated by individual action. Disputes of this kind can only be settled by friendly consultations between both master and man, imbued with the spirit of mutually imparting facts, with a view to render assistance to each other; if this,in connexion with the efforts of mutual and disinterested friends, cannot be accomplished, we say then let men and masters part; offer no opposition; the men, however great or small their number, to be supplied with means of existence until they obtain other situations of work from the funds of the Society; and the employers to obtain other men as best they may; and we contend that this unassuming quiet plan of operations, is, according to its number of members, accomplishing, and will continue to accomplish, infinitely more real good to the trade, in all its ramifications, at a minimum expense to its members, than any other plan of operation by any other society, however much vaunted or boasted of, and therefore deserves to be well supported by the operatives of the trade in general.

'The history of strikes in the aggregate confirms the opinion that they are a serious evil to all concerned and to the public in general; the right to combine is one to which the artisan, operative as well as employer, are fully entitled. Combinations are capable of producing great advantage, and supply important deficiencies; the labour of the operative is his capital, and he is justified in disposing of it to the greatest advantage, and protecting it from injury or depreciation; but he is justified in no more; he must stop there; he has no right to assail or interfere with others; the moment this line is transgressed by either master or man, that moment a complete change is effected in the character and operation of the body; from a positive good it becomes a positive evil.

Document 3

A.J. Mundella's evidence to the Royal Commission on Trade Unions, 14 July 1868. *Source: Tenth Report of the Commissioners appointed to Inquire into the Organization and Rules of Trades Unions and other Associations* (London, 1868), Minutes of evidence, pp. 73–6

19,341. (*Chairman.*) I believe that you have come to state to the Commissioners your experience with reference to arbitration? – I was requested to communicate something to the Commission on the subject of arbitration as we practise it at Nottingham. And I divided it in this way: Firstly, the state of the relations betwixt masters and workmen in the hosiery trade (which is my own trade) prior to the establishment of a board of arbitration and conciliation; secondly, the circumstances under which that board was established, and its influence on those relations; and, thirdly, the application of such boards to other branches of industry. That occurred to me as the proper order. In speaking of the first point, the state of the relations betwixt masters and workmen in the hosiery trade prior to the establishment of a board of arbitration and conciliation, I may say that that goes far beyond my recollection, because although I was born, so to speak, in the hosiery trade, and have been engaged in it ever since I was six years old, yet the dreadful state of the relations betwixt labour and capital is a matter of history. . . .

. . . Well, in 1860, we had in a single branch three strikes, one of which lasted 11 weeks. There was rather a good demand for the American trade; when the time came for the delivery of our goods, we had no goods to deliver, the men having been out 11 weeks. The manufacturers came together to consider what we could do to completely change this state of things. We resolved to do something as we considered it in self-defence. I may say here that of course the one branch that was out was supported by the branches that were at work. It was only the Sutton branch as we call it, the wide hand frames, which require rather a skilled class of men, that were out, still a number of steam power men and narrow hand frames, and glove hands, all contributed their quota to maintain these men while they were on strike. It was proposed that we should lock out the whole of them, that is to say, that if these men would not come to work on our terms, we should cease to give them any kind of work, and we would stop the steam power frames also. We knew what this meant; it meant throwing the population on the streets, and we should have had a dreadful state of commotion. We were sick of it, and some of us thought that better means might be adopted.

19,344. What was the real subject in dispute? – The men asked a large advance of wages in one branch.

19,345. Upon that the whole subject turned? – Yes, upon that the whole subject turned. As I say, some of us thought that we might devise some better means of settling the thing. I had heard of the Conseils de Prud'hommes in France, and with one or two others I built up a scheme in my imagination of what I thought might be done to get a good understanding with our men and regulate wages. The result was that a handbill was issued (I have one of the original bills here) inviting the men to a conference. At a meeting of hosiers it was arranged that a number of middle men and workmen should meet together, at least we invited them to meet together with us, to consider the suicidal character of their proceedings, and three employers were deputed to confer with the workmen. We say at the end of the bill, 'We hereby invite the workmen in the branches referred to, to depute persons to take part in the conference, and to arrange with us the time and place of meeting. Signed A.J. MUNDELLA, THOS. ASHWELL, J.H. LEE,' those being three of the largest manufacturers. We met, and we debated in our Corn Exchange for two or three days.

19,346. (*Lord Elcho.*) Do you know what steps the men had taken? – The men consulted together and put out a handbill. They said that it seemed a fair proposal and they would meet it.

19,347. How did they choose their men? – They chose the leaders of their trades unions undoubtedly. We three met perhaps a dozen leaders of the trades unions, and we consulted with these men, told them that the present plan was a bad one, that it seemed to us that they took every advantage of us when we had a demand, and we took every advantage of them when trade was bad, and it was a system mutually predatory. And there is no doubt that it was so; we pressed down the price as low as we could and they pressed up the price as high as they could. This often caused a strike in pressing it down and a strike in getting it up; and these strikes were most ruinous and injurious to all parties, because when we might have been supplying our customers our machinery was-idle, and the probabilities were that some part of our trade was going to our rivals in France and Germany, for we have constant competition with France and Germany, and we suggested whether we could not try some better scheme. Well, the men were very suspicious at first; indeed it is impossible to describe to you how suspiciously we looked at each other. Some of the manufacturers also deprecated our proceedings, and said that we were degrading them, and humiliating them, and so on. However, we had some ideas of our own, and we went on with them; and we sketched out what we called a board of arbitration and conciliation. What we were going to do was very indistinctly prefigured in our own minds, except that we had agreed that to this board we would refer all questions in dispute, and that an equal number of workmen and manufacturers should be elected annually, the manufacturers by their body and the workmen by theirs, and that we would bind ourselves to agree to the decision of the board; of course the parties selected to sit on the board being manufacturers and workmen in equal numbers.

. . . the men are convinced by their own senses of the justice of what we say and by their knowledge of the laws that govern trade, because this system has been a complete educational process for our men; they know as well as we do whether we can afford an advance or not; they know whether the demand is good or bad, and at what prices the article can be made in France or Germany; and they are accustomed to consider the effect of a fall or rise in cotton just as we do; and when they think that things are going well they ask to share in the benefit, and when they think that things are going wrong they are willing to take lower rates.

19,359. They have, in fact, confidence in your board? – They have now. At first it was difficult to inspire that confidence, as we did not confide in each other; there were not above half the manufacturers that came into it at first, but when we put our names to these statements the others could not for shame stand out, and now we have only three or four who hold aloof, for there are men in our trade as there are in every other trade who for the sake of a few shillings a week would not hesitate to put a whole district in confusion – masters who are perfectly indifferent as to be effect upon the trade in general, so that they can gain a little more.

19,360. (*Lord Elcho.*) What number do the ten men on your board represent? – Fully 20,000 men.

19,362. (*Mr. Roebuck.*) Ten persons representing the employers on the board were chosen by the employers? – Yes.

19,363. (*Mr. Harrison.*) Who has a right to vote for them? – The employers who are members of the Hosiers' Association.

19,364. Those outside of that association would not have the right? – We have only about three such.

19,365. And the ten men's representatives are selected by the men's different unions, are they not? – They are selected by the men's unions; and I believe the non-unionists voted for them in the first year. I believe it was by universal suffrage that they were chosen, they actually polled the number of votes. So many men were nominated, John So-and-so had so many thousand votes, and so on; and the nine with the highest number of votes were appointed.

19,366. Who had the suffrage? – Every man who worked at the trade.

19,367. Did they take the votes at central voting houses? – I think the votes were sent to the secretary of the trades unions.

19,368. Then the vote was collected by the trades unions putting themselves at the head of the working men of the town? – Yes, we could have done nothing without the organization of the union, and it was to deal with that we adopted this plan.

19,369. What proportion of the men are in the union? – The great bulk.

19,370. Do you suppose that you could have got hold of them without such an organization as that of the union? – No; when we proposed to the men the formation of a board of arbitration they took our proposal back to the trades unions for consideration, and the trades unions determined to give it a trial. Here is the way in which it is worked in the lace trade. The third rule of the board of arbitration and conciliations for that trade is this: 'The board to consist of eight manufacturers and eight operatives, three of each to form a quorum; the operatives to be elected by a meeting of their own body, the manufacturers to be elected by a meeting of employers. The whole of the deputies to serve for one year, and to be eligible for re-election.' Now here is the men's circular: 'The committee earnestly request that a delegate be elected from every workshop, and those factories or shops numbering more than ten workmen are requested to send one delegate for every additional ten workmen, to meet in the office, Rigley's Yard, on Thursday evening next, the 4th day of July, at 7 o'clock, when it is intended to choose eight workmen according to the above-named scale' (that is to say, that every ten men should choose one, and that out of that number they should choose the eight who should represent them) 'to meet the same number of employers to draw up a code of laws, and to form the board for the ensuing year.'

19,371. (*Lord Elcho.*) That is irrespective of whether they belong to the union or not? – That seems to be irrespective of whether they belong to the union or not. But this is my experience, that the men who are not in the union are always glad to take the advantages gained for the men by the union, and if you will deal with the leaders of the trades unions they will be glad for you to do so. If we were to attempt to adopt the principle which Mr. Nasmyth has been recommending to you this morning of dealing only with one man at a time I think it would be most unfair to the men.

19,372. (*Mr. Roebuck.*) I think Mr. Nasmyth's remark on that point applied to the contracts between employers and employed? – That is the rock on which I think employers split; and I think that Mr. Nasmyth only stated very boldly and frankly what many employers – indeed, the majority of employers – secretly feel; that is this, that they will not have anything to do with deputations at all, they want to deal with men one at a time. Now so long as there are 20 or 30 factories working in one town, and the men in one factory are getting 16s. a week and the men in the other factories 16s. 6d. a week, the 16s. men will not stand it, but they will form a combination with the 16s. 6d. men to get the extra 6d. and they will deal with you by their representatives, and they have a right so to do; because if I take men one at a time I being a large employer can trade upon their necessities and weed out the men that have any independence, and screw the rest down to any terms I may please. That is the rock on which too many of the employers split, and so long as we wish to make a world to please ourselves, and will not take it as we find it, I believe that we shall have these strikes and lock-outs. I see no way to avoid that state of things, but allowing men to avail themselves of the principle of association; although I believe there have been many wicked things done under it, and I always denounce in the strongest way I can any outrage, any intimidation, anything illegal or irregular, any opposition to machinery, any objection to work a particular class of stone; for instance at Bradford I have done so. I there told the men plainly what I thought of them and got them to go home and erase their rules the next day; yet I am quite sure that the men on the whole have benefited by their trades unions.

19,373. (*Mr. Hughes.*) You say that you quite admit the right of the men to deal with their employers by their representatives? – That is the only way of avoiding these difficulties.

19,374. And you have had great experience of the representatives of the men in your part of England? – Yes.

19,375. What sort of men have you found them to be? – I will tell you what has been the effect of our board of arbitration. The very men that the manufacturers dreaded were the men that were sent to represent the workmen at the board. We found them the most straightforward men we could desire to have to deal with; we have often found that the power behind them has been too strong for them; they are generally the most intelligent men; and often they are put under great pressure by workmen outside to do things which they know to be contrary to common sense, and they will not do them. They have been the greatest barriers we have had between the ignorant workmen and ourselves, and I know that is so. I have found it in my correspondence with trade union secretaries and leaders; all over England I have found that so. I know that they are opposed to most of the evils that pervade the trades unions, but there are some that are not so; it is quite clear that this Commission has developed that.

19,376. So that you consider them to be genuine representatives of the working men? – Yes, generally I do.

Document 4

Working-class advancement post-1850. *Source*: B. Wilson, *Struggles of an old Chartist* (1887), in D. Vincent (ed.), *Testaments of Radicalism: Memoirs of Working-class Politicians 1790–1885* (London, 1977), pp. 241–2

In March, 1885, I mentioned to Mr. John Culpan and Mr. Joseph Foreman that I should like us to have a meeting of the few old Chartists still living as soon as the reform bill was passed, and it was agreed that I should make all the necessary arrangements. I had a number of circulars printed as follows: –

SALTERHEBBLE, JUNE 29th, 1885.

DEAR SIR, – You are cordially invited to meet a few old Chartist friends to take Tea and spend a Social Evening together at Maude's Temperance Hotel, Broad St., Halifax, on Tuesday Evening next, July 7th, to commemorate the passing of the Reform Bill. Tea on the Tables at Half-past Six. Hoping you will be able to make it convenient to be present.

Yours truly, B. WILSON.

The following account is taken from the *Halifax Courier*. – 'Unique Gathering of Old Politicians. – Twenty-two members of the old Chartist Association of this town met at Maude's Temperance Hotel to spend a Social Evening in celebration of the incorporation in the law of the land of the principal portion of the Charter. The chair was occupied by Mr. John Culpan, who was secretary when Mr. Ernest Jones was a candidate for Halifax in 1847, and also all the time Mr. Jones was in prison for advocating measures which have now a place on the statute book. An excellent repast having been served, the chairman delivered an address of unusual interest; he reviewed the progress of the people from 1844 to 1885, and related remarkable incidents of each epoch of social advancement and political triumph; his very suitable observations were listened to with evident pleasure, and on their conclusion the old veterans shook the chairman cordially by the hand. Mr. Joseph Foreman then moved – "That the best thanks of this meeting be given to Mr. Gladstone and his government for passing into law those principles which we have endeavoured during a long life to enjoy." He congratulated the assemblage on their fortune in living to see the realization of those things for which a comparatively weak and despised class they struggled forty years ago; formerly persecuted and taunted as revolutionists and levellers, they were now freely acknowledged as law-abiding citizens not that they had changed their attitude but because the opinions for which they suffered now prevailed. The motion was seconded by Mr. Geo. Webber, one of the Chartist speakers of '48 and who gave some reminiscences of the old days. The resolution passed with manifestations of enthusiasm. Mr. B. Wilson moved, and Mr. Shackleton seconded, a vote of thanks to the two Liberal members who have given Mr. Gladstone and his government continuous support. This was also cordially adopted, the company rising to their feet. The ages of those present averaged upwards of 65 years, and varied from 62 to 76. At the time of the

Chartist agitation they were all poor working men earning low wages, not the least interesting part of the speeches therefore was their account of the hardships the working classes had to endure within living memory, enabling younger politicians to make a useful and instructive contrast. Their humble origin nevertheless, the majority of those attending the meeting have become men of business and in some cases employers of labour, and a few by economy, industry, and temperance have secured a competency for their old age. Public exultation may be paraded once in a while when it is considered that merely because of their early efforts to improve the condition of their fellows, they were denounced as the unwashed scum and the like. Tuesday's proceedings was diversified by songs and recitations, and the party enjoyed themselves till a late hour.'

Document 5

'Account of the Strike and Lock-out in the Building Trades of London 1859–60' by T.R. Bennett and G.S. Lefevre. *Source*: National Association for the Promotion of Social Science, *Report of the Committee on Trades' Societies and Strikes* (1860, reprinted New York, 1968), pp. 56–7, 58–9, 60–1, 63–4

. . . a Conference met in September, consisting of seven members of each of the three trades.

This Conference drew up a memorial, which was signed by the Chairman and Secretary of each of these three trades, and presented to the masters on the 18th of November.

'To the Master Builders of London and its Vicinity.

'GENTLEMEN, – We, the operative carpenters and joiners, stone masons and bricklayers, beg to lay before you this memorial, praying for a reduction in the hours of labour.

'From daily experience in our avocations, we are convinced that owing to excessive hours of labour our worth as artisans is depreciated, both in a mental and physical point of view.

'We justify ourselves in taking this position on the ground of our having an equal right to share with other workers that large amount of public sympathy which is being now so widely extended in the direction of shortening the hours of labour.

'The fact is well known that the present hours are too many to afford either rest from exhaustion or time to improve the intellect, so as to acquire the knowledge and skill requisite for the rapid progress of invention; that continuous exertion without recreation must engender those evils we deplore; that owing to this continuous exertion, premature incapability must necessarily ensue, whereby our value in the field of labour is materially affected, and we ourselves are eventually left a heavy burden upon the public.

'Further, Gentlemen, your memorialists regard this question as a purely public one: a question which does not in the remotest degree affect the employers' profits, other than as it has a tendency to increase them; and the public, benefiting as it does by the introduction of machinery, will not, we feel assured, deny to us under your sanction a like participation.

'The object we are desirous of attaining by this memorial is, a concession from our employers of one hour per day, *and the present rate of wages to continue;* by such a concession you will relieve your memorialists from the evils they at present suffer, and yourselves from those future evils consequent upon our own.

'We beg leave also to suggest, that the employers will do well to have regard in all future contracts to the *nine hours per day,* for we are so sanguine as to consider the consummation of our desire inevitable.

'Trusting, Gentlemen, that our memorial will receive that consideration which is due to our wants, is the wish of yours respectfully, the carpenters and joiners, stone masons and bricklayers.

'Signed on behalf of the Trade Committees: –

Carpenters and Joiners .	{ MATTHEW BENN, *Chairman.* { GEORGE POTTER, *Secretary.*
Stone Masons	{ EDWIN DANIEL, *Chairman.* { R.W. GREY, *Secretary.*
Bricklayers	{ WILLIAM BLACKBURN, *Chairman.* { HENRY TURFF, *Secretary.'*

A copy of this memorial was sent to every master builder in London . . .

About a month after this, the painters and plasterers joined in the movement, making altogether five trades, all of whom were thenceforward represented each by seven members at the Conference.

. . . meeting held on the 20th of April, and attended by about seventy masters, including those who were, as well as those who were not, members of the Association.

The following resolutions were passed unanimously.

'Moved by Mr. Charles Lucas, and seconded by Mr. Myers: –

'That in the opinion of this meeting it is not expedient to accede to the request of the workmen contained in their letter of the 19th

March, because the present arrangement of hours is the most convenient to all parties, and does not involve such an amount of time as to bring the building workmen at all within the limit of those on whose behalf the public interest has been excited, and its benevolence aroused (the hours being from six in the morning to half-past five in the afternoon, with one hour and a half interval for meals); and because much public inconvenience would result from the discontinuance of work at so early an hour as half-past four, involving, as it would do, the stoppage of all machinery, plant, and cattle, at an early hour.

'Moved by Mr. Dummage (of the firm of W. Cubitt and Co.), and seconded by Mr. Kelk: –

'That if the builders were to admit the principle sought for by the workmen, they would take upon themselves the responsibility of taxing the public more than 10 per cent, and establish a regulation which must necessarily govern labour and its value with all other trades throughout the country; that, acting upon this impression, this meeting records its opinion that there is no sufficient reason at this time to justify such an advance as is demanded by what is called the nine hours' movement. During the past few years the desire of the master builders to meet every reasonable demand has been evinced by the fact that they have given up, without reduction of wages, one hour and a half on each Saturday afternoon, and so lately as the year 1853 they agreed to an advance of 10 per cent on the wages then paid, by reason of which the skilled workman on an average now receives 33s. for $58\frac{1}{2}$ hours' labour.

'That for these reasons, amongst others, it is the opinion of this meeting that the request for nine hours, to be paid for as ten hours, ought not to be acceded to.'

About this time the labourers of the various building trades joined the Conference, and seven of their body were appointed delegates, making up the number of the Conference to forty-two.

On the 11th of May another meeting of the building trade was held in Exeter Hall, and the Conference were again instructed to communicate with the master builders. On the 26th of May the following ultimatum was sent by Mr. Potter on their account.

'AN ULTIMATUM.
To the Members of the Master Builders' Association.
'GENTLEMEN, – At a large meeting of the Building Trades held in Exeter Hall on the 18th instant, your resolutions were discussed, and after deep consideration we were unable to see that you have

definitely answered our letter of March 19th, and we are unwilling to believe that you seriously entertain the intention of taking on yourselves the responsibility of causing the public disaster which was threatened by several of your body at your meeting on the 20th April.

'We therefore, being influenced by the most friendly feelings, once more appeal to you to consider our claim, and we respectfully request a decisive answer from your meeting on the 9th June next, *whether you will concede the nine hours as a day's work.*

'I remain, Gentlemen yours respectfully,
On behalf of the United Trades,
GEO. POTTER, *Secretary.*'

The following reply was sent by the order of the Builders' Society.

'*June* 10*th*, 1859.

'SIR, – Your letter of the 26th May was laid before the Builders' Society yesterday, and I am desired to remind you, that when you addressed to this Society your letter of 19th March, the Society felt that the question was too important to be dealt with by them, and it was therefore determined to convene a meeting of the Builders of the Metropolis. This meeting was held on the 20th April. Your letter was submitted to the consideration of *that* meeting, and the resolutions *then* unanimously passed were forwarded to you in due course – that it appears to this Society, that the concluding paragraph of *those resolutions does very distinctly* answer the request contained in your letter of the 19th March, and repeated in that of the 26th May.

'I am desired further to say that no "*threat*" has been held out, and should any such "*public disaster*" occur, as that to which you allude, the responsibility must rest with those who may occasion it.

'I am, Sir, yours obediently,
GEO. WALES, *Secretary to Builders' Society.*
'To Mr. Geo. Potter.'

The strike having thus commenced, a public meeting of the Metropolitan Builders was convened on the 27th of July, at the Freemasons' Tavern, at which nearly two hundred of the principal members of the London Building Trade attended. . . .

Complaints were then made by the members of the trade, of the tyranny and dictation of the Trades' Unions, and a firm determina-

tion was announced to liberate the trade from the thraldom with
which it was threatened by a strike . . .

After much discussion, it was resolved, 'That the metropolitan
builders are compelled to close their establishments on the 6th of
August; but taking into consideration the great number of men who
wholly discountenance the Conference, a Committee of twenty be
appointed to consider the best means of opening the doors to such
men as may be willing to come to work, independent of, and not
subject to, the dictation of any society interfering with the labour of
the working man.' . . .

. . . when by means of Trades' Unions, Conferences, and the
simultaneous action of strikes, working men seek to compel their
brother operatives and their employers to regulate their mutual
agreements solely at the dictation of an irresponsible extraneous
body, and to deprive both labour and capital of their undoubted
right of independent judgment and entire liberty of action, it is clear
that the tyranny of combinations must be resisted by the firmness
and unanimity of those who are threatened with the infliction of
their mandates. When trades' societies combine, it is essential that,
in self-defence, their victims should unite; and your Committee, as
a condition precedent to all attempts to grapple with the difficulty
relegated to them for solution, regard the immediate establishment,
for mutual protection, of an Association of Metropolitan Master
Builders as absolutely indispensable.

'Your Committee therefore recommend that the gentlemen
present at this and the former meeting do constitute themselves into
a society to be called the "Central Association of Master Builders,"
to which any employer of workmen engaged in any business connected with the building trade should be eligible by the votes of a
majority of the members present at the meeting at which he is
proposed.

'Your Committee further submit that the following (among
others) should be adopted as fundamental rules immediately ob-
ligatory and binding upon each member: –

'That no member of this Association shall engage, or continue in
his employment, any contributor to the funds of any Trades' Union
or Trades' Society which practices interference with the regulations
of any establishment, the hours or terms of labour, the contracts or
agreements of employers or employed, or the qualification or terms
of service.

250

'That no deputations of Trades' Unions, Committees, or other bodies, with reference to any objects refered to in article 3, be received by any member of this Association on any account whatever; it being still perfectly open to any workman, individually, to apply on such subject to his employer, who is recommended to be at all times open and accessible to any personal representation of his individual operatives.

'That no member of this Association shall engage or continue in his employment any workman whomsoever until the person engaging such workman shall have stipulated with and obtained from him his distinct agreement and formal assent to the conditions embraced in the following form of engagement, which shall be read over to every such workman, and a copy whereof shall be handed to him before entering upon his work: –

' "I declare that I am not now, nor will I during the continuance of my engagement with you become, a member of, or support, any society which directly or indirectly interferes with the arrangements of this or any other establishment, or the hours or terms of labour; and that I recognise the right of employers and employed individually to make any trade engagements on which they may choose to agree.'

'That no member of this Association shall permit dictation interference, or direct or indirect tampering with the management of his establishment, or the engagement, or conditions of the service of his workmen; but that, in the event of a strike or turn out occurring in the establishment of any member of this Association from reasons or from causes which shall, in the opinion of the executive committee, entitle the employer so assailed to its countenance and support, it is hereby, and shall continue to be distinctly understood, that all the members of the Association shall sustain, according to their power and ability, such member in upholding the objects of the Association; it being expressly understood and declared, that no acts shall warrant the interference of this committee except such as it is the declared object of the foregoing provisions to prevent.'

'Your Committee further recommend, that all works on which the metropolitan Builders are engaged within the circle of the London Postal District shall be discontinued Saturday next, the 6th August current, and that it shall be intimated to each workman that, so soon as Messrs. Trollope and Sons have resumed their works, the other Master Builders will re-open their works on a new agreement, as contained in the subjoined notification, which shall also be posted up where it can conveniently be done, at each place where works of members are in progress.

Document 6

The death of Richard Pilling. *Source*: Ashton-under-Lyne *Reporter*, 5 December 1874, p. 5

On Monday one of the old landmarks of Ashton historic Radical-ism was removed from our midst in the death of Mr. Richard Pilling. For some time he had been failing in health, the feebleness of old age has crept gradually upon him, and he breathed his last on Monday morning, having very nearly completed his 75th year.

Mr. Pilling was a native of Bolton, and in 1832 he removed from that town to Stockport. He was somewhat prominent among the working men for the part he took in the agitation for the reform bill. Subsequently he joined the Weavers' Association in Stockport, and took an active part in the agitation against the reduction of wages. Subsequently he became identified with the Chartist movement, and through the opposition he excited among the employers gener-ally in consequence of his trades unionism and Chartism he was denied employment in the town, and in 1840 he had to leave the town. He came to Ashton, but his zeal in the cause of his class was not abated by the hard treatment, he had endured. He now became identified with the short time movement and advocated on the platform the Ten Hours Bill. The bill first passed as an Eleven Hours Bill for 12 months, and then it was to be 10 hours. The masters exerted themselves to secure the continuance of the 11 hours, and they endeavoured to get the females in their employment to sign for this. At this time Mr. Pilling was in Ashton, and he and Joseph Leach, from Manchester, addressed a meeting of females in Stockport on this subject, and at this meeting Mr. William Herbert, then of Stockport, presided. In fact, throughout his life he has al-ways been conspicuous for his advocacy of working class move-ments, and he and his family suffered materially in consequence. He was imprisoned for Chartism about 1839 or 1840; and when Bright, the policeman, was shot in Bentinck-street on August 14, 1848, Mr. Pilling and others fled to America, lest they, being so prominent among the working men should be arrested for riot. It is, however, stated and believed by many that Mr. Pilling was not in town at the time, others say he left the same night. In the great six weeks' strike in 1842 when the operatives in Ashton and Stalybridge turned out and a mob of rioters came from Stalybridge and stopped the Ashton mills by drawing the plugs of the boilers, Mr. Pilling's name was, justly or unjustly, connected with the transactions and his name had always this black mark placed against it by the factory masters. Mr. Pilling remained in America about two years. He returned to

Ashton in 1850–24 years since, last Ashton Wakes – and since that time he has never been employed in any of the factories of the district, and has had to eke out a living the best way he could. In the agitation for the incorporation of Ashton, which was accomplished in September, 1847, he took an active part, and ever since his return from America he has exerted himself strenuously at election times in the Liberal interest. Throughout his life he was a sincere and consistent Radical in politics. At the last municipal election in Ashton he delivered a characteristic speech, full of hard hits and humorous sallies. It is feared by some of his friends that the excitement of the election was too much for his enfeebled frame, and that it has had the effect of hastening his departure from our midst.

Document 7

Orange demonstration in Manchester. *Source: Manchester Guardian*, 16 February 1869

Last evening, a meeting, which had been announced as a Protestant demonstration, was held in the Free-trade Hall. It had been extensively advertised that Mr. Johnston, M.P. for Belfast, Mr. M'Keowne, M.P. and other leading Orangemen, would be present; but they did not attend. Mr. W. Murphy, who wore an orange scarf, came upon the platform with the Chairman (Mr. Booth Mason), and was received with cheering and the performance of 'Rule Britannia' by a company of performers who were advertised as the Protestant band. A large number of persons paid the charge that was demanded for admission.

The CHAIRMAN . . . had the honour to be the deputy grand master of the Orange Association in England. The civil and religious liberties of the people were in danger from a combination of Cardinal Cullen and his associates with the Radicals, the infidels, and the Unitarians. – (Cheers.) Orangemen had had some little faith in Mr. Disraeli's Government; and they had hoped that when the Government reverted to the ancient constitution of England, and placed the people in power, the result would be favourable to them. The elections in Lancashire had shown that the people knew how to use their power. – (Cheers.) It was by the united exertions of the Orange Association, the Orange Institution, and the Protestant Electoral Union, that those great results had been accomplished. – (Cheers.) Mr. Gladstone had been kicked out of Oxford for not being a Churchman, and he had been kicked out of Lancashire for not being a Protestant. – (Cheers.) The Satanic ambition of the Premier reminded him of the individual of whom Milton said that he

'Would rather reign in hell than serve in heaven.'

(Cheers.) A thief was a thief, whether he was prime minister or peer – (cheers); – and the robber and spoliator of the Irish Church must be a thief. – (Renewed cheers.) Orangeism represented 500,000 men, armed men; for they must remember that the Bill of Rights gave to all Protestants the privilege of bearing arms. – ('Hear, hear,' and cheers.) Therefore, if Mr. Gladstone wished to spoliate the Irish Church he would have to ask 200,000 armed Irish Orangemen. – (Cheers.) He would have also to ask a great army of English and Scotch Orangemen – (loud cheers); – and he would have to ask a vast army in the Canadas (cheers); – and a vast number in the army and the navy too. – (Prolonged cheers.) If Mr. Gladstone wished to break up the British empire, or if he liked to 'cry havoc, and let loose the dogs of war,' the sooner he started the better. – (Great cheering.)

At the conclusion of the Chairman's speech the band played an Orange air, which seemed to work the assembly up to a great pitch of excitement. Old women rose and waved their umbrellas, and orange hankerchiefs with portraits of William III. upon them, whilst the men cheered vociferously and gave rounds of 'Kentish fire.'

Document 8

Mid-Victorian partnership and patriarchy. *Source*: W. Marcroft, *The Inner Circle of Family Life* (Manchester, 1886), pp. 8–11, 15, 16–18, 24–5, 26–7

IV. – CHOOSING OF A LIFE PARTNER.

THE young man, in looking out for a woman to make him a partner, has need to look into the affairs of the family of the intended wife. The inner circle of the family home is much as a garden; wasteful habits, like weeds, come into practice and grow without teaching or sowing. Is the family of the intended bride extravagant or careful of the means on which they live? Is the family of a healthy stock, industrious and courteous in their manners? Are they a reading family? good books are intelligent companions. In the mere spending of money there is not needed much ability – the whole trading community will help persons to do that. Are there good home regulations? for they have an influence to strengthen the weakest temperaments to their best effort, and hold the strongest of temperaments to their duty.

In good home life the father supplies the money and trusts the mother to expend it. The mother brings around her the daughters to help her to lay out the money to the best advantage, thereby to encourage an intelligent conversation as to the purchasing of the cheapest and the best of food, so as to give strength and health to the body. Do the daughters take part in the cooking of the food? Also observe do the daughters enjoy the taking an active part in the management of the home, in bread baking, washing and darning, and appear familiar to the work.

In the articles of clothing there ought to be taste combined with cleanliness and adaptability. There should be much of the clothes making done at home; re-arrangement of clothing to be often seen, the mending of clothes and the knitting of stockings occupying the spare moments of the mother and daughters. However well to do be the family, the habits of industry and carefulness are the charms of family life; they are as scattered seeds of usefulness, to be reaped in after years.

In what I have related as needful for the young man to do, so the young woman has need to observe in the conduct and in the home of the intended young man, the expected husband. It is said that 'Love is blind;' that may be so, if the choice is formed by the mere whim of the moment, when only the passions rule. To marry is the most important event in human life; therefore the young man and the young woman should bring to their judgment their most serious reflections, and ask themselves, Do the probable conditions exist in us, the two persons, that ought to make life comfortable and the home happy?

V. – HOME! SWEET HOME!

The home is said to be the Englishman's castle. Is it to be a castle of order, peace, and cleanliness, or a castle of confusion, disturbance, and filth? Young men, make your choice. Each can be had at the same price. In the home of poverty, where intelligence, industry, and carefulness are ever in action, happiness and cheerfulness are intertwined in mutual hope and resignation to make the best of the circumstances in which the family are placed. The mere home of great wages is too often one of negligence, the husband of hard toil supplying an abundance. The sight of the home of dirt and disorder troubles him; he seeks a second home, where cleanliness, civility, and friendship – these are the nets laid to catch wandering animals.

Beauty commands attention everywhere, and is appreciated by men as well as women. A clean and tidy woman is the prettiest sight on earth; but a dirty, slovenly woman is the most offensive thing in creation.

A few minutes' earlier rising in the morning would enable the wife and mother to light the fire with patience, prepare the breakfast, clean the hearth, and put each article in the house in its proper place – to wash her face and hands, comb her hair, and make tidy her clothing. Thus, on the husband coming to breakfast, order and cleanliness and kind words might welcome him to contentment – the table covered with a white cloth, the pots clean and placed in nice order, the food all ready for the keen appetite, the wife speaking inviting words of kindness, telling the husband of some happy event.

The morning well started makes the household duties throughout the day an amusing, pleasant recreation. Wives ever have it present in the mind that other people are interested, and make it a part of their business to make their houses more agreeable to the husband than does his wife. Life should ever be one of courtship, ever trying to make dulness into brightness, sorrow into gladness, and making ourselves acceptable in the sight of one another.

To enable the wife to perform the many obligations of family life in a cheerful manner, the husband should be at home as much as possible. The wife has need of the husband's advice and companionship. It requires the husband and wife to act in union to make home a place of sweetness, joy, and contentment. The natural tendency of a woman is to be clean and modest.

Home is the heaven gained in female life. There she makes a world as she wills it; order, cleanliness, regularity, and comfort are the four points of her compass. The husband is the altar of her worship, and to guide her children to do right is the pleasure of her life.

Wives and mothers, trust not to your daughters or to your servants; your presence is the sun of light and warmth that can alone cause home to be a little heaven below. Then the song of songs may be sung with the fervour of a felling heart and a full chorus of voice –

> Home! home! home! Sweet home!
> Wherever I wander, there is no place like home.

VI. – SAVING HABITS AND THOUGHTFUL PREPARATIONS.

THE young man, before deciding to marry, should have saved an important sum of money, considering his wages, say from £50 to £100, and the young woman from £25 to £50. Mutual love or affection is but one of the many requirements in the affairs of a married life. There is need of adaptability to circumstances. And as money is a necessity, and the possessor commands respect and attention in all places and conditions of life, so money is a needful requirement to ensure a contented and a happy home.

The young man that is sober, industrious, and careful, with a good moral character, and can earn an average weekly wage, say from twenty to forty shillings per week, is in such a position that he need not fear to approach for courtship a young woman, or even a lady of any rank or station in life. The industrious, sober, and prudent young man holds a fortune in his conduct. In a well-to-do family the daughters are generally well acquainted with the duties of a wife and a mother, and are, in modesty, as approachable as a young woman in humble life. The old grandmothers say the young man has all the unmarried young women in the world to choose from. He may, in modesty, use his best judgment in the selection of the woman most suited to his mind.

IX. – HOUSEHOLD MANAGEMENT.

THE first mutual agreement in my new home was to place a sovereign in my young wife's hand, to enable her to buy the food and other needful requirements, and when the amount was expended she was to ask for another £1. The remaining spare money was deposited in the savings bank at Rochdale. When the sum saved came to five or ten shillings I could be seen walking to Rochdale, three miles from Heywood, at the hours from five to seven o'clock on the Saturday evening, to deposit the amount saved. On my return the bank book would be often looked at, and calculations made how long it had taken me to save a certain sum, and how long it would take to save another given sum, and when the amount came to be so much, what the interest would be, and in what number of years the income from the money would be £1 per week. 'Then,' I exclaimed, 'both of us, William and Jane, would be independent.'

X. – EXTRAVAGANT LIVING.

THE cost of living for myself, my wife, and one child, since I came to Oldham, had been over £2 per week. I called my wife to my side, read over to her the amounts, and commented on the random and extravagant way in which we had lived, what we had saved in money, and what we ought to have saved. I wept, and she cried, and for a time both were speechless; at last I said, 'Well, what is to be done? conduct like this is a disgrace to us both.' She said, 'Do you think I have wasted the money, or given it away?' 'No, but the money is gone; we both are to blame for thus living without a system of order and arrangement.'

'The plan that comes to my mind at present is to give you a sovereign every Saturday at noon, and find you a book to set down what you spend it on during the week; if more than a sovereign has been spent, then I will pay you the additional sum, as well as the £1. If less has been spent, then I pay you up to the sovereign.' 'Well, I will try any plan, so as to be agreeable. Who will pay the rates?' 'I will pay them, besides allowing you the £1.'

The plan agreed upon went on several weeks, she not being a good reckoner. When Saturday came there was generally something wrong through neglect of the amount not being set down. I said, 'Do not be so agitated; all will come right amongst honest people.' By a patient calling over of the items, the missing things were remembered; a penny or twopence of an error was looked over, no more to be mentioned.

The reckoning up on a Saturday often caused tears to be shed and a timidity of action during the whole of the week. I then said, 'Mother (we agreed to adopt the custom of calling the husband father and the wife mother), I do not like this crying nearly every time the week's reckoning has to be done; therefore I want you to try another plan.'

XI. – HOME MANAGEMENT BY CONTRACT.

'How much will you contract for to find all the food needed in the house for myself, yourself, and the one child? Also your own clothing, and the child's clothing, the gas and coals, pay the rent and all other household requisites (except my clothes), and any additional furniture that may be required – you to buy it, and to repair or replace the wornout bedclothes and other useable things? I will give you a few days to make out what you can manage the affair for.' The mother said, 'I have already thought of a sum, and am prepared to tell you now.' 'Well, how much is it?' 'Well, if you will pay any doctor's bills that may occur, pay the rates, and when we may have any increase of family you will allow something extra in my weekly allowance, I will undertake to try eighteen shillings per week, if paid every week all the year round.' I said, 'I will allow you nineteen shillings per week, so as to encourage you to work out your own plan of family management.'

To facilitate comfort at home, I agreed that on the washing days on Mondays, and the cleaning days, Saturdays, I would not expect any regularly-prepared meals; whatever was convenient for the mother to get ready, the same food should do for me. But the mop, brushes, and dolly tubs were to have done their work when I came home in the evening, and especially so on the Saturday at noon. I also agreed not to make a practice of ordering what the dinners or other meals must be; whatever was suitable for the mother should be agreeable for me. And the same plan was carried out in bringing up the children; and I said, 'Let there be no locking up of provisions; let us all feed alike, and eat at the same table; if I, or the children, or you be sick, then the simplest of food is the best, which requires but little cooking. For food never buy liver, lungs (known as 'leets'), or the heart, the pancreas (known as sweetbread), or the kidneys, tripe, or any intestines or blood-prepared foods. These articles are the apparatus by which the food is manufactured to build up and to supply the waste of the body. So that if there be any disease in the body of an animal, it will be in the afore-mentioned parts. Therefore they are not fit for human food. By so living we shall have no need of vaccination; the eruptions of the skin are generally the effect of the liquids and foods the body is fed with. Whatever sort of food is bought, let it be of the best quality, for in the average it is the cheapest.'

I further resolved to be more at home in the evening, thereby to keep mother company, to read and sing for her, as I did in the early time of our married life. The neglected home once again became a happy home.

A new class of songs began to be sung. I had decided to try the sober plan of becoming a teetotaler. My wife Jane also agreed to be teetotal. We were often seen at teetotal meetings. Every book that could be had was read by the father for the mother about the evidence of teetotal people being healthy, strong, and living long. The plan of living by a method went on very smoothly. No reckoning up of items on the Saturday. The weekly nineteen shillings were ever paid and received with a cheerful smile.

XVI. – REGULARITY AT HOME.

To enable the mother to bring up a family of children with discipline and regularity, the father must feel the responsibility, and make it a duty to interest himself in the arrangements of the family home. Therefore every book on household matters that I could get I read for mother. I perused with much careful attention Graham's 'Science of Human Life,' Fowler's 'Complete Works,' Nichol's 'Hydropathy,' Samuel Thomson's 'Botanic Medical Guide,' Buchan, Culpepper, and other medicinal works.

Every evening, after the retiring of the children, the mother and myself made it a constant habit to sit before the fire at least half an hour, as a consideration committee, to talk over the occurrences of the day, our present position and requirements, and our future intentions. Thus many a difficulty was by mutual exchange of opinion made easy to carry out.

At the co-operative society I allowed mother to have the whole of the dividend on the purchase of goods at the store, which sum she put to her saving fund.

In the training of the children I induced mother to never frighten them, for I have a painful remembrance of an event which took place at the time when my mother and I were in the poorhouse at the top of Hebers, near Middleton. A big, half-sane boy took me with him to a well on the road-side for a canful of water. When he had filled his can he took hold of me and said he would show me how they drowned dogs. He held me by the legs and ducked me head first into the well. The talking of 'boggarts,' 'black Sams,' and other persons of dread, have had a lasting effect of fear on my mind up to the present time, though now over sixty years of age.

The mother of my children never threatened them to do this or that, or frightened them for doing that which she did not like, or to do that which she wanted. She ever appealed to their sense of right; and in the making of promises was ever faithful to her word. On the minds of our children it had a strengthening effect. In the whole of the time in the bringing up of my family a candle was never asked for on their going to bed at night, did they retire singly or collectively; thus each child had an undaunted mind.

In one of the evening conversations mother reminded me that the children now required fully the amount of her weekly allowance. 'Well, what do you propose in addition?' 'Well, I think, as the children have commenced to work, I ought to have their wages in addition to what you allow me.' 'I have no objection to that if you attend to all their other expenses, and allow them a little spending money, and a small sum to be put into the Penny Savings Bank at the Co-operative Society.' The mother agreed to do so.

The mother was much assisted by information from books, to know what kind of food to buy, and in what manner and variety it should be eaten at the same meal. Flesh meat was only used as a palatable, to give a flavour to vegetable food. Cassell's *Working-man's Friend* was read aloud at the family table, so that the children as well as mother could know the valuable opinions of other people, how to live well and cheap, to be happy, healthy, and strong, and to live a long life. The articles in Cassell's *Working-man's Friend*, named

'Martha Save Penny,' were read by the daughter in the presence of the whole family with much pleasure and profit, and many a plan of hers was successfully tried. 'Rough and enough' is a good motto in food supplies for children.

The mother and the children were educated to a conviction to be careful, which I deemed much better than being forced absolutely to practise.

XVII. – DINNER-TABLE HABITS AND EXERCISES.

MR. SAMUEL BAMFORD, the Middleton Peterloo hero of 1819, has said in his book of 'Early Days': 'There was no talking allowed at the table when the food was being eaten.' The same custom was adopted in our family; everyone calmly submitted to the food placed before them.

At the family table every Sunday at noon, for a great many years, when the dinner was over, the multiplication table was run through by the family as each sat at the table, up to the numbers 12 times 12, forwards and backwards, which by constant practice could be run up in three minutes and down in four minutes. Sometimes difficult words were tested to be spelt, and sentences parsed, questions asked and answered, and articles read bearing on family management. The time allowed for the Sunday's exercises was generally about one hour.

Document 9

Women's rights and wrongs. *Source: The Co-operator*, 22, 29 August, 5 September and 17 October 1868, reprinted from *Papers on Social Subjects* by Robert Harper, 'an occasional contributor to *The Co-operator*'

'Women's Rights' is a phrase which our country often hears from across the great waters, but which has not yet obtained any special signification here. Robert Owen and others have endeavoured to show how intimately women are associated with progress in all that relates to morality and refinement; but little has been done in the way of organising any special means of securing the full application of women's peculiar gifts, and superior organ of sweetness, to the general human progress. Dr. Doddridge used to say that 'Women are our superiors in most things besides physical strength;' and it is not a little remarkable that nearly all the great reforms which the world has seen in later times, have been materially assisted by the Co-operation of women. Do we not often see men of powerful intellectual capacity work long and earnestly at a subject, which the keener instinct of the woman sees through at a glance?

Are we not continually reminded of the fact that the greatest saviours of the world are women, inasmuch as they are the mothers of the world, and wield a power, in virtue of that capacity, which men cannot possibly attain unto? Dr. Doddridge has written on this topic, and has told some very useful truths; but the doctor was scarcely sufficiently aware of the great power of the human mother for good or evil. The sacred relationship which is implied in the term mother, is the holiest known to mankind – the most loving, and therefore the most Godlike of which we have any conception. Now, seeing this is so, does it not become a question of the most vital importance, that our future mothers of the race should be in all things such as their sacred office seems to dictate?

The question of women's rights is, however, capable of discussion and illumination from other sources than those already named. The simplest peasant woman has rights which hitherto have been ignored in all countries, and in none more completely than our own. These rights refer – first, to the social status she ought to hold; and, second, to the social influence she ought to wield. Regarding the first, she cannot be said to have advanced in the least since the period of the Crusades, inasmuch as there still exists an unrepealed law, which permits a man to sell his wife, in open market, with a halter round her neck. Regarding the second, it is clear that whatever improvement a general increase of civilisation may have produced, the general influence of women in society is very little advanced from even periods more remote than the Crusades. The law still regards women as infants; and although a brutal husband may now be punished for physical barbarity, the multifarious modes of inflicting cruel suffering upon women, for which the law has no penalty, are altogether a shame and a reproach to a civilised community.

The cumbrous question of the political franchise for women, though just begun to be agitated, is as yet very little understood, and still less appreciated. The sons of toil and labour are generally in a condition of Cimmerian darkness on this subject; and until they are well and sufficiently educated on this matter, nothing very decided will be done.

It were not difficult to show that, in regard to all that relates to legislation for women, they themselves should unquestionably have a voice; while in all that relates to the moral censorship of society, women would be of unmeasured utility, in virtue of their keener sense of the suffering which immorality entails. The wisest of womankind, perhaps the purest, and certainly the most loving, have been those who saw the necessity there has always been for women to become more distinctly associated with the progress of society in all useful reforms. The wonderfully accelerated ratio of progress in later times, makes the fact more transparently clear – that the employment of women in all the social business of the world is the question of questions, and demands our most serious investigation.

During the last century and a half, there has been no question before the public mind of this country which has so loudly called for its most serious and considerate attention. During that period many profound questions have been discussed, analysed, and decided; but there has been none embodying such momentous consequences to the future of the country, as this question of women's rights. These consequences may be in the highest degree beneficent and ameliorative in their character, or they may be socially suicidal, as we determine on our line of national and social procedure regarding this question.

Scarcely one of the questions which have agitated the public mind of later years has been of the same deeply radical nature, or cast such a formidable horoscope of the nation's future. The welfare of the entire human race may be said to be involved in this question; and any proceedings by this nation cannot be otherwise than influential in the progress of the rest of the human race.

We purpose in the present paper to place before the public mind some few of the evidences of the vast importance of the question, derived from the physiological and phrenological departments of human knowledge. The first series of facts we shall name in this connection, is the congeries of facts relating to hereditary descent. The serious mind becomes here awed by the contemplation of vicious tendencies inherited, deep-seated diseases propagated, and most awful ignorance perpetuated, by the untaught, unhealthy, and immoral women who are the mothers of the next generation. This set of considerations is of so portentous a character that we cannot dwell upon it without painful feelings of misgiving and anxiety on account of our future.

The next single fact to which we shall call attention, is the fact that, summer and winter alike, we are suffering a deeply deplorable evil to exist in our midst, which saps the very vitals of the young – and not the young alone; which murders its thousands – probably its ten thousand annually, and which is a plague and a curse, which no man or woman of ordinary humanity can contemplate without a shudder. This is the one mighty wrong inflicted upon women, which cries aloud to be redressed, which utters its curses upon society, as society walks our streets at mid-day, and which, in the solemn hours when nature is at rest, sends forth its victims to the worse than slave market of the streets.

There is one other fact on this part of our subject before we pass on – viz., the fact that our institutions are all governed by men; whereas it is clearly demonstrable that the capacity of women for positions of trust and discretion is in no case less – but in many cases greater – than that of men. The amazing egotism which has led to the existence of the present mighty inequality, has in it something wonderful, and not at all complimentary to the male portion of the community.

Dr. Doddridge wrote on the treatment of the poor women in the workhouses of the country, and set forth very vividly the injustice of punishing old people for the crime of being poor. Something of the same kind requires now to be done in respect to the treatment of some of the sewing women, who do an amount of work, and do it under conditions so vicious and deplorable, that the remuneration they obtain is simply an inhumanity and a wrong, which loudly calls for redress. Whatever be the fate of any attempts to obtain the elective franchise for women, there is unquestionably an amount of justice and of expediency in the demand, which commends it to the candid and impartial considertion of the whole community. Doubtless it will be said that women are not intended to be equal with men in all relations of life, and that 'man is naturally the head of the woman,' &c. We would like to inquire whether, supposing the cases to have been reversed, and that man was, at this advanced period of civilisation, putting in a claim to the franchise, he would not have thought it rather a begging of the whole question to be told that 'woman is the natural head of the man.' The real truth of the case is, that many men who are at this moment married to women, are so inferior to those women in all that relates both to intellect and refinement, that had it not been for the schooling they have received from their really 'better half,' they would have cut but a sorry figure in society.

Now, on coming into a closer acquaintance with this subject, we find that it has relations which we never suspected, and ramifications which possibly may lead us to different views on the whole matter, from those with which we commenced the investigation.

The department which we propose next to venture upon is the one connected with Schools. There exists here a most lamentable deficiency of means and methods by which to secure anything like a useful education for the women of this generation, and therefore the mothers of the next. Superficial and cursory, the education (so-called) at present is at once ruinously expensive and wretchedly bad. The simple expedient of advertising a set of so-called accomplishments, seems to be deemed a sufficient inducement to send young persons to places called schools, where nearly everything useless is taught, and everything valuable is omitted. There is here a most solemn and startling wrong, of which the general public is either simply ignorant, or to which it is painfully indifferent.

Could some master-mind picture in true and vivid colours the moral apathy, the intellectual imbecility, and the truly shocking, soul-crushing vanity, which characterise the teaching in many of the best girls' schools, it were no mean service to the general public. Scarcely one of these much-vaunted seminaries but simply considers its duty done when it has taught its pupils the so-called accomplishments current at the period, and given to them what is called a finished or distinguished air. Now, probably no course of educational training could possibly be more vicious or harmful than this. The very points in the female character which most need to be checked are held in abeyance, and are hereby fostered and developed into extravagant growth and baneful luxuriance. The morning of life is precisely the best time in which a sound and useful education ought to be imparted. There is then the necessary freedom from care and from household employments, which makes this period by far the most favourable for the instilment of solid lessons of common sense, which may be of service to the individual for the remainder of her life. During the years which precede a young girl's marriage, there are subjects of most vital importance to her when married, which she ought now to be thoroughly taught. Who, that has any experience at all of the world, has not noticed the amazing ignorance of some young mothers on subjects connected with their new circumstances, and the beloved treasure committed to their charge? Surely here is a wrong, which most deeply appeals to the parents whose children are now being educated, to be put right.

Sacred as all subjects are which treat of the modes of the divine operations in any department of His universe, there can be no indelicacy in thoroughly instructing a girl, who, in all probability, may become a mother, in all the scientific knowledge relating to such a condition. Certainly no right-minded person will see any impropriety in such a course, inasmuch as the sure way to prevent all secret curiosity on such subjects is to place the necessary information, in a pure form, within the normal pale of a commonplace education.

The last point which we propose to introduce in the present paper, is one which may, perhaps, be considered by some persons superfluous or indecent; nevertheless, at the risk of being thought coarse, we shall not flinch from the duty of unveiling a wrong which appeals to the most manly and sympathetic feelings of the male portion of society. We refer to the painfully common occurrence of women brought to an early grave by excessive child-bearing. – [There are well-grounded fears that the Princess of Wales will be another victim. Considering her youth, and what she has suffered, we say, with mingled sorrow and respect, that instead of the recent address of congratulation, Parliament ought to have passed a resolution of condolence with the Princess.] – Doubtless many will suppose this to be a subject quite beyond the pale of social discussion: we do not admit that theory. The real rights and wrongs of women are co-extensive with the whole of their relations with men, and with each other; and he who has the hardihood to lay bare a scathing blighting evil in any of these relations, is the true friend of women, and not the enemy of anyone worthy the name of man. It is certain, then, that hundreds of women are annually sacrificed by the selfishness or ignorance, or both, of the men whom they call husbands. The evidences which any surgeon in practice could furnish on this subject, would startle those who are not aware of the extent of this evil. So common is it, that the surgeon ceases to take note of the circumstances; he knows, from repeated experience, that warning is of little use in the case; that some men are so void of common humanity that they will not make the least sacrifice, but simply leave to what they call 'Providence' that which is a physiological certainty, and thus rob their children of a mother's care, and themselves of the satisfaction which some small sacrifice for such a purpose would most certainly have produced.

We cannot enter further into this part of the subject, but must leave it to the conscience and *common sense* of the husbands of society to suggest a remedy.

We have now said probably sufficient on the rights and wrongs of women for one paper; but the subject has yet many ramifications into which we may possibly venture on a future occasion. At present we commend the matters herein mooted to those whom they concern, simply suggesting a few moments' thought to prove whether they really are so or not, and any labour we have taken will not have been in vain.

THE PROPERTY OF MARRIED WOMEN.

The select committee of the House of Commons, to whom the Married Women's Property Bill was referred, have agreed to a special report. From the lateness of the session, they have not been able to conclude their inquiry. The legal evidence taken by the committee shows that the courts of common law and the courts of equity administer two distinct systems of law with reference to this subject, and are guided by entirely different principles. In the former, the married woman is not, in respect of property, recognised as having a legal existence independent of her husband; whereas, on the other hand, the courts of equity have been occupied from a very early period in elaborating a system under which the wife may, by ante-nuptial arrangement, escape from the severity of the common law. But, much as they have done to mitigate the common law, these courts have failed in many respects, through fear of pushing their decision to a legitimate conclusion. The report proceeds: –

Evidence has been given as to the effect of the law which gives the wife's earnings to her husband. Very numerous cases of hardship occur: it is not uncommon for the husbands to take the wives' earnings to spend them in drinking or dissipation. The law at present gives protection for the wife's earnings only in the case where the husband has deserted her. It has been stated that the extension of such protection orders to the case of women whose husbands are intemperate, reckless, idle, or cruel, would be a very insufficient remedy, inasmuch as few women, while continuing to live with their husbands, would come forward to claim in public a protection which would involve giving publicity to their domestic grievances, and an application adverse to their husbands. In many cases, also, the protection ordered would be too late, as it often is in the case of desertion. The small fund which the wife has saved before or after marriage is swept off before the application can be made. On behalf of the wives of labouring men, it is urgently claimed that the only proper course will be to give them an absolute property in, and control over, their own earnings and savings. The evidence of Mr. Ormerod, the president of a working man's Co-operative society at Rochdale, is of great interest on this point, as it shows what have been the steps taken by his society to secure the shares of married women who are shareholders in the society, from the claims or control of their husbands. The means adopted are of doubtful legality, and it is stated that it would be a great disaster if it should turn out that the society is unable to prevent improvident husbands disposing of these shares, or taking the interest of them. Your committee have further taken evidence as to the changes made in the United States and Canada within late years in this branch of the law. It appears that till these changes took place, the common law of England and the rules of our equity courts prevailed in those States. Objection, however, was made to the state of the law on the part of persons with small fortunes, and of women earning money by their own exertions; and now, throughout the greater number of the American States, and in Canada, the common law has been altered, and women, after marriage, retain their separate property, with power to contract, and to sue and be sued in respect of it as if they were single. . . .

Looking, therefore, to the result of this experiment, and to the general tendency of the provisions of equity, your committee is of opinion that a change in the law of this country, with reference both to the property and earnings of married women, is necessary. It does not appear to be necessary to make any alteration in the liability of a husband to maintain his wife, in consequence of such a change in the law with regard to the property of married women. A married woman living apart from her husband can only bind him for what is necessary, and her possession of property of her own, *pro tanto*, negatives the authority arising from necessity. A married woman living with her husband has an authority which, in spite of some fluctuation and uncertainty of judicial decisions, seems to be regulated by the general principles of the law of agency. Agency is a mixed question of law and fact, and the courts will give due weight to such a fact as the possession of property by a married woman without any express statutable direction. Other questions of importance arise in settling the details of such a measure; – whether, for instance, the poor-law liability of the father for the maintenance of the children should be extended to the mother; whether the change should be confined to future marriages only, or should be applied to existing marriages, where after-acquired property is concerned; whether the restrictions imposed by the Massachusetts code on alieniation of property by the wife should be adopted; whether the wife's power to contract, convey, and take by conveyance, should be extended to contracts with, or conveyances to or from, her husband, or be limited to third parties, as appears to be the case in the American States, whose legislation has been referred to; and whether at the death of the wife intestate, any part of her personalty should go to her next of kin, or the whole to her husband only. These questions, however, require more time for discussion

than your committee at this period of the session have been able
to devote to them: they therefore recommend that a select committee be appointed in the next session of Parliament for further
inquiry.

THE 'SATURDAY REVILER,'

AND THE

WANT OF CO-OPERATION FOR WOMEN.

. . . The *Saturday Review* of the 12th instant, in an article on Co-
operation, remarks: – 'the contributors to Mr. Pitman's journal
discuss other and greater matters than the prices of soap and
sugar. . . .

. . . quoting from the *Co-operator* a remark of mine, that 'Co-
operation is most wanted in domestic affairs,' the writer almost
seems to take the idea in the light of a good joke; it is, of course, too
absurd to be thought of seriously – it would never do for a moment.
If women were only to begin to think of Co-operating, they would
become independent, and could no longer be kept in subservience
by the men. And yet he admits that my views 'are such as some
women of the middle class would perhaps find harmonious with
their own.' Does he not feel just a little too sure that very many of
the middle class, and a still larger number of the working class, are
even now quite ready for the change, and only need the way pointing out? Does he not know – and may not any who will only look
plainly see – that there are thousands upon thousands of women
who are more than wearied by their long, long waiting for justice,
ever and still ever deferred? whose spirits are goaded on to the very
verge of hate for their oppressors, their warm and often too-gener-
ous hearts surcharged and oppressed by the scorn they cannot help
but feel for the despicable cowardice that heartlessly tramples upon
their dearest rights, and wantonly insults both their understanding
and their feelings, solely because – shall I say it? – because they are
women! and are therefore supposed to be less able to defend themselves physically than if they were of the other sex? Need I give
proofs? Take up any newspaper, daily or weekly, and you will find
plenty of them. Read the Revising Barristers' replies to the women's
demands for the franchise, some of which are positively a disgrace
to the age, with all our boasted enlightenment and so-called civilisation! And if these are not enough, then read the *Saturday Review*. Do
we not find it common to add insult to injury, where only women
are the sufferers?

269

What, I ask, short of Co-operation, will remedy this state of things? Without it will the generality of men ever become more generous? The very fact of a woman depending upon a man for her daily bread gives him a power over her he could not otherwise acquire; and in all but the very best natures the man is thereby rendered egotistical, conceited, and unjust. We know that some men tell us they can love better those who are dependent upon them. Yes – with such love as they ought to have for children; but as men are not children, neither are women, and therefore cannot appreciate their condescension or their patronage. So long as women are brought up to look to marriage for their future homes and means of subsistence, and men to seek out wives to minister to their little comforts – many of them not blushing to ask their wives to brush their shoes – is it any wonder that the offspring of such false unions should prove the selfish beings we usually find them? In their turn, as falsely educated, the boys generally become ludicrously pompous and offensive; the girls too often mere slaves or hypocrites, not unfrequently miserable, sometimes perfectly reckless, caring little for anything but change – a natural consequence of the anomalous position they occupy; for they feel they could do so much, and might be, oh, so different!

I repeat, then, Co-operation is most wanted in domestic affairs; for do we not know that half-a-dozen women, with the proper means and appliances, could cook for a whole community of 1,000 or 2,000 persons with much greater ease and pleasure than each woman now cooks for her own separate family. The washing, cleaning, sewing, and all other domestic drudgery, may be just as easily disposed of by Co-operation and machinery. Then think of the amount of wasted energy and labour under the present system. Sum up, if you can, this annual loss of wealth to society; and let the women more especially remember how much time would be at their disposal for higher and more ennobling employments. The better training of their children would, of course, become a special object of interest. And again – by such combination or Co-operation, with what ease this might be effected. The fine arts would no longer be neglected, neither would any useful invention that would lighten labour or add to the general good. Besides taking their full share in all the duties and responsibilities of life, as nature intended them to do, women would so help each other to enjoy life, instead of, as at present, wasting their energies, and doing violence to their common sense, by vieing with each other in following foolish fashions on the one hand, and on the other, looking up to and waiting on the men; while it is only requisite for themselves to unite and lead the way.

Alice Wilson.

Manchester.

Document 10

'Roughness' and 'respectability'. *Source*: J.K. Walton and A. Wilcox (eds), *Low Life and Moral Improvement in Mid-Victorian England: Liverpool through the Journalism of Hugh Shimmin* (Leicester, 1991), pp. 41–4, 239–43

1   AN HOUR IN A GROG SHOP

There is not one of these – not one – but sows a harvest which mankind *must* reap. Open and unpunished murder in a city's streets would be less guilty in its daily toleration than one such spectacle as this. – *Dickens*

How bitterly cold it is! How keenly the wind swirls through the narrow court! There are no sounds of revelry there now. Doors are shut, windows are stuffed. Here and there a shimmering gleam lights up a snow-rimed window sill. An hour ago, mother and children crouched around the small fire, and footsteps were eagerly listened for. It is Saturday night. Father is expected home with the wages. The remains of the thin candle have sunk in the socket of the iron holder. It is no use applying at 'the little shop' for anything more now; as 'a clean book' cannot be shown. The children, wearied out, fall asleep. Mother throws over them what rags she can muster, and taking her youngest child to her bosom, and covering it as she best can with her tattered shawl, she steals out, gently drawing the door after her, and is now off in search of her husband.

From four houses out of six in this court, on this night, *seven* wives have gone to look for their husbands. The men are shipsmiths. In two instances, for months at a stretch, the weekly earnings of these men amounted to *ninety shillings*! – yes, often have they drawn five pounds a week; and yet they had scarcely a decent article of furniture in their houses, and nothing worthy the name of a bed to lie down upon.

Would you know how this state of things came to pass? Would you cease to theorise for a time, and *stoop* to look at facts? Follow then one of these wives; keep close up with her as she hurries along.

271

Stand behind her as she pushes open the gin-palace door, by pressing the body of her babe against it! Look there! look there at the bright lights, the costly decorations, the beaming visages behind the bar, the steaming mixtures which are handed to the jabbering crowd, and think of the dark court, the dull misery-stricken house; the wife lean and vixenish, the children pallid and ragged. Can you see any connection between these?

One brazen door after another is pushed open – no husband is met with. Crossing Scotland-place you hear this: 'Haven't you found him? I found my chap, and good-humoured enough he was, too, for once. I got more than I expected from him; come and have two pennoth.' With compressed lips, from which bitter curses have just issued, muttering wrathful imprecations, and threatening vengeance, is it surprising that the shipsmith's wife yields to the solicitation of her neighbour? They go to have 'two pennoth'; and in this locality, as in many others, they have not far to go in order to reach a gin shop. Oh! what thanks are due to the magistrates for the kindness and consideration shown in providing these refreshment houses for their humble brethren! Oh! what paeans of praise will flow forth from wives driven to desperation, and children driven to crime, in consequence of the facilities afforded to their protectors for dallying with this body- and soul-destroying vice!

'Have a glass, Mary, have a glass; two pennoth is right enough when you can't get more, but have a *glass* now, it'll do you good this cold night. Dick, two glasses of whiskey.'

The young man thus familiarly addressed smilingly complies with the request, and the women toss off the drink before one can see who surrounds them. They have a good deal of talk before they think of going further, and their threats of vengeance are hurled about. At the door they meet a tall, swarthy man, whom they recognise, and elicit from him, after much to do, as the creature is far gone in drink, that 'Bill is tossing for quarts of ale at ——.' Away the women go. It is not far off, come along with them.

At the door of every gin shop which had been passed, stood puny young shivering children, in filth and tatters. 'Please give me a 'apenny,' or 'please buy a box of matches,' uttered in a drawl, first called attention to these sorrowful and pitiful objects. And no one who felt the weight, worth and influence of home – no one who gazed on the blear eyes, wan faces and stunted forms of children driven by parents to wear out their lives in such a manner – no one who had not torn off rudely the tender silken cords of a mother's love, which had been twined round the heart in infancy and childhood, and even yet, in vigorous manhood, vibrate when touched –

no man, with right conceptions of the duties, obligations, responsibilities and hopes of life, could witness such scenes without fully endorsing the burning words of Charles Dickens: – 'There is not one of these – not one – but sows a harvest which mankind *must* reap. Open and unpunished murder in a city's streets would be less guilty in its daily toleration than one such spectacle as this.'

After a slushing tramp, we reach one of the largest, and certainly the most costly vaults in the town, and it is now, every department of it, filled with dirty, ragged, miserable-looking men, women and children. The wife, fired with whiskey, and tightening her shawl around her babe, goes from division to division; at length she sees the object of her search – her husband, the smut of the forge never removed from his face. He is engaged in 'tossing' who pays for all.

'Two out of three, or sudden death,' roars the half-maddened mechanic.

'Sudden death,' is the reply.

'That's the style – no two ways,' says a bystander.

'I'll give you sudden death!' screams out the wife; and a torrent of indescribable abuse is hurled upon her husband and his companions, as if there and then the awful threat were being put into execution. This has the effect of interrupting the lively and profitable game to which many workmen devote some portion of their time and their money on Saturday evenings – tossing for quarts. Of course there are 'sponges' around, who fawn and flatter, in order that they may be permitted to imbibe their share of the quarts; so that what a man spends on drink for himself is a very small proportion to what he squanders on others.

The woman wearies herself in a little while with foul speech and idle threats, and when her volubility subsides, the husband and she become more reconciled. She 'takes a drop of something hot', has some money doled out to her, and in half an hour, or less, she is gone to market – to the shop – to her home and her children. But her husband is still at the bar of the vaults. He has been here two hours; and here we will stay a while with him.

Leaving for a time the smith and his companions lighting their pipes and preparing to dispose of 'another quart', come on into the next compartment. Seven women are here, forming two groups; some have bonnets on and baskets with them, and all are very talkative. The presence of a stranger in nowise disconcerts them, nor interferes with their conversation; on the contrary, they seem to like it, and, as a cigar which we have asked for does not seem to be forthcoming, a very stout woman in a cotton bedgown, loosely worn, her hair matted and twisted about her head, takes up a pint pot and says, 'You luk as if a spot of hot fourpenny ud do you good – here tek a sup.' This calls forth a roar of laughter from the groups, and is joined in heartily by the ruddy-faced waiter with the pork pie hat, who had looked suspiciously on us several times before. Fire of this sort soon exhausts itself, if it be borne coolly, and the women become friendly and very communicative. We soon know who their husbands are, what they earn, what they spend, and what they 'allow for the house'. We are told their peculiarities, their weaknesses, their loves, and likings; and one woman volunteers a statement, that if we wish to hear a good song, we must hear her husband, who is now at the *Goose Club*, where there is a 'free and easy'.

A little girl, without shoes, scarcely any garments on her, comes in with a quart jug destitute of handle. She places the jug on the marble counter, and has to stand on tip-toe to do this. She then places the money beside it, and never utters a word! The women recognise her, and speak very cheeringly to the tattered child, who replies to their questions, and then stares wildly around at the gilded cornices – the panels – the ceiling – the chandeliers – so glittering and bright. In the meantime the waiter has taken away the jug and half filled it – has swept the coppers into the till – and with a shout of 'There you are, Kitty,' pushes the jug towards where the child stands, and then proceeds to supply 'four two-pennoths' which are being bawled out for by some men in the next compartment. There was a slight expression of pity on two of the women's faces, as they looked on the child creeping out, shivering with cold, and carrying a pint of ale to its mother!

Through one division after another we roamed for an hour – girls, boys, women, old men, robust villains, slender mechanics, oyster men, stay-lace women, dog fanciers, street musicians, a comic vocalist ready to entertain a group with song or recitation for 'a drink' – all these were met with. Some were drunk and raving, others were in that dangerous state said to be 'ready for anything'; loungers slouched about, leering wistfully at working men, whom they saw draw money from their pockets to pay for drink; and when we reached the smith again, he was being ejected from the place for using abusive language to the barman. None were more active in thrusting the man out than he who had taken his money, supplied him with drink, and thus instigated him to commit a breach of the peace. What oaths these men hurled at each other; and when we saw the smith skulk away from the policeman who had been called in to protect the dandy barman – the thought crossed us, What about this man's wife? What about his children? 'There is not one of these – not one – but sows a harvest which mankind *must* reap. Open and unpunished murder in a city's streets would be less guilty in its daily toleration than one such spectacle as this.'

32 AN HOUR IN A CO-OPERATIVE STORE

Last week the improvidence of working men was illustrated by describing 'An hour in a Grog Shop,' the aim is now to shew the providence of working men by a visit to the Co-operative Store. Dick Stubbs with his stout cheerful little wife, and what he calls his 'big little family', live in a neat cottage house in Toxteth Park. It is a picture of domestic happiness to see Dick, after he has had his tea, rolling about the floor playing with his children. Of course his wife 'fairly dies' with laughing at them, and of course his wife, children, and home are all the world to Dick. But Dick was once 'a wastrel', he was not a great drunkard, but he took 'a good sup', and this made him indifferent to home joys, reckless, and improvident. Dick likes to tell how 'his eyes were opened', and on this point a week or two ago we heard him in very plain terms declare how much working men might do to help themselves, if they would only practice a little self-denial, and said he, 'Come to the Store any Saturday night and see for yourself. We make no bounce. We spend no money in advertising; we don't *palm* the papers to report even our annual meeting at length. We work hard, but don't *talk* much; and you'll not be likely to know much about us, unless you come and see.'

Such were the concluding remarks of Dick Stubbs, with whom we had been conversing on work men's savings and work men's earnings. Co-operation was his great panacea for the healing of the nation's social wounds; and he was zealous and truthful in his advocacy of it. Being thoroughly convinced, by practical experience, that anything which will tend to the formation of provident habits amongst working people, must ultimately prove extremely beneficial, we readily accepted the invitation to spend an hour on a Saturday evening in the Co-operative Store, in Camden-street.

Most people have heard of the Co-operative Associations of Rochdale, of Leeds, and of other manufacturing towns; but with reference to Liverpool, it is much as our friend says, the mere existence of the society is little known, certainly not as much as it ought to be. What the association aims at is, 'The improvement of the social and domestic condition of the members, by raising a sufficient amount of capital to establish a store for the sale of provisions, clothing, &c., to the members only.'

The Liverpool Co-operative Provident Society has, for the convenience of its members, branches in different parts of the town. In the South, Warwick-street; in the North, Virgil-street; and in the East, Lord-street, Edge-hill. These branches are open on stated nights in each week, and are supplied with goods packed up and ready for delivery, from the Central Store, Camden-street.

The capital is raised by shares of £1 each; and each member is required to take not less than five, nor permitted to hold more than £100. The payment is brought within the means of any working man, being not less than threepence per week for every five shares. There is an entrance fee of one shilling. Thus, *any who can pay this entrance fee, and who can contrive to save threepence per week, may become a member*, and is at once entitled to the advantages which the store offers for the purchase of good, and, so far as the vigilance of the officers can secure, unadulterated groceries, clothing, &c., with honest measure and weight, at a fair and reasonable price.

To shew the progress made by the association, a few figures only are necessary. In 1851 there were 34 members, the capital was £60, and the receipts on sales amounted to £317. In 1860, there were 1,200 members, the capital was £2,200, and the receipts £15,000. The magnitude of the operations involves the employment of a manager and permanent staff in the Central Store; and it is gratifying to learn, that after defraying the cost of management, and paying five per cent. per annum to the members upon their accumulated capital, a sum has always been left to be divided amongst the members to the extent of their purchases, the average profit being about 1*s*. 4*d*. in the pound.

But, we can fancy a working man saying on reading this, 'It may be all very well, but instead of a dry yarn why don't you tell us how the system works, that's what I want to know.' Well, have patience, my hearty. Here is Dick Stubbs and his wife coming along Lime Street, with the intention of getting the week's supply of groceries, and some 'extra goods' at the Central Store in Camden Street, let us join them and Dick or his wife (she is the talker) will soon show how the system works.

To reach this Central Store Dick and his wife have walked from Toxteth Park, and they have on their way passed the doors and flaming lights of *forty-three* public houses! No small temptation for a working man, on a bitter cold night, with money in his pocket and not very thickly clad. But Dick has found that he cannot eat a cake and have it, and he is so far on the right track as to forego present pleasure for future good. He could easily have spent three or four weekly subscriptions to the Store fund whilst walking this distance. Three two pennorths of rum for himself and wife would have amounted to four weeks' subscription, and this would be considered a very 'small Saturday night allowance' by hundreds of men and women.

Business is brisk at the Store – the manager and assistants seem hard at work supplying the wants of working people in the way of groceries and provisions. The place is not very well lighted, neither are the fittings of the recognised fancy class. Whilst setting themselves boldly against any useless expenditure in this way, it would be a great mistake if the committee should go to the other extreme. Utility and neatness may be combined without extravagance and there *is* an educational effect to be secured by this means whatever people may say to the contrary. The gradual expansion of the business has something to do with the awkward appearance of the shelves and the mode in which they are 'pieced out' sets all conventionality at defiance. On the one side, butter, bacon, cheese, &c., are being disposed of, at the other tea, coffee, sugar, &c.

Here is Dick's stout little wife; she brings with her a list of articles which she requires, this she hands to one of the assistants, together with her pass book, and her goods will be looked out. Some of them, (such as butter, cheese, &c.,) she selects – the amount will be entered in her book, and her list be filed as a check on the storekeepers. The list of articles is printed and supplied by the society, and the working man or his wife can fill in the quantity of each article they require at their leisure and at home. Cash is paid for all groceries.

But whilst we have been looking about this lower room of the Store, we have observed women, most of them very neatly and comfortably dressed, leave their orders and pass up stairs. We learn that they are bent on a supply of 'extra goods', and we follow them. Here is a really fine room, well fitted, neatly arranged, the goods tastefully displayed, and an air of solid comfort and substantiality, which is very pleasing and suggestive. This is the drapery department, and women seem very much at home here. Husbands are standing by, whilst the home comforts for wives and children are being measured and chosen. The stock comprises everything in the way of clothing which working people require, and the go-to-meeting suits for both sexes seem to have received due consideration. This department was set on foot to counteract the rapacity of 'Scotchmen', whose dealing with working men's wives have earned for them such unenviable notoriety. In a few weeks these co-operatives will have, in the rooms above the drapery department, shoemakers at work, and will manufacture their shoes on the premises; indeed there seems to be hardly any limit to the extent to which they may push their operations, if they be conducted with the same sagacity and prudential foresight, which would appear to have secured their progress thus far.

But the term 'extra goods' requires explanation. In most Co-operative Stores cash payment is required for every article, and purchases may be made by the general public. In this, the sales are confined to members, and *credit is given on 'extra goods'*. That is, articles of clothing or coals. Here is our friend Dick. He has paid up five shares, of one pound each, and is therefore in a position to obtain four pounds worth of extra goods on credit. His wife may have a good shawl, frocks and flannel for the children, and he may have a pair of shoes or whatever he stands most in need of; or he may have a couple of tons of coals, and his repayments must be made at the rate of one shilling per week. And mark, there is no interest charged for this; if he pays up his instalments regularly he receives his full share at the division of profits. This is a feature novel in Co-operative Societies, and if it can be successfully worked, may, in many cases prove extremely useful.

But as we see it, the great advantages of a society of this nature, beyond the obtaining provisions of good quality, weight, and measure, is to be found in the facilities which it offers for *saving*. It requires a great effort on the part of a working man or his wife to save at all. Now here is a fulcrum which gives the *start* and makes the progress steady and easy. When a man has five pounds in, he feels a degree of independence to which thousands are strangers; and besides, should any misfortune occur, the cash is always attainable for use; indeed it is not an unusual thing, as the manager told us, to find workmen at pressing periods withdrawing their money to meet extra demands made upon them. It may be that many members of the society could be steady, frugal, and industrious without any such aids, but numerous cases were given which go to show the Co-operative Association has been mainly instrumental in *raising men and their families*, socially and morally, and this from what has been shewn can be easily understood.

From reflection on the hour spent in this store we are firmly of opinion that if all working men could be induced to concern themselves about the *right use* of wages as much as some are led to concern themselves about the *rate*, they would be placed in a more manly, honourable, and independent position, and might then *possess* what now they in many cases only *talk* about.

But if all have not learned true wisdom on this matter, it is pleasant to know that some have. The Tortoise clumsily built, awkward in its movements, perseveringly travelled on whilst the Hare, its boastful opponent, slept. In like manner, whilst Social Science philosophers after their boastful talk, are sleeping, a few working men – men with little to say, and 'small very' to look at, have passed them by, and so far as solving what is termed the great problem of Social Economy is concerned – have won the race. All honor to such men, and success to the Camden-street Co-operatives!

Document 11

Employer 'driving', 'free' labour and trade union 'coercion'. *Source*: *Textile Mercury*, 22 September 1894

ALLEGED 'DRIVING' IN WEAVING SHEDS

(To the Editor of *The Textile Mercury*.)

Sir, – As this subject appears to be occupying to a large extent, if not actually agitating, the minds of a large number of Lancashire weaving operatives, and as there is manifestly a great deal of misapprehension thereon, it has been thought advisable to address a few lines for insertion in your valuable paper with the hope of elucidating the matter, and thereby creating a state of affairs wherein employer and employed may work together for common good. No one at this time of day will require to be told that competition compels the manufacturer to carefully watch every detail of the various operations in his mill, and to see that no leakage or waste of material takes place therein. It is also of equal importance that there should be no superfluous hands, nor what is known as fitting square pegs in round holes. Added to all this, it is necessary that the workpeople should be as highly skilled as possible; and a certain degree of competency is absolutely necessary. To make the latter point quite clear, it is only requisite to remember that all the fixed charges in a mill or shed, such as interest on capital, or rent, rates, and taxes, and the like, have to be paid, whatever amount of production is obtained therefrom, and that there is a minimum production per loom which becomes a *sine quâ non* of a paying manufacturing concern, whatever the state of trade may be. It is perfectly true that this minimum will vary with the percentage of profits, but this in recent times has become so small that the average production can no longer be neglected.

At the present time the disparity between what may be termed the best and the worst weavers in a loom-shed is greater than perhaps in any other period in the history of weaving. Personally, we believe this to be the result of many weavers of the present generation having been very imperfectly trained, owing in a great measure to the fact of more perfect and automatic machinery being employed, which has tended to render many operatives to a large extent careless of their own technical development. The consequence is that the disparity before named produces a corresponding variation in the amount of wages earned by different weavers in the same shed with precisely the same kind of work. Not only does the inferior weaver earn less money, but he or she is compelled to go through a far greater amount of personal labour and discomfort than another who may be earning twice the amount. Indeed, it may be said that in weaving on piecework (and the remark is probably equally true in any other trade) the wages will be somewhere about in inverse ratio to the bodily labour bestowed. This to an outsider may appear somewhat paradoxical, but it comes about in this wise: The greatest quantity of cloth produced is when the fewest stoppages from broken yarn or other causes occur. The good weaver is nearly always simply watching the looms driving along; on the other hand, the inferior weaver is mostly to be found, with several looms stopped, piecing ends, the breakage of the threads being in most cases the result of inattention. This involves not only small production and consequent low wages, but also very defective pieces of cloth, as every stoppage for such purpose practically means a fault, of greater or less importance, as the case may be.

Now, a weaver of the incompetent class referred to naturally feels worried when any pressure, however gentle, is brought to bear upon him or her with a view of bringing the standard of produce ion nearer to that of better-trained comrades; and, instead of dealing with this difficulty in its true light, a certain section have begun to propagate the idea of what they term 'driving' in weaving sheds on the part of the manufacturer. They imagine that their employers desire to drive them to work under slavish conditions, to the detriment of their health and comfort, forgetting that such a state of affairs would be utterly detrimental to the interests of any manufacturer. And it is absurd to conclude that any manufacturer in these days would either desire or feel it advantageous to stoop to such a course of procedure. On the other hand, what the manufacturer does wish, and doubtless has a right to expect, is that a reasonable average production per loom, as well as the standard of quality, should be kept up; and surely all workpeople and manufacturers alike must strive to achieve this result, unless we are to loose our place amongst manufacturing communities. To this end we beg to suggest a simple and rational solution of the difficulties of the second or third rate weaver – whether that classification results from general incompetency, from ill-health, or from natural slowness of disposition – which would not be objected to, so far as we know, by the manufacturer, and yet at the same time would remover all appearance of what is called 'driving.'

At the present moment the best weavers, with the assistance of a 'tenter,' work six looms, and all the others are, of course, ambitious to do the same thing, but for one reason or another they cannot obtain an equal average production. Let them, therefore, be content to weave with four or a less number of looms, by which means, considering they will be able to discard the services of the 'tenter,' they will have better opportunity for concentrating their attention upon the less number of looms, and their wages will not only be no less than at present, but probably substantially increased, while at the same time the quality of their work will be improved.

This remedy for what is termed 'driving' is exceedingly simple, and we believe would be to the mutual advantage of all concerned; and we most cordially invite the trade-union officials to co-operate in advising this course to be followed. They may do this all the more readily for the reason that it may be made a stepping-stone for the advancement of even the most incompetent or weakly weavers; as by this means the incompetent will have opportunities of improvement, and the weak a chance of regaining their health and strength; after either of which events the management of a greater number of looms can be again resorted to.

In conclusion, we would like to point out that the difference between a highly competent and a very poor weaver consists almost wholly in the one having a careful regard to minute trifles or technical details, which the other, unfortunately, does not think worth attention. Perhaps one of the most important of these trifles is the condition of the shuttles employed, the least roughness, or scarcely-to-be-observed crack or splinter in them – especially in some classes of goods – being sufficient to keep a weaver employed in piecing ends for a whole afternoon. In like manner, a trifling disarrangement of the weft-fork, an undue weighting of the warp-beam, a too tight or too greasy driving-strap, unnecessarily hard picking resulting from short picking bands, and numerous little things of that character, will, to the non-observant weaver, cause great hindrances. Weavers should not forget that little difficulties with regard to shuttles are more common nowadays, inasmuch as the good old boxwood of former times is not so available for shuttle-making, and any other wood, unless it is rendered artificially hard by compression, is very liable to develop minute chips of a detrimental character. Indeed, if they will carefully watch and tend their shuttles, they will do a very great deal to avoid what they now fancy to be 'driving' in a weaving shed. – Yours, etc,

ROBERT PICKLES, Limited.

Cairo Mills, Burnley, September 17.

FREE LABOUR AND TRADE-UNIONISM.

In the annual report of the executive of the National Free Labour Association, which will be presented at the annual conference to be held in October (having been postponed from Monday last, the date originally fixed for the gathering), some statistics are given concerning the present position of free labour in Great Britain. It is stated that up to the end of August last no fewer than 228,000 seamen had been registered as free labour men, and a large number of these were known to have previously belonged to 'Wilson's Union.' In the metropolitan docks the demand for free labour tickets has been so great that it has been necessary to limit their issue according to the actual number of men for whom employment could be found. 'The aggressive attitude of Messrs. Burns, Mann, Tillett, and Wilson, with their "new unionism," has,' the report proceeds, 'resulted in their utter defeat, and has converted Southampton, Plymouth, Cardiff, and Dublin, as well as Hull, into free labour ports.'

Discussing the present strength of the trade-unionists, the report says that out of 9,786,073 male persons of 20 years of age or over, who are working for their living in the United Kingdom, only 1,109,014 are members of trade unions, leaving 8,677,059 to be described as free labour men, non-unionists, 'blacklegs,' 'scabs,' 'knobsticks,' or anything else but trade-unionists. Since the great dock strike 'persistent and cruelly unjust efforts' have been made to force unwilling men to join the trade societies, many of which are run on purely party grounds or to further the socialistic schemes of the union leaders. 'But what success,' the report continues, 'has attended the efforts of Mr. John Burns? The voluntary and compulsory additions to trade unions between the 1891 and the 1892 returns left a total of 18,000 less than the desertions. The numerical strength of the unions has gone back in spite of his great efforts, and confidence in the management of the agitators and self-seekers has been shaken among those who remain true – voluntarily, or under dread of the consequences. We believe in the need of combination, but not in the 11 per cent. being allowed to coerce 89 per cent. of the workmen of the country.'

The report also deals with the question as to what effect trade-unionism has on the trade of the country, and on this point it says: – 'The value of fixed capital laid idle by the strikes in various trades during 1891 amounted £9,493,000. But the most fearful indications of the evil wrought by strikes which occurred in 1891, 1892, and 1893, are shown by the exports from Great Britain during the three quarters of each of those years ending September 30. The totals were – in 1891, £187,475,396; in 1892, £170,480,788; in 1893, £165,393,621, or a difference of nearly £22,000,000 between 1891 and 1893.' Notwithstanding this diminution in production, the bill of the nation for food and drink imported has, the report adds, not stood still, or diminished, but, on the contrary, has increased, and Great Britain has been paying this bill, not out of income from material produced, but out of capital.

The following manifesto, dealing with the recent Trade Union Congress, has been prepared by the National Free Labour Association, and will be issued in the course of a few days: –

'After the series of ridiculous farce enacted at the late Trade Union Congress at Norwich, we invite your attention to the policy now entered upon by the leaders of the "new" trade-unionism, and ask you to compare their wild theories with the sturdy common-sense of the well-tried and veteran Labour leaders who have served you so well in the past.

'At the recent congress at Norwich the following resolution was actually passed: –

' "That, in the opinion of this congress, it should be made a penal offence for an employer to bring to any locality extra labour, when the existing supply was sufficient for the needs of the district."

'Now, we ask you to consider the full meaning of this insolent demand. (*a*) It means that no employer will be able to give you work unless you belong to a trade union. (*b*) It means that no British workman shall be free to work, except he receives the precious permission of the trade-union officials. (*c*) It means that an insidious attempt is being made to coerce you into joining the trade unions.

'But that is not all! The congress, which professed to have for its object the freedom of labour, has a curious idea of that policy, for it resolves to urge upon the Government the advisability of reintroducing the Employers' Liability Bill, with the clause which forbids workmen to make better terms with their employers than he Law Courts would enable them to do.

'Fellow workmen, we do not think you will call this freedom; we thing you will call this tyranny, and that, too, in one of its worst forms.

'Has now every workman the right to make terms with his employer as to insurance against accidents? We think you will say, Yes, undoubtedly; but the trade-union officials say, No, let us destroy these mutual insurance societies in order that we may wield more power over the destinies of their members. And we therefore maintain that a congress of trade – union officials which advocates the passing of a measure forbidding "contracting-out" has no right to profess to champion the rights of labour, but that it has grossly misrepresented the opinions of the vast majority of the working classes.

'Evidently wishing to cap these demands with something more ridiculous still, the congress passed a resolution affirming the deairability of nationalishing, not only the land, mines, and railways, but all the means of production, as if there were the slightest chance of this wild dream ever being realised. If newspapers had been included in the list of things the congress wished to nationalise, would not there have been a tremendous outcry raised by those journals which are at the present moment engaged in supporting these trade-union officials? And yet there is far more sense in the theory of nationalising the Press that in that of nationalising the land and its minerals.'

Document 12

Accommodation between capital and labour (a) Presentation to a Manchester employer. *Source: Typographical Circular* (the organ of the Typographical Association), September 1899. Kindly supplied by Pat Duffy, who is researching the printing trade

On Saturday, July 22, an interesting presentation took place at the Gutenberg Works, Pendleton, the day being the 70th birthday of the proprietor, Alderman James F. Wilkinson, J.P., C.C. The works were closed at noon, and the employés met together in the warehouse, which had been tastefully arranged for the occasion. Mr. R.H. Bowman (manager) took the chair, and was supported by Mr. H.R. Powell. Alderman Wilkinson was accompanied by Mrs. Wilkinson and Miss Wilkinson. The Chairman, in opening the proceedings, spoke of the pleasure it gave him to preside, and said what a blessing it would be if gatherings such as these could be brought together oftener between employers and employés. Mr. James Wright, who has been with the firm for 46 years, said that a great many changes had taken place during that time in the works. When he commenced, in 1853, black clouds were hanging over the place for a short time, but Mr. Wilkinson's indomitable perseverance and energy turned it to bright sunshine. Several other old hands spoke feelingly of their long and pleasant years under their employer. Mr. Powell then asked Mr. Wilkinson to accept, on behalf of the whole staff, a gold keyless $\frac{3}{4}$-plate centre-seconds watch (by Russell, of Liverpool), along with an illuminated book, signed by everyone employed in the works – over 160. Mr. Wilkinson, in response, spoke of the pleasure it gave him to meet them all. He was glad to say that, through all his long life, he had never had any difference with his workpeople, he found all in his employ did their duty, and that was the secret of everything working smoothly. Speaking of the establishment he hoped it would continue to prosper and grow, and ever keep to the standard of its motto – 'Praestantia et celeritas' (highest excellence with speed). He thanked them heartily for the beautiful watch, which would remind him, whenever he looked at it, not only of the present occasion, but it would ever tell him that the sands of time were slowly but surely passing along. Mrs. Wilkinson and Miss Wilkinson also addressed the meeting.

Document 13

Accommodation between capital and labour (b) Trade negotiations. *Source*: G.P. Reviers, 'Recollections drawn from Sixty-two Years in the Printing Craft', *Monotype Recorder*, 32:4 (winter 1933). Kindly supplied by Pat Duffy. T.E. Naylor was chair of the London Labour Party and later MP

The Labour Leaders I have met are shrewd, able men, who can state their case well. They hold their briefs from their constituents, and whether they agree with them or not, nobody can tell, for they fight the case as though they did. They are absolutely loyal in their advocacy, although I am sure (knowing the men) they cannot always agree with their instructions.

For about three years negotiations were proceeding over the London Piece Scale for 'Monotype' Composition. The Committee of the London and Home District Monotype Users' Association, of which I am Chairman, acted as a Sub-Committee of the Labour Committee of the London Master Printers Association in this matter, and it was my duty to preside over the meetings. Every point was carefully discussed by both sides, and many times we reached a temporary deadlock; but we never lost our tempers on either side of the Table. The difficulties were very great, owing to the small amount of reliable information as to output. That produced by Mr. Cahusac and Mr. Chaney was not only valuable, but reliable, and its accuracy was not challenged by the other side. They did, however, claim it to be exceptional. We fought for a long time over the price per thousand, and, finally, it was decided to leave the solution of that problem until the end with a view to each side having plenty of time for investigation and consideration. We then discussed the scale, clause by clause, line by line, and one clause would often take more than half a day. We adopted the plan of first passing by any clause upon which agreement could not be reached and accepting those we could accept, after a little give-and-take. Thus a certain amount of headway was always being made. Having got through the scale in this fashion, we came back to the contentious clauses one by one. The intervals between the meetings gave both sides an opportunity of considering the other man's point of view, and, what is more, saved either side from getting too heated over the arguments. It enabled us to maintain that good feeling which is so desirable. Gradually, agreement was reached, except for the price per 1,000.

Both sides put up a suggested figure, and the matter was then referred back to the Labour Committee of L.M.P.A. and to the L.S.C. Neither side agreed, and the matter was sent back for further consideration. My own view, and that of my Committee, was that 4d. per 1,000 was a fair price; but the other side could not agree, and ultimately the price was fixed at $4\frac{5}{8}$d. uncorrected. After some years' experience, I still maintain my figure was the proper price to pay. To Mr. Timberlake, the Chairman, and Mr. Naylor, the Secretary, of the L.S.C., I must pay my tribute for the courtesy and ability they displayed in conducting the negotiations for their Society. I am sure they would be the first to admit that on our side of the Table there was evidenced a strong desire to be absolutely just and fair. I owe a debt of gratitude to my Committee for their assistance, especially the two gentlemen I have mentioned for the great help they gave me.

Document 14

The issue of Labour representation. *Source: Report of the Conference on Labour Representation held in the Memorial Hall, Farringdon Street, London, E.C., on Tuesday, the 27th February 1900, at Twelve o'clock (Noon), and Following Day, in accordance with the Resolution of the*

Selected documents

Trade Union Congress at Plymouth, September 1899, reprinted in *The Labour Party Foundation Conference and Annual Conference Reports 1900–1905,* Hammersmith Reprints of Source Documents 3, National Museum of Labour History, pp. 8–10, 12–13, 18

THE Conference on Labour Representation convened by the Parliamentary Committee of the Trades Union Congress, acting upon instructions given by the last Trades Union Congress at Plymouth, was opened in the Memorial Hall, London, on Tuesday, February 27th. Invitations to send delegates were issued to the Trade Unions and Co-operative Societies of the United Kingdom, the Independent Labour Party, the Social Democratic Federation, and the Fabian Society. The invitations were accepted by all the various organisations, with the exception of the Co-operative Union, who, in the absence of any mandate from their last annual conference, were unable to pledge their organisations. Preliminary meetings were held by selected representatives of the various organisations. Messrs. Woods, Steadman, Thorne, Bowerman, and Bell represented the Parliamentary Committee; Messrs. Hardie and J. Ramsay Macdonald, the Independent Labour Party; Messrs. Taylor and Quelch, the Social Democratic Federation; and Messrs. Pease and Shaw, the Fabian Society.

This Committee agreed upon the agenda, which, after alterations by the Parliamentary Committee, was issued as follows: –

AGENDA.

1. – OBJECT OF CONFERENCE.

A resolution in favour of working-class opinion being represented in the House of Commons by men sympathetic with the aims and demands of the Labour movement.

2. – LABOUR MEMBERS IN THE HOUSE OF COMMONS.

A resolution in favour of establishing a distinct Labour Group in Parliament, who should have their own Whips and agree upon their policy, which must embrace a readiness to co-operate with any party which, for the time being, may be engaged in promoting legislation in the direct interest of labour, and be equally ready to associate themselves with any party in opposing measures having an opposite tendency.

3. – CONSTITUTION OF COMMITTEE.

The Executive Committee shall consist of twelve representatives from Trade Unions, ten from the Co-operative Societies, providing they are represented as a body at the Conference, two from the Fabian Society, two from the Independent Labour Party, and two from the Social Democratic Federation. Such members shall be elected by their respective organisations.

4. – DUTY OF COMMITTEE AT ELECTIONS.

In the case of elections, the Executive Committee appointed for this purpose should collect information respecting candidates pledged to support the policy of the Labour Group, and recommend the United Labour Party to support them.

5. – DUTY OF COMMITTEE.

This Committee should keep in touch with Trade Unions and other organisations, local and national, which are running Labour candidates.

6. – FINANCIAL RESPONSIBILITY.

The Committee shall administer the funds which may be received on behalf of the organisation, and each body shall be required to pay 10s. per annum for every 1,000 members, or fraction thereof; also, that it shall be responsible for the expenses of its own candidates.

7. – REPORTING TO CONGRESS, ETC.

It should also report annually to the Trades Union Congress and the annual meetings of the national societies represented on the Committee, and take any steps deemed advisable to elicit opinion from the members of the organisations to which the Committee is ultimately responsible.

8. – STANDING ORDERS GOVERNING THE CONFERENCE.

BASIS OF REPRESENTATION.

Societies, by whatever name they may be know, shall be entitled to one delegate for every 2,000 members or fraction thereof; and they must pay ten shillings for each delegate attending the Conference, and forward their names and addresses seven days prior to the date fixed for the meeting. No credential card shall be issued to any society not having complied with the foregoing conditions.

VOTING.

(1) The method of voting shall be by card, to be issued to the delegates of trade societies according to their membership, and paid for (as per Standing Order) on the principle of one card for every

1,000 members or fractional part thereof represented. (2) Such cards to be issued to delegates by the Secretary to the Parliamentary Committee before the meeting of the Conference.

There were altogether 129 delegates present, representing 568,177 organised workers.

REPORT.

OPENING PROCEEDINGS.

Mr. J.T. Chandler (Manchester), who, in his capacity as chairman of the Parliamentary Committee, presided at the opening of the proceedings, said the Parliamentary Committee had convened the Conference in accordance with instructions given them by a resolution passed at Plymouth. The object of that resolution was very clear. It was hoped by its movers that this Conference might be able to devise some scheme whereby they could unite the various forces of the Labour organisations throughout the country in a determination to focus their efforts upon the return of a much larger number of members of Parliament in sympathy with the Labour cause and prepared consistently and persistently to advocate it in that assembly. In giving effect to the resolution the Committee felt it would be a great advantage to the Conference if before the meeting they were able to ascertain the views of several of the Labour organisations which would be invited to take part in the proceedings. Consequently they communicated with the Co-operative Union, the Independent Labour Party, the Social Democratic Federation, and the Fabian Society. The Co-operators were unable to see their way to take part in that meeting, owing, as he understood it, to their moving in the direction of Parliamentary representation in their own particular way; but the other three organisations sent representatives to meet the Parliamentary Committee, and they discussed the situation and devised practically the outlines of the scheme upon which in their wisdom they thought the Conference ought to proceed. It was not expected that the outline of a scheme which they had before them would in any way bind the Conference. This was submitted to a full meeting of the Parliamentary Committee, and certain amendments and alterations were made before the scheme was issued in its present form. He could only express a hope that the outcome of their deliberations would be that they would evolve a scheme which would command the support of the Trade Unionists and of the nonunionists of the country, and that as a result they would have a much larger number of friends in the House of

289

Commons in the future than they unfortunately had at the present moment. (Cheers.)

Alderman WILL THORNE (Gas workers) moved that Mr. W.C. Steadman, M.P., be elected chairman of the Conference. He explained that Mr. Chandler was not a delegate to the Conference.

Mr. VOGEL (Waiters) formally seconded the proposition, which was carried unanimously.

Mr. STEADMAN, M.P., having taken the chair, said he recognised the position to be one of an important and honourable character. He was one of those Trade Unionists who believed, until the last ten years, that the workers of this country could attain their object in securing better conditions by voluntary efforts through their trade organisations. But the dispute which occurred in his own trade ten years ago for a reduction of the hours of labour had convinced him that the leaders of the advanced movement who believed in political action were right and he was wrong. (Cheers.) Therefore he was now as ready as any man to take political action to redress the grievances under which the workers suffered. He gave way to no man in his desire to see labour better represented in the House of Commons than it was to-day. They had an illustration of the need that very day. The miners had secured a good position for the Eight Hours' Mines Bill, which came on Wednesday in the House of Commons, and, while certain members were going to move and second that Bill, a large mine owner sitting in that House was down on the paper to move the rejection of that Bill. He had been a member of the House of Commons but a short time, but he had been there sufficiently long to know that every interest was represented and protected in that House (especially when privilege and monopoly were attacked) but the interest of labour. The great industrial army of the country, the men who were endeavouring to raise mankind not by the shedding of human blood, but by the peaceful conquest of the ballot-box, were the only class who were insufficiently represented in the House of Commons. He hoped the result of the conference would be a practical one. For the first time in the history of the Labour movement all sections in that movement were drawn together in that Conference, with the exception of the Co-operators, and the reason of their absence was that at their last Conference no mandate was given them to send delegates. Whether they formed a Labour Party or allied themselves to other political parties in the House of Commons, let them be represented by men of character, men who had borne the heat and burden of the day, and he hoped whatever opinions delegates might hold in dealing with the resolutions and amendments, they would deal with them in an honest and straight-forward manner. (Cheers.)

Mr. KEIR HARDIE (Independent Labour Party) moved, as a further amendment: –

RESOLUTION 2.

That this conference is in favour of establishing a distinct Labour Group in Parliament, who shall have their own Whips, and agree upon their policy, which must embrace a readiness to co-operate with any party which for the time being may be engaged in promoting legislation in the direct interest of labour, and be equally ready to associate themselves with any party in opposing measures having an opposite tendency; ...

The amendment left no doubt as to its meaning. It aimed at the formation in the House of Commons of a Labour Party having its own policy, its own whips, and acting in all that concerned the welfare of the workers in a manner free and unhampered by entanglements with other parties. (Cheers.) Each of the affiliated organisations would be left free to select its own candidates without let or hindrance, the one condition being that, when returned to Parliament, the candidate should agree to form one of the Labour Group there, and act in harmony with its decisions. In this way they would avoid the scandal which in the past had pained earnest men on both sides of seeing Trade Unionists opposing Socialists, and *vice versa.* (Cheers.)

MR. WARDLE (Railway Servants) seconded the amendment ...

Mr. ASPINWALL (Miners) thought it would be a mistake to confine the action of the Labour members to labour questions. He wished to know where they would find a constituency in the kingdom which would return a man to the House of Commons whose action was to be confined to a few labour questions.

Mr. PETE CURRAN (Gasworkers) said it was time to have a separate Labour Party in Parliament, and for the organisations to have control of the members of that party. They found after adopting resolutions at the Trade Union Congress there were so-called Labour members ready to work with the capitalists against them in Parliament.

Mr. JOHN BURNS, M.P., said he was going to support Mr. Hardie's amendment, qualified by what he was going to say. There was a distinct Labour Group in Parliament, definitely organised for the past four or five years, of which Mr. Woods and himself were

291

Whips. They had not called themselves independent, they had not worn Trilby hats and red ties, but they had done the work. He would, however, warn the Conference against too much dictation. The Labour Party were not united on all questions. Look at the war. They were not united about that, but he was glad to say that eleven out of the twelve Labour members were dead against that. (Loud cheers.)

Mr. CLERY: A point of order. I protest against Mr. Burns introducing this kind of thing here. (Cheers.)

Mr. BURNS, resuming, said there was the Miners' Eight Hours Bill, and on the following day three Labour members would vote against it and two for it, and the other Labour members would support the two. (Cheers.) But he did not know that those three men could be excluded from the counsels of labour. (Cheers.) They were men of capacity and ability and character. (Cheers.)

Mr. TILLETT (Dockers) and Mr. DAVIS (Gasworkers) having spoken, Mr. Keir Hardie's amendment was put and carried unanimously.

The conference then adjourned until 10 the following morning.

VOTES OF THANKS.

On the proposition of Mr. KEIR HARDIE, a vote of thanks was heartily accorded to Mr. Steadman, M.P., for presiding.

The CHAIRMAN, in responding, expressed the hope that the work of the Conference would result in the consolidation of the Labour movement, so that in the near future labour would be better represented in the House of commons than it was to-day.

This concluded the business of the Conference.

Document 15

Poverty and insecurity. *Source*: C. Booth, 'Condition and Occupations of the People of East London and Hackney, 1887' *Journal of the Royal Statistical Society*, 51 (1888) 276–9, 288–9, 293–4, 305

I. – *INTRODUCTION*.

THE paper I have the honour to present to the Royal Statistical Society to-night is a continuation of that read in May last year, in which I described the population of the Tower Hamlets. I have now extended the same system of inquiry to the Hackney School Board Division (comprising the registration districts of Shoreditch, Bethnal Green, and Hackney), with its 440,000 inhabitants, and am able to deal in all with a district containing 900,000 inhabitants . . .

Before làying the tables which divide the population by occupation and class before the Society, I wish to refer again to their basis, and to state my confidence in its validity. My information is obtained from the School Board visitors. Of these there are in all 66 in the district. These men are intelligent, and without any bias that I have been able to trace. They are in daily contact with the people, and have a very considerable knowledge of the parents of the school children, and especially of the poorest among them, and of the conditions under which they live. . . .

. . . I am . . . embarrassed by the mass of my material, and by my determination to make use of no fact to which I cannot give a quantitative value. The materials for sensational stories lie plentifully in every book of our notes; but even if I had the skill to use my material in this way – that gift of the imagination which is called 'realistic' – I should not wish to use it here. Of destitution and hunger there is enough, of struggling poverty still more, and of drunkenness, brutality, and crime only too much; no one doubts that it is so. My object has been to attempt to show the relation which poverty, misery, and depravity bear to regular earnings and comparative comfort, and to describe the general conditions under which each class lives. I do not come forward with any sovereign remedy for the evils which exist. My facts have not been gathered to support any view. I claim only that, to avoid foolish action, as much as to forward wise action, it is first of all necessary to take a large view, and understand in every sense the relation which different classes bear to each other.

My arbitrary division of the people into 'poor' and 'very poor' has been criticised; but I am glad to know that the criticism comes from both sides. A great authority (Dr. Leone Levi), whose untimely death I and all of us are now grieving for, thought that with 20s. a-week a family could not be considered poor; while an evening journal 'doubts if Mr. Booth has adequately realised the struggles and privations of even the best paid of those who figure in his tables – whether he has taken account of the scantiness of their food, their clothing, their bedding,' and adds that my entire pamphlet on the Tower Hamlets 'reads too much like a complacent and comforting bourgeois statement of the situation.' In reply to both criticisms I can only say that I have tried and am trying to learn how the poor live, and have studied and am studying the manner of life of those I place above the line of poverty, but frankly admit that my knowledge is incomplete. I shall, however, return to this part of my subject, and need only say now that I see no reason to change my definition of poverty, which I will here repeat. By the word 'poor' I mean to describe those who have a sufficiently regular though bare income, such as 18s. to 21s. per week for a moderate family, and by 'very poor' those who from any cause fall much below this standard. The 'poor' are those whose means may be sufficient, but are barely sufficient, for decent independent life; the 'very poor' those whose means are insufficient for this according to the usual standard of life in this country. My 'poor' may be described as living under a struggle to obtain the necessaries of life and make both ends meet; while the 'very poor' live in a state of chronic want. It may be their own fault that this is so; that is another question, about which also I shall have something to say by and by; my first business is simply with the numbers who, from whatever cause, do live under conditions of poverty or destitution.

V. – *THE CLASSES*.

A, *The Lowest Class*, I put at nearly 11,000, or $1\frac{1}{4}$ per cent. of the population, but it must be clearly understood that these people are beyond enumeration, and mostly outside of the School Board visitors' books. I described this class in my last paper, and I need not repeat the description here.

B, *Casual Earnings*, very poor, add up almost exactly to 100,000, or $11\frac{1}{4}$ per cent. of the whole population. I beg that I may not be quoted as asserting that there are 100,000 *men* of this class. The numbers in great poverty are serious enough, without a resort to this most common form of mis-statement. Widows or deserted women and their families bring a large contingent to this class . . .

C, *Intermittent Earnings*, poor, are 74,247, or $8\frac{1}{3}$ per cent. of the whole population.

D, *Small Regular Earnings*, poor, are 128,887, or nearly $14\frac{1}{2}$ per cent. of the population. It must not be understood that the whole of these have quite regular work; but only that the earnings are constant enough to be treated as a regular income, which is not the case with the earnings of Class C. Of D and C together we have 203,134, and if we divide this number equally to represent those whose earnings are regular and irregular, which would be to place the standard of regularity a little higher than has been done in this inquiry, we should have equal numbers of each grade of poverty – 100,000 of B of casual, 100,000 of C or intermittent, and 100,000 of D or regular earnings, out of a total population of 900,000, or one-ninth of each grade.

E, *Regular Standard Earnings,* above the line of poverty, are 376,953, or over 42 per cent. of the population.

F, *Higher Class Labour,* and best paid portions of the artisans, together with others of equal means and position from other sections, amount to 121,240, or about $13\frac{1}{2}$ per cent.

G, *Lower Middle Class,* are 34,392, or nearly 4 per cent.

H, *Upper Middle Class,* are 44,779, or 5 per cent. The large proportion of the upper, as compared to the lower middle class, is entirely due to Hackney. For East London proper the figures are 32,205 for G, as against 12,387 for H.

Grouping these classes together, A, B, C and D are the classes of poverty sinking to want, and add up to 314,175, or 35 per cent. of the population, while E, F, G and H are the classes in comfort rising to affluence, and add up to 577,364, or 65 per cent. of the population.

Separating East London from Hackney, the same system of grouping gives us for East London 269,361, or 38 per cent. in poverty, against 439,314, or 62 per cent. in comfort, and for Hackney by itself 43,257, or 24 per cent. in poverty, against 139,607, or 76 in comfort.

The most poverty-stricken district (St. George's) has 23,246, or 49 per cent. in poverty, against 24,332, or 51 per cent. in comfort. It will be noted that this is also the smallest district, and it is possible that an equally large area not less poor might be found by dividing one of the larger districts.

VI.   THE QUESTION OF POVERTY.

Omitting Class A, which rather involves the question of disorder, we have Classes B, C and D as containing the true problem of poverty. I propose to study some aspects of this problem.

In the table I divide the population approximately, according to age, sex, &c., in each of these classes. Of this large total (303,196), I should say that the 100,000 of 'very poor' are at all times more or less 'in want.' They are ill-nourished and poorly clad. But of them only a percentage, and not I think a large percentage, would be said by themselves, or by any one else, to be in 'in distress.' From day to day and from hand to mouth they get along; sometimes suffering, sometimes helped, but not always unfortunate, and very ready to enjoy any good luck that may come in their way. They are, very likely, mostly improvident, spending what they make as they make it; but it has been truly said, 'the improvidence of the poor has its bright

	Very Poor.	Poor.		Total.
	B.	C.	D.	
Married men	16,705	12,822	23,110	52,637
Their wives	16,682	12,760	22,990	52,432
Unmarried men	7,195	5,505	9,955	22,655
Widows	6,495	4,119	5,776	16,390
Unmarried women	5,191	3,986	6,749	15,926
Young persons, male	4,812	3,565	6,164	14,541
" female	4,623	3,363	5,833	13,819
Children	29,000	20,880	36,032	85,912
Infants	9,359	7,247	12,278	28,884
	100,062	74,247	128,887	303,196

side. Life would indeed be intolerable were they always contemplating the gulf of destitution on whose brink they hang.'[3] Such are the very poor. Some may be semi-paupers, going into the 'house' at certain seasons, and some few receive out-door relief, but on the whole they manage to avoid the work-house. On the other hand, the 200,000 of 'poor,' though they would be much the better for more of everything, are not 'in want.' They are neither ill-nourished nor ill-clad, according to any standard that can reasonably be used. Their lives are an unending struggle, and lack comfort, but I do not know that they lack happiness.

It will be seen that just as I draw a distinction between the 'poor' and 'very poor,' so I draw one also between Poverty, Want, and Distress. Want, as I use the word, is an aggravated form of Poverty, and Distress an aggravated form of Want. The distinction is relative: I recognise a degree of poverty that does not amount to want, and a degree of want that does not amount to distress.

Taking the estimated percentages of poverty as given in the tables, and the population of 1881, we get a total of 963,943 poor in London, or, with the population of to-day as our basis, rather more than 1,000,000. This number does not include in-door paupers or other inmates of institutions.

If the proportions of Classes A, B, C, and D amongst themselves are similar in all London to what I make them in the East End, we get in round figures the following division of a population of 4,000,000, again excluding in-door paupers, &c.: –

A (loafing)	50,000	
B (casual earnings)	300,000	Classes in poverty
C (irregular „)	250,000	sinking to want
D (regular „ low pay)	400,000	
E („ standard earnings)		
F (higher class labour)		Classes in comfort
G (lower middle class)	3,000,000	rising to wealth
H (upper „)		
Total	4,000,000	

Document 16

Impressions of working-class life and leisure. *Source*: C. Booth, 'Sundays, Holidays and Amusements', in *Life and Labour of the People in London* (London, 1902), final volume, pp. 47–56

Many accounts have been given us concerning life on Sunday, both in the streets and in the homes. 'The day,' says one, speaking of his own poor neighbourhood, 'is comparatively quiet but for the costers shouting all day long in the poor streets. The shops, with few exceptions, are shut or only partly open. In the homes the men lie abed all the morning, mend rabbit hutches and pigeon lofts in the afternoon, and go for a walk in the evening. Their objection to going to church,' this witness adds, 'is stronger than ever.' 'Those of a rather better stamp take the "kids" for a ride on the tram;' and for these and some of a rather higher class too, a picture is drawn of the man in bed with his paper on Sunday morning and his wife cooking the dinner. A deacon of a Congregational church gives the following description of the people in his neighbourhood: 'They get up at nine or ten, and as he passes to his chapel he sees them sitting at breakfast half-dressed or lounging in the window reading *Lloyd's Weekly Newspaper*. After they are washed and dressed the men wait about until the public-houses open, and then stay within their doors till three o'clock, when they go home to dinner, which meanwhile the women have been preparing. At half-past twelve, as he returns from chapel after the morning service, the minister often meets women laden with baskets of provisions from the street-market near by, on their way home to cook the dinner. After dinner the men, if they have drunk much, may go to bed, but the better sort take a stroll. In the evening the young people pair off for walking out, while the elders may perhaps go to a concert or Sunday League lecture.'

Here is another more summary description: 'The church bell, they say, wakes them: they get up, adjourn to the public-house from one to three, dine soon after three, sleep, and either go again to the public-house in the evening or to the Park.' This comes from Mile End, but is echoed almost exactly from Stockwell (*vis à vis* on the map): 'Up at twelve to be ready for the "pubs.," which open at one; dinner any time between two and four, then sleep, and then off with wife and children to hear the band on the Common.'

By way of contrast I may add the account given by a Baptist minister in South London of the church-goers' Sunday: 'The evening service is best attended; families come then. In the morning the man often comes without the wife, leaving her at home to cook the dinner. Sunday dinner, the meal of the week with his people, for which all the family are gathered together, takes place between 1 and 2.30. Some children are late for Sunday school at three because dinner lasts so long. After dinner, when the children go to school, the men sleep, though this has been broken into to some extent by the men's P.S.A.* meeting lately inaugurated, to which fifty to seventy come, over a hundred being on the books. [The P.S.A. is an Evangelistic service, with instrumental and vocal music, hymns, solos and a short address.] Tea at five, and then the evening service, which all attend.'

Secular amusements on Sunday are said to have increased to such an extent as to have become a nuisance to those who like a quiet rest on that day. The brakes that drive past laden with pleasure-seekers have generally each their cornet-player, and this custom has gone so far that some suburban local authorities are making by-laws to check it.

The decent occupations, interests and pleasures encouraged, or provided, by the efforts of the 'Sunday Society' are even more directly aimed at the improvement of the uses to be made of the Sunday holiday than are the efforts of the religious bodies, and they have been rewarded with considerable success. The victory won over the narrower Sabbatarian has been attested by the success of the Society in securing the opening of public museums on Sunday afternoons. Crowded audiences of respectable non-church-doing people welcome the Sunday concerts and other entertainments offered by the National Sunday League; whilst the Sunday Lecture Society's meetings are well attended, as are also the Ethical Society's lectures and concerts. The concerts given at the Albert Hall and at the Alexandra Palace draw crowds. Moreover the clubs provide

* Pleasant Sunday Afternoon.

Sunday amusement for some thirty or forty thousand people in winter.

In the way of Sunday pleasuring much is spent on themselves alone by the men, who leave their wives and children at home. The thoughtless selfishness and indifference of men of all classes are denounced, and the consequent lack of home life is mentioned as a blot. The clergy hold the upper classes especially responsible for sapping the foundations of religion by making Sunday a day of pleasure. 'Sunday is becoming the great holiday,' said one of them, and mentioned the stream of bicyclists, but at the same time bore witness as to his own following that 'our faithful people are very faithful, and our earnest people very earnest.'

A more agreeable and perhaps quite as true a view of the life of the people is that 'Sunday is the great day for visiting; families go off to see their relations, whilst others are receiving theirs at home.' 'In the morning they do not get up in time for church; in the evening they receive or visit their friends, and in summer go to the park or the common.' With some of a different class we hear that 'Sunday is spent in lounging about or gardening, and in the evening you hear the tinkle of the piano and the mandoline.'

Holiday making is spoken of as 'one of the most remarkable changes in habits in the last ten years,' and the statement is applicable to all classes. 'The amount saved by working men is little compared to what is spent in this way' and yet, in the opinion of this witness (a superintendent of police), 'they save more than they used to.' 'The district' (says one of the Hackney clergy) 'is almost deserted on Bank Holiday. The women go off as well as the men.' 'A great change,' says another witness, 'has come over the people'; instead of 'spending so much in the public-houses, they go for 'excursions of all kinds' and the result is recognised as a distinct improvement. But it is partly in connection with this that the public-houses have acquired a new use, it having become customary for young men to take young women there, when out on pleasure together. The change of habit in holiday making has thus helped to introduce a practice that was formerly never thought of – a change in fashion as regards what it is proper to do corresponding to that as regards smoking in the streets, which fifty years ago was inadmissible. This use of the public-houses has been fostered by the fact that other places of refreshment are usually closed on general holidays as well as on Sundays, but there are some signs that a change is coming in this matter; tea rooms having been opened, as many of them certainly should be.

Excursions in brakes are without end. One of these noted consisted of sixteen vehicles, containing all the girls from some large works with their young men, as to whom all that the milkman, who was looking on, could say, was, 'Well, they dress better, but their manners are about the same.' The manager of another large works at which many girls are employed, said: 'It is useless to open the works on the day after Bank Holiday, or even for two days.' Very rarely does one hear a good word for the Bank Holidays. The more common view is that they are a curse, and, as already stated, the mischievous results from a sexual point of view due to a general abandonment of restraint, are frequently noted in our evidence. But the rough crush must act as a safeguard of a kind, although 'nothing,' says one witness, 'can surpass the scenes of depravity and indecency' that sometimes result. From other points of view, too, there is some reason to think that their establishment was a step in a wrong direction. The religious festivals at Christmas and Easter, with perhaps one national day (which among them all we have not got), make perhaps a sufficiency of fixed points. Beyond these it would certainly be far better that each trade, or each business establishment, should arrange holidays to suit its own convenience and the seasons of its work, and this freedom might even be extended to each individual. The spirit of pleasure in London does not appear to need fostering so much as wise guidance. It is only as enforcing holidays when otherwise they might not be taken at all, that the atmosphere of a general holiday may be accounted as good.

'To keep the Sabbath holy' is worth a great effort; and for this purpose Sunday labour should cease, so far as possible, but when this high reason does not apply it seems folly to plan that all, except those whose work is such that they are over pressed to meet the needs of the holiday makers, should take holiday on the same day. Those who cater for amusements, and the sellers of drink, are busier than ever; but other shops are closed very inconveniently, and it is said that though drink is always obtainable, food, too often, is not.

The closing of banks on these fixed days is inconvenient and quite unnecessary. The staff of every bank is arranged on a scale which allows for holiday absences.

The convergence on Saturday as a weekly half-holiday is on another footing, and though it may be abused, as in the case of men who spend half their week's wages before coming home, it more properly and more generally enables the wife to do her week's marketing in good time and still have leisure and money left for the evening's enjoyment; shops and markets in the poor districts and places of amusement everywhere being in full train of activity. With a richer class this half-holiday is valued as making 'week end' outings possible.

The demand for amusement is not less noticeable than that for holidays, and supply follows. To 'What shall we eat, what drink, and wherewithal shall we be clothed?' must now be added the question, 'How shall we be amused?' To this an answer has to be found. Even to the police it has presented a problem. 'What,' they ask, 'is to be done with young fellows? Every evening crowds of them come back from their work and loaf about the streets; they join in with whatever is forward, and are an embarrassment if there are no places of amusement for them to go to.'

And from something more than the police point of view, what can be made of it? 'It is a good thing for people to clean themselves up and go out,' says a vestryman of long standing, who holds that not half enough local amusement is provided, and who declines to accept as adequate the efforts of the religious bodies in this direction. Unmistakably, taste is more critical, and, beyond this, any attempt to 'improve the occasion' is resented. 'Concerts and entertainments given by the Church are poorly attended,' said a North-West London vicar, but added that if let for some benefit, when a concert of the usual music-hall type would be given, the hall was always crammed.

Passing by the ordinary mission entertainment, of which the failure is patent, and considering only professional work, there has been a great development and improvement upon the usual public-house sing-song, as to the low character and bad influence of which there are not two opinions. The story of progress in this respect may be traced in many of the existing places which, from a bar parlour and a piano, to an accompaniment on which friends 'obliged with a song,' have passed through every stage to that of music hall; the presiding chairman being still occasionally, and the call for drinks in almost every case, retained. But the character of the songs on the whole is better, and other things are offered: it becomes a 'variety' entertainment. The audiences are prevailingly youthful. They seek amusement and are easily pleased. No encouragement to vice can be attributed to these local music halls. The increase in the number, as well as size of these halls, has been rapid. The profits made by the proprietors have been great, and the favourite performers, being able to appear before a succession of audiences, passing rapidly with their repertoire from hall to hall, can be and are very highly remunerated. The performances also can be continually varied, for the supply of artistes is without end. The taste becomes a habit, and new halls are opened every year: soon no district will be without one. Then theatres follow. But meanwhile, and especially in poor neighbourhoods, the old-fashioned style of sing-song still continues in force.

In the central districts all places of amusement are very largely supported by the rich or by strangers visiting London. People from the outskirts come occasionally, but it is the music hall or theatre of their own neighbourhood that they frequent, and of which the influence has mainly to be considered. It is, perhaps, too much to ask that the influence of music halls and theatres should be positively and entirely good; at any rate no one claims that it is so. If it is not directly, or on the whole, evil, or if one can hope that it takes the place of something worse, a measure of improvement may be indicated. This can, I think, be claimed. It is not very much. A tendency in the direction of the drama, which is certainly an advance, may be noticed in music-hall performances, and it is to be regretted that questions arising from the separate licensing of play-houses should check the freedom of development in this direction amongst the halls. Excluding the dramatic pieces or 'sketches,' the production of which is hampered in this way, the attractions most usually offered are those of a low form of art or of blatant national sentiment, neither of which can be carried further without becoming worse; or of displays of physical strength and skill on the part of acrobats and gymnasts, or of performing animals; all representing, indeed, a background of patient and unwearied effort, but involving, it cannot but be supposed, not a little cruelty in the training of children and animals necessary to secure the rewards of popularity. But the 'variety' of the entertainments increases. In addition to conjuring and ventriloquism, which are old fashioned, we have now, for instance, the cinematograph and various forms of the phonograph, and there has been much development in the forms of stage dancing.

Limitations in the form of entertainment apply less to the halls in Central London, where, for instance, beautiful and elaborate ballets are produced. These fashionable resorts have the best of everything that can be offered, and the performances, consequently, reach a perfection which silences criticism in that respect, though in some cases there may remain ground for attack on the score of encouraging vice. In these palaces of amusement even music is not neglected. The orchestra at the Alhambra is very famous, whilst those at the Empire and the Palace are also excellent. But in the minor halls, development is never in the direction of music. Strange as it may sound, anything that can rightly be called music is seldom produced at a local music hall. The only exceptions I call to mind are a performance of Lancashire bell ringers and the vagaries of a musical clown on his violin. In this respect, the efforts of negro minstrelsy have been far superior. Perhaps music might some day find its way in through operatic sketches, if these were encouraged.

The taste for music, and for good music, in all classes, is undoubted. 'People' (says a London Country Councillor) 'will not put up with any sort of music; they appreciate good music, and insist on having it.' 'They appreciate the best music you can give them,' remarks the Superintendent of a Wesleyan Mission. They may not be so ready to pay for it, but they find pleasure in hearing it, will take trouble to go where it is given, and will pay a little – will pay to enter the enclosure near the band stand, or for a reserved seat when the rest are free. Good music would seem to be amongst the things which can with safety be supplied collectively, and in this matter, as in others, the London County Council are showing the way. Voluntary effort in the same direction is exemplified by the People's Concert Society and by the choral societies and orchestras connected with many of the churches, Polytechnics and Settlements.

Over this matter Sunday becomes the bone of contention. On the one side it is said that to supply such attractions outside tends to empty the churches, or if given inside to lower the flag of religion; and on the other that the churches can, without going beyond their *rôle*, 'hold their own,' and never will do more, and that it is from the delights of the public-houses and the charms of the streets, and from homes that fail to delight and lack all charm, that the people are drawn to Sunday concerts or to the parks when the band plays. In confirmation of the latter view we were told at Greenwich that at the outset publicans readily set forth in their windows the bills announcing the times at which the band performances took place, but that they do so no longer. One of them (it was added) had said that his takings had been reduced £7 or £8. But we have also heard much of the increasing difficulty of holding the young people at church or Bible-class when the band is playing, and some, no doubt, are drawn from both directions.

Document 17

Attachments, boundaries and exclusions. *Source*: R. Hoggart, '"Them" and "Us"', chapter 3 of *The Uses of Literacy* (Harmondsworth, 1958), pp. 53–4, 60–1

Presumably most groups gain some of their strength from their exclusiveness, from a sense of people outside who are not 'Us'. How does this express itself in working-class people? I have emphasized the strength of home and neighbourhood, and have suggested that this strength arises partly from a feeling that the world outside is strange and often unhelpful, that it has most of the counters stacked on its side, that to meet it on its own terms is difficult. One may call this, making use of a word commonly used by the working-classes, the world of 'Them'. 'Them' is a composite dramatic figure, the chief character in modern urban forms of the rural peasant – big-house relationships. The world of 'Them' is the world of the bosses, whether those bosses are private individuals or, as is increasingly the case today, public officials. 'Them' may be, as occasion requires, anyone from the classes outside other than the few individuals from those classes whom working-people know as individuals. A general practitioner, if he wins his way by his devotion to his patients, is not as a general practitioner, one of 'Them'; he and his wife, as social beings, are. A parson may or may not be regarded as one of 'Them', according to his behaviour. 'Them' includes the policemen and those civil servants or local-authority employees whom the working-classes meet – teachers, the school attendance man, 'the Corporation', the local bench. Once the Means Test Official, the man from 'the Guardians', and the Employment Exchange officer were notable figures here. To the very poor, especially, they compose a shadowy but numerous and powerful group affecting their lives at almost every point: the world is divided into 'Them' and 'Us'.

'They' are 'the people at the top', 'the higher-ups', the people who give you your dole, call you up, tell you to go to war, fine you, made you split the family in the thirties to avoid a reduction in the Means Test allowance, 'get yer in the end', 'aren't really to be trusted', 'talk posh', 'are all twisters really', 'never tell yer owt' (e.g. about a relative in hospital), 'clap yer in clink', 'will do y' down if they can', 'summons yer', 'are all in a click [clique] together', 'treat y' like muck'.

There has been plenty of violent action by the authorities in England, especially during the first half of the nineteenth century. But on the whole, and particularly in this century, the sense of 'Them' among working-class people is not of a violent or harsh thing. This is not the 'Them' of some European proletariats, of secret police, open brutality, and sudden disappearances. Yet there exists, with some reason, a feeling among working-class people that they are often at a disadvantage, that the law is in some things readier against them than against others, and that petty laws weigh more heavily against them than against some other groups. . . .

Towards 'Them' generally, as towards the police, the primary attitude is not so much fear as mistrust: mistrust accompanied by a lack of illusions about what 'They' will do for one, and for the complicated way – the apparently unnecessarily complicated way – in which 'They' order one's life when it touches them. . . .

B.   'US' – THE BEST AND THE WORST OF IT

In any discussion of working-class attitudes much is said about the group-sense, that feeling of being not so much an individual with 'a way to make' as one of a group whose members are all roughly level and likely to remain so. I avoid the word 'community' at this stage because its overtones seem too simply favourable; they may lead to an under-estimation of the harsher tensions and sanctions of working-class groups.

Certainly working-class people have a strong sense of being members of a group, and just as certainly that sense involves the assumption that it is important to be friendly, co-operative, neighbourly. 'We are all in the same boat'; 'it is no use fighting one another'; but 'in unity is strength'. One's mind goes back to the movements of the last century, to the hundreds of friendly societies, to the mottoes of the unions: the Amalgamated Society of Engineers, with 'Be United and Industrious'; the Provisional Committee of the National Union of Gas Workers and General Labourers choosing, in the late nineties, 'Love, Unity and Fidelity'. And the 'Love' in the last recalls the strength which this sense of unity acquired from a Christian background.

The friendly group tradition seems to me to have its strength initially from the ever-present evidence, in the close, huddled, intimate conditions of life, that we are, in fact, all in the same position. You are bound to be close to people with whom, for example, you share a lavatory in a common yard. That 'luv' which is still the most common form of address, and not only to people in their own class, by tram and bus conductors and by shop-keepers, is used automatically, but still indicates something. To call anyone 'neighbourly' or 'right sociable' is to offer a high compliment; a club may be praised because it is a 'real sociable place'; the most important recommendation for lodgings or seaside 'digs' is that they are 'sociable', and this outweighs overcrowding; and a church is just as likely to be weighed in the same scales.

Index

Index

Index

Index

Owen, Robert 42, 261
Owenism 33

Paris Commune (1871) 192
Patriotic Fund 58
Peel, Robert 6, 96
Pelling, Henry 9
Penn, Roger 125, 136
Pennybacker, Susan 154
Pickering, Paul 24, 90
picketing, legalities of 50–1
Pilling, Richard 252–3
Platt, John 231
Platt Brothers and Co. 231
Plug Plot riots (1842) 36, 67
Pollard, Sidney 28
Potter, George 249
poverty 220, 292–7
power-loom weaving 28
Preston
    Conservatism in 95
    lock-out 67
Primrose League 183, 199, 202, 203
printing trade 63, 284–5
    strikes 236–9
Progressive Alliance 185, 186, 194, 195
Pugh, Martin 199
Purvis, Martin 47

quarrying 63

radicalism 80–1, 94
    independent 190–2
    see also Liberalism
railway strike (1911) 169
Reach, Angus Bethune 131, 132
Rechabites 61
Reform Acts and Bills 27
    (1832) 6, 33
    (Second) (1867) 26, 36, 89, 100, 182,
        183, 186, 189, 190, 205
    (1884) 182, 183
    (1918) 148, 182
Reform League (1865) 78, 88, 94
Reform Union (1864) 94
Reid, Alastair 9, 10, 11, 79, 80, 81, 147,
        186, 188, 189, 190, 193–4, 195,
        197

Reynolds's Newspaper 191
respectability 30–1, 115–37, 112
    Chartism and 123–4
    gender differences 136–7
    in home life 32, 113, 118–21, 254–61
    middle-class 121–2
    of women 116, 118–21, 122–3
    working-class 32, 112–13, 122–6,
        271–9, 304–5
    in working-class communities 128–
        36
revisionist historiography 9–11
Revolt of the Field 167
riots
    anti-Catholic 97, 98, 99, 102
    Hyde Park (1866) 27
    Plug Plot (1842) 36, 67
    see also lock-outs; strikes
Roberts, Elizabeth 119, 220
Roberts, Robert 216–18, 219, 222, 225
Rochdale
    Conservatism in 95
    Liberalism in 86, 91–2
Rochdale Pioneers 29, 44, 46, 47
Rose, Sonya 10, 222
Ross, Ellen 119, 220
Rowbotham, Sheila 11
Rowntree, Seebohm 156, 220
Royal Commission on Trade
        Unions 239–44
Royle, Edward 190
Royton, Lancashire 53, 54
Royton Temperance Society 55
Russell, Lord John 88
Rutherford, John 106

Sacred Month 27
Salford
    housing 216–18
    poverty 220
Salisbury, Lord 183, 184, 185, 204
Savage, Mike 66, 125, 150, 226
Saville, John 1, 4, 35, 44
SDF (Social Democratic
        Federation) 184, 191
self-help 30–1
sewing schools 118
Sheffield outrages 50

310